ARCHITECTURE AS INFRASTRUCTURE

ARCHITECTURE CHINA

CONTENTS

News

Architecture as Infrastructure

Li Xiangning
Editor-in-chief, Architecture China
Professor, College of Architecture and Urban Planning, Tongji University

The history of architecture as infrastructure does not go back a long time. It was with the birth of modern metropolis that the phrase "architecture as infrastructure" emerged as an approach, mainly in the integration of architecture into the physical network of a city. Basically, infrastructure is composed of physical structures such as roads, railways, bridges, tunnels, electrical grids, and so on—all of which are not essentially categorized as architecture. The expansion of modern cities and their industrialization breaks the boundary of architecture and infrastructure; emerging new techniques in civil engineering accelerate the fusion of these two originally separated fields. Hence, it becomes crucial to further the research on "architecture as infrastructure," or "infrastructure as architecture" in the context of urbanization.

In the last two decades, China became the most known test site for the fast construction of cities and suburban areas around the world. This phenomenon has brought about fierce discussions on the acceptance of infrastructure in the traditional research field of architecture; new practices in major cities such as Shanghai and Beijing also help to further blur the boundary of infrastructure. New typologies of infrastructure are being included into the scope of contemporary Chinese architecture and new practices prove the legitimacy of a common ground for a coalition of infrastructure and architecture. Against this background, the Winter 2020 Architecture China promotes some relevant reflections that include a series of recently built projects that can be grouped as exemplary cases of architecture as infrastructure in China.

In this Issue's Essays, two scholars share their own observations on architecture as infrastructure. Zhang Bin, the principal architect of Atelier Z+, writes on infrastructure as an emerging new field for architecture. As an active practitioner in Shanghai, Zhang Bin provides a broad view of how architecture participates in shaping publicness through its connection with infrastructure, in the process, highlighting the type of new concerns for an architect when faced with the rapid urbanization of a metropolis such as Shanghai. The recently completed Wetland Research and Education Center is a response to one such concern. Tan Zheng, associate professor from Tongji University, provides his study of the interrelationship of urban architecture and infrastructure from the beginning of modernity. He argues that the potential of infrastructure could be injected into architecture through the attempts of theoretical studies by scholars such as Stan Allen, Keller Easterling, Stephen Graham, Simon Marvin and Dana Cuff. Both essays launch a critical reflection on the global role that infrastructure has played in the past decades' urbanization.

The main section, In this Issue, explores the 11th Horticultural Exposition of Jiangsu Province and the infrastructure and building projects that are being completed to set the stage for the event. It also delves into the "dirty business" of toilet design and construction with architectures that successfully counter the negative perceptions of the lavatory through creativity, in Toilet Revolution. Projects Highlight showcases built projects in China that stand as good examples of architecture as infrastructure.

Situated at the suburban Tangshan County of Nanjing, the site for the 11th Horticultural Exposition of Jiangsu Province was originally an industrial area for railways. It was renovated to create habitability and the area is today regarded by the municipal government of Nanjing as a test for other major modern transformations of former industrial areas. Hosting the 11th Horticultural Exposition of Jiangsu Province necessitates a variety of strategies for combining infrastructure and architecture and the constructions for the exposition hold little back. The built projects for this horticultural expo, which include pavilions, museums, transformed stations, hotels, and art colonies are planned within the left network of the original railway industry in combination with nature.

The Toilet Revolution in contemporary China responds to the interaction of top-down policies and changing urban contexts, and it was the passing of one such federal policy that expanded the toilet revolution into urban and rural communities, providing a common point for campaigns aimed at renovating cities and revitalizing rural villages. The included design proposals, which are all unbuilt, showcase different strategies adopted by architects in response to the imposed policy and the basic needs of local inhabitants. This article opens a window for our readers to look into the circumstances of the practices related to urban infrastructure in contemporary China.

The selected projects in Projects Highlight hail from recently built constructions of Shanghai architects. In the last two decades, the renovations along the riversides of Huangpu River have changed the waterfront landscape tremendously. Riverside Passage and Ash Gallery are two of the most distinct projects among these renovations and they each display their respective strategies for intervening a once industrial site. Interestingly, Pocket Plaza and Wetland Research and Education Center, when juxtaposed with the urban development of Shanghai, display two design strategies that are almost two extremes—one is a tiny, high-density renovated open space in the old district and the other is a suburban large-scale building cluster expanding in dialogue with nature. The Visitor Center of Changping Future Science City narrates a different urban story set in a different city altogether, making impressions at its Beijing site.

Throughout this issue, readers will be reminded that the interrelation of architecture and infrastructure remains tight as well as loose. It should also not be overlooked that together with “architecture as infrastructure,” exists an “infrastructure as architecture.” Though it is not spoken of in detail in this issue, it stays in no way insignificant. As architecture is turned into an inclusive container to fit the urgent demands of present, and future, contemporary situations, rest assured, more new meanings and associations will be found among familiar terms we thought we had already learnt.

Shaping Publicness: Infrastructure as an Emerging New Field for Architecture

Zhang Bin
Atelier Z+, Principal Architect

Infrastructure and Urbanization in China

China's enormous urbanization and flooding demographic migrations since the 1980s have led to consistent, yet fragmented spatial production driven by the local government's reliance on land-leasing revenues. This is exemplified by the development and construction of numerous new towns with socially stratified gated residential areas and their insular commercial, cultural, educational, and public service facilities. The interconnection of these islands is supported by China's exceptionally well-developed infrastructure: high-speed railways, airports, roads and bridges, telecommunication networks, and other large installations. However, in terms of the microcirculation that sustains everyday life, we have largely failed to build community networks with a high sense of identity and participation, which has also been the reason for—and the dilemma of—grassroots governance in recent years. Through the anti-urbanity of mega-urbanization, we constructed bubble-like experiences of urban life that contributed to the alienation of the individual. Inspired by Chinese urbanization, the German philosopher Peter Sloterdijk called this contemporary urban environment "a global Individualgesellschaft." Within this context, the expansion of infrastructure has played a significant role in the acceleration of socio-economic activities and the change in the spatial distribution between urban and rural areas, temporarily relieving the demographic and communicative pressures of rapid urbanization. But this exceptionally well-developed infrastructure has also often fragmented organic urban communities and worked against rapidly changing urban needs. The term "infrastructure" refers to the material and technical facilities designed to allocate public resources, coordinate public relations, and improve the public environment, which are the physical conditions for the survival and development of society. Furthermore, it is the material basis for the mobility of modern society, which guarantees the efficient global allocation and flow of materials, human resources, capital, and information. Infrastructure can be broadly divided into gray municipal infrastructure and green environmental, ecological, and life-sustaining infrastructure.

Gray infrastructure is defined as a municipal network of roads, bridges, energy, communications, water, and other utilities necessary to ensure the proper functioning of an industrialized economy. It pursues the efficient realization of a predefined single function and often manifests itself with a hidden, functional, and aloof appearance, which tends to neglect the social, aesthetic, and ecological aspects that infrastructure should possess. As a consequence, gray infrastructure oftentimes causes the fragmentation and obstruction of urban public and community spaces, which in turn affects the overall contribution of infrastructure to the built environment.

Green infrastructure is the support system of natural life in an area, hosting a variety of naturally-occurring and self-regenerating ecosystems and landscape elements. For example, an interconnected network of open spaces that sustain natural species, preserve natural ecological processes, and protect air and water quality, such as waterways, wetlands, woodlands, wildlife habitats, greenways, parks, nature reserves, farms, pastures, and wilderness. With its ultimate goal being the sustainability of the ecological environment, green infrastructure has sociological and economic value.

Since the progression of the digital age in 2013, people's lifestyles, as well as their interaction and consumption patterns, have been undergoing profound changes. This has left traditional communities based on autonomous local living spheres—an already underdeveloped social segment in China—with little chance to flourish. The public lives and interactions of young people have become increasingly dependent on social networks centered on mainstream consumption and shared identities, and the rapid development of digital technologies and capital has inevitably reinforced the aforementioned new urbanity of alienated individuals, while adding new pressures on our everyday spatial environment. With this technological progress, infrastructures such as transportation, logistics, and mediums of communication have become more and more powerful. Separated into relatively amiable user interfaces and underlying logistical systems that disregard the existing urban fabric, modern technology reinforces the spatial alienation of individuals.

The situation is exacerbated given that at the same time, China has also entered a phase of transformational development based on the renewal of existing spaces and resources, thanks to a phase of investment-driven and growth-oriented urbanization. Thus, faced with profound lifestyle changes, social stratification, and the crisis of local culture—within the context of globalization—urban renewal of these existing spaces needs to return to the core of human needs and focus on the re-identification of local culture and the re-establishment of social relations. Instead of merely seeking to maximize the exchange value of spatial resources, it is necessary to emphasize the concerted development of social equity, the natural environment, traditional culture, and real-world social networks, while maximizing a space's use value and reshaping local publicness.

Landscape Urbanism and Landscape Infrastructure

Theoretical and practical discussions of landscape urbanism first emerged in Europe and the United States—the result of having experienced the energy and ecological crisis, and the failure of modernist urban planning since the 1990s. Landscape urbanism defines landscape as a worldview and a set of values that address the relationship between all people and places, instead of a technique for aesthetic expression and representation. It is the carrier of all natural and human processes, whereas buildings, infrastructure, and open spaces are only a continuation of the landscape—mere undulations of the earth's surface. Landscape urbanism interprets the city as an ecosystem. By building and improving landscape infrastructure, the functions of traditional infrastructure are combined with the social and cultural needs of the city. The landscape acts as a vessel for the city to develop and extend, reshaping the relationship between nature and people. As a supporting pillar for urban life, landscapes can synergize and integrate single-use gray municipal infrastructure with green infrastructure, such as ecological corridors, greenways, river networks, and parklands, which pass through various natural processes to become landscape infrastructure. Landscape infrastructure continues the fundamental sustainability principles of green infrastructure, while exploring the inherent connection and potential integration of landscape structures and infrastructure to better respond to the needs of ecological, social, and economic development.

As China enters this new phase of urbanization characterized by the renewal of existing space and the pursuit of high-quality development—while also facing land resource constraints, high urban density, and the need for sustainable development—it is imperative to replace traditional single-use infrastructure that interrupts urban public and community spaces. By carefully adopting the development paradigm of landscape infrastructure, which aims to coordinate the development of urban open space systems as a whole, we can maximize the functions and benefits of each infrastructure element such that the ecological, communication, and non-motorized traffic systems in a region are included. As a multifunctional medium and vessel, landscape infrastructure catalyzes and synchronizes the integration and optimization between various ecological processes and municipal works by providing a common platform for their interaction. Its ability to enhance open spaces and public life manifests itself in our altered perception of the city, not only as a highly functional machine, but also as a mixture of different lifestyles.

It is encouraging to note that in recent years, a number of landscape infrastructure projects have emerged in China's major cities with the goal of integrating urban public space resources and revitalizing communities and public life. They range from ecological restorations, landscaped flood control facilities, country parks, greenways, and waterfront public spaces to non-motorized traffic systems and the revitalization of industrial relics, and are often a combination and symbiosis of multiple landscape and infrastructure systems. This new kind of infrastructure changes people's perception of traditional infrastructure as hidden, aloof, and functional, presenting itself in a dynamic, public, and integrated form. In a palpable fashion, it becomes the vector for new behaviors and an aesthetic object in the urban space. Landscape infrastructure serves as a medium for a new publicness of the city and also expands the boundaries of architecture by becoming a new way for Chinese architects to participate in social processes.

Infrastructure Architecture

The built environment is the human and material ecosystem constructed by modern infrastructure, and both tangible and intangible domains such as landscape, communication, energy, and logistics exert a significant influence on the built environment. Buildings become endpoints and nodes of globally networked infrastructures with specific scale and dimensions. The study of infrastructure expands the boundaries of classic modernist architecture, which focuses on the physical environment by incorporating landscape, communication, energy, logistics, and property rights that affect the built environment. Since 2000, following the emergence of three distinct phenomena—namely the economic crisis in the West, a number of infrastructure collapses, and the growing fragmentation and alienation of urban communities—architecture has started to reflect on the failure of neoclassical liberal political and economic strategies to resist the trend toward symbolistic architecture, and to criticize the detachment of architecture from the shaping of urban spaces and creating social values. This gave rise to the discourse of infrastructural urbanism and infrastructure architecture. Architecture's interest for infrastructure represented an exploration into the implications of modernity in the wake of modernism. The close connection between infrastructure and public policy dictated that it become an important new opportunity for architecture to intervene in urban public life, aligning infrastructure architecture with the ideals of modernist architecture.

During the first 30 years of rapid urbanization and infrastructure development, Chinese architecture circles were unable to share the West's pain of the erosion of architecture from the public sphere, given the different rates of construction and economic development. However, on entering the current development period characterized by the renewal of already existing space and the decline in large-scale construction activities led by the public sector, the re-construction of space had to adopt more decentralized, gradual, complex, and sophisticated approaches when faced with simultaneous transformations in capital, technology, and media. As issues such as landscape infrastructure, the revitalization of industrial heritage, and transit-oriented urban development enter the Chinese architectural discourse, architecture will have to learn from the latest developments in the areas of environment, resources, performance, and materials in order to increase the efficiency of public spaces and the built environment (thereby also transforming the unknown sentiments of Chinese architecture circles in those initial years to become more apparent). To this end, a more comprehensive approach is needed to discuss the fundamental experiences of modernity within the public realm, such as mobility, accessibility, freedom, and density.

Infrastructure architecture shifts the focus from architecture's intra-disciplinary knowledge to a broader study of the built environment, concerning itself with the reshaping of the entire human habitat, including the various systems of built objects, and the topographical, climatic, ecological, and media environments they affect. At the same time, infrastructure architecture responds to questions of human subjectivity, exploring not only the persistent contradiction between the objectification of human beings and the personification of machines—including manufactured artifacts such as buildings—but also the human attempt of attaining freedom through technology and its resulting conflicts. Infrastructure organizes and operates a complex system of flows and exchanges, and by learning from infrastructure, buildings can be expanded from solidified functional objects to more stimulating and nurturing systems, to abstract tools for nourishing a city's collective potential.

If we perceive architecture as twofold: as an understanding and expression of existence and nature, and as an intervention of, and a reflection on social production, then the integration of architecture and infrastructure is, in fact, highly relevant to this discipline's core concerns. For architecture, the explorations of infrastructure into areas such as nature, topography, and catalysts can offer significant new insights.

Nature

The combinations of natural and human-made, and green and gray, which are associated with landscape infrastructure represent a new concept of nature and ecology that no longer distinguishes between natural and human-made, but instead, understands nature as a product of human society, politics, and economy. Nature can thus be categorized into four tiers: the first is virgin nature; second, nature transformed by human productivity and life; third, nature as an aesthetic reproduction of the first and second nature; and fourth, nature as damaged and later ecologically restored. The practice of landscape infrastructure relates mostly to the second and fourth forms of nature. Second nature is the landscape form produced by superimposing human activities on first nature; it is the result of mutual adaptation between humans and nature. Second nature is also an important part of the human habitat and a carrier of human history and culture. And fourth nature is essentially a post-industrial subject. It discusses how to revive damaged nature through regenerative natural processes or proactive ecological restoration in the face of nature's over-exploitation by human activities. The recent emergence of new types of landscape infrastructure in China, such as country parks, wetland conservation and restoration sites, river management and waterfront greenways, and the revitalization and reuse of industrial ruins, forces us to expand our understanding of nature and rethink its meaning. Only then will we be able to avoid simplistic and symbolistic approaches in our practice and explore the diversity of ecology and nature.

Topography

Modernist architecture redefined the relationship between architecture and site by placing self-evident forms of architectural organization above the landscape's complexity, leading in turn, to the rise of the Megastructure movement. With the emergence of landscape urbanism, however, topography that examines the undulations of the earth's surface entered the architectural discourse. It defined a series of urban design practices that created artificial topographies, reorganized space and directed pedestrian flow, evolving into a new design language. Focused on dissolving the dichotomy between structure and site, and restoring the continuity of the built environment that modernism had neglected, topography has become a comprehensive spatial form that includes landscapes, buildings, and various other structures. Large-scale infrastructure nodes are the very medium for creating continuity beyond the limits of single buildings, for example, transportation hubs, revetments, large public buildings, and other pedestrian-friendly spaces that are combined into an accessible network to form a new anthropogenic terrain.

Catalysts

Architecture is not only a neutral space that houses certain activities, but also a tool that shapes new ways of living, inspiring social change. In a number of urban renewal practices, infrastructure can serve as a catalyst, shifting its role from a purely functional necessity to a vehicle which influences the patterns of urban mobility and the ways in which people gather. Infrastructure is a set of technologies, protocols, rules, and social relations that can take on an "active form," which can trigger a chain reaction in a defined area, change spatial protocols, and induce spatial behaviors. Applied in this way, architecture can overcome its singular function as formal games, as well as cross the boundary between information and symbol to generate social benefit. Based on the premise of the built environment as systematized infrastructure, the concept of the catalyst can reshape architectural methodology. The far-reaching effect of infrastructure as a spatial intervention proves that the social impact of architecture has a lot of space to grow.

Publicness

The underlying reason of why infrastructural operations of various types and scales have entered the contemporary Chinese architectural discourse can be found in the central preoccupation of modernist architecture, or in how publicness in the present is shaped and how people are connected. After more than 30 years of rapid development, architecture in China has reached a decisive crossroad: on one hand, technological development has reinforced the connection between power and capital, creating a foreseeable future defined by solitary and fictitious human existence sustained through invisible infrastructure that has lost genuine spatial publicness. This illusion of a secure existence is most certainly indicative of humanity's completed alienation. On the other hand, if we hope to avoid a future of atomized humans, spatial design practitioners need to re-engage with their profession's main concerns, actively take part in public life, use spatial interventions as a medium to promote discussions of publicness, and keep contributing to the creation of public spaces that support social life and its aspirations. A city's vitality is embedded in the network of people's daily lives, with the respect and support that urban spaces can provide to communal life. Therefore, cities should encourage freedom, diversity, and intellectual innovation. The essence of public space revolves around the rights of people and the connections between them, so it should be both inclusive and open. Beyond its material appearance, the quality of a public space is defined by its ability to accommodate publicness and a rich urban life, not only on special occasions, but also in terms of its compatibility with everyday life, and its openness and respect for different people. This publicness must be formed within an ecologically, naturally, and socially sustainable framework through pluralistic and collaborative mechanisms. In order to form a connection between social structure, civic culture, and the physical space, and to nurture diverse forms of public life and urban culture, it is necessary to not just consolidate the fragmented urban space, but to also foster life in the city, a cultural atmosphere, and regional identity.

According to the Spanish sociologist Manuel Castells, evolving urban structures, urban landscapes, and architectural patterns, as well as local and global spatial networks all adhere to the two basic spatial forms of information societies: a static "space of places" and a dynamic "space of flows" for traffic, goods, capital, and migration. Although infrastructure itself is static, it organizes and manages a complex system of flows, movements, and exchanges, and should be understood as an abstract tool rooted in the urban surface matrix while fostering the public potential of a city. As a complex urban event-structure, this new type of infrastructure integrates public services, public landscape, and public space to establish a new relationship with the public sphere to achieve a dynamic balance between "spaces of places" and "spaces of flows"—to become the living matrix of cities through an inclusive and open attitude and to provide a structural, yet flexible, basic condition for the subsequent evolution of the urban landscape, which not only stimulates the daily activities of its users and optimizes the allocation of spatial resources, but also enhances its own topological capacity and ability to connect with the surrounding environment, mending the urban life system, bridging urban fault lines, and healing the city's scars. This opens up the potential and possibility for a positive evolution of the urban structure. Precisely in this context, architecture's intervention in infrastructure can enable the expansion of the discipline's focus from singular, solidified visual objects to more inspiring and nurturing systems. Architecture can also leverage its interdisciplinary experience to act as a leading spatial designer and professional coordinator in the practice of infrastructure to unlock its potential of publicness. We cannot expect architecture to single-handedly initiate lifestyle changes and the creation of publicness as it did at the dawn of modernity in the industrial era. Instead, given new social and technological contexts, it is important that practitioners proactively integrate with finance, the internet, and other professions in their efforts to reshape publicness and serve as a fundamental corrective force that prevents excessive human alienation.

If China's post-pandemic social development depends on a renewal through the voluntary integration and organizational evolution of—as well as the cooperation and mutual assistance between—all social strata, then a "re-localization" that aims to overcome the spatial and social isolation caused by the rapid urbanization of the last 30 years, as it also restores social production and life interrupted by the pandemic becomes imperative. This re-localization addresses the possibility of social and spatial restoration in the context of: an impossible survival of traditional communities in China, the dramatic separation of people brought about by the rural-urban dichotomy, and the cultural re-identification that is required for the self-organization of communities in the digital age.

We need to establish localized forms of communal cooperation outside of the emerging digital infrastructure dominated by the consumerist ideology of power and capital. New technologies should be used to foster sustainable, self-managed, and healthy networks of local life. Embodied by infrastructural integration, the renewal of existing space is an essential element and public tool of re-localization. During the progressive self-renewal of a city, the bottom-up spatial production exemplified by the temporary and creative reuse of urban blind spots by the local community is an important channel by which the people embrace and adopt large-scale urban infrastructure into their daily lives, as well as a social process in which spatial design professionals can participate. In our spatial operations, we should encourage all temporary appropriation, adaptation, and modification of these giant closed-off systems in order to foster their disintegration, liberalization, and opening, rather than fetishizing their increased security brought about by new technologies. This will also require us to re-examine the values of our discipline.

In *The Human Condition*, Hannah Arendt borrowed from the ancient Romans to illustrate the qualities of the human condition, forcing us to consider how spatial design professionals can support the restoration of degenerated public spaces and everyday life: "'to live' and 'to be among men' (*inter homines esse*) are synonymous—just like 'to die' and 'to cease to be among men' (*inter homines esse desinere*)."[1]

Notes

1 Hannah Arendt, *The Human Condition* (Chicago: The University of Chicago Press, 1958) 7-8.

Looking at Urban Architecture in the Perspective of Infrastructure

Tan Zheng
Associate Professor, School of Architecture and Urban Planning, Tongji University

Cities are the result of the interaction, dislocation, collision, and juxtaposition of two forces: form and flow. The research on "form" encompasses the physical features and working mechanisms of the urban morphology that gradually solidify and dominate social relations. The research on "flow" includes not only the technological and social forces that constantly challenge the existing physical features of a city, but also the factors that string cities together in one shared global space. Beginning the nineteenth century, transport infrastructure emerged as the dominant factor impacting the existing urban morphology, with railroads, highways, and subways expanding the geographical scope of cities and their modes of operation, and also changing the shape of communities and buildings. In the twenty-first century, new human networks constituted by social media, the Internet of Things (IoT), and global logistics chains have further affected the physical order of the built environment and its corresponding social behavior, forcing urban researchers to reflect on the nature of communities in the context of modern technology, and to explore the possibilities of their evolution in light of new infrastructure.

Infrastructure and Modernity

According to Merriam-Webster's English Dictionary, the word "infrastructure" refers to: "The basic equipment and structures (such as roads and bridges) that are needed for a country, region, or organization to function properly." In the academic discourse of urban studies and architecture, infrastructure is a collective term for service facilities that aim to allocate public resources, coordinate public relations, and improve the public environment. On its official website, the American Planning Association lists four major types of infrastructure: transportation, water supply and drainage, energy, and communications. According to the *13th Five-Year Plan for the Nationwide Construction of Municipal Infrastructure*, jointly published by China's Ministry of Housing and Urban-Rural Development and the National Development and Reform Commission in 2017, municipal infrastructure includes a total of seven sectors: urban transportation systems, urban underground pipeline systems, urban water systems, urban energy systems, urban sanitation systems, urban green space systems, and the smart city—the last three are not mentioned in the American Planning Association's definition. In recent years, public services such as education, health, and sports are also often referred to as "infrastructure," but they rather represent arranged social institutions. To avoid confusion, the subsequent analysis follows the general definition of the term infrastructure in terms of contemporary urban studies, which focuses on its physical and engineered elements.

Infrastructure in English is composed of the words "*infra*," Latin for "below," and "structure." Infrastructure is often hidden from the eye, while the substances, energy, capital, and information it transmits are in constant flow. As a network-like system without a standardized form, infrastructure cannot be perceived in its entirety, which is why certain methods are usually employed in its research: looking at single components of the overall infrastructural network, turning it into a diagram that can be analyzed, or applying it in practice and gaining insights from its daily operation. Infrastructure needs to be deconstructed, interpreted, and gradually made visible through interaction. In recent years, "infrastructure" has become a research area of common interest for Western architects and urban planners, precisely because it is a manufactured framework that manifests the movement of energy, matter, and information within the city. Infrastructure connects the macroscopic regional or urban level with the mesoscopic neighborhood or building level, while also prompting a series of research methods that simplify urban problems, thus qualifying it as a point for research.

In the sense of urban anthropology, the spaces of infrastructure in the city constitute "institutions"—spaces such as subways, airports, ports, and streets act as installations that simultaneously provide services, define behavior, and exert control. Pierre Patte's 1769 section of a Parisian street represents the first time that an architect placed architecture and the local water facilities into an integrated system. Patte not only showed the characteristics of the city's street infrastructure, including its layout and sewerage, in a classic cross section, he also revealed the close relationship between the city's spaces for interaction and the working mechanisms behind them—the fountain at street level and the underground drainage installation belong to the same system. Their pipes are connected under the street, with the water for the fountain being provided by drinking water pipes located within a main water pipe. The cultural meaning of this urban fountain space relies on its technical under-structure. During the industrial revolution, infrastructure was gradually integrated into the urban landscape and the city's boulevard and park networks constituted a system of facilities that purified the city and maintained the health of its citizens. Urban scenery and infrastructure became one.

The Multiple Perspectives of Infrastructure Architecture

Given the twofold dimension of infrastructure—urban and architectural—and the complex movement of substances, energy, and information it contains, its behavioral mechanisms are difficult to describe using the understanding and terminology of classic architecture. Therefore, over the last two decades, scholars of urban studies have attempted to create a body of academic terms for infrastructure that architects can understand and apply: Stan Allen's "thick 2D" and "infrastructural urbanism;" Ignasi de Solà-Morales' "terrain vague;" Keller Easterling's "organization space" and "extrastatecraft;" Stephen Graham and Simon Marvin's "unbundled infrastructure;" and Dana Cuff's "infrastructure as catalytic." These concepts share a common focus on how cities as expressions of human society can coexist with infrastructure as an engineered system. They are often referred to as "infrastructural urbanism." The fundamental concerns of infrastructural urbanism can be summarized as follows: how infrastructure integrates into human society; how it becomes an organic part of the human social organism; and how space influenced by infrastructure enables high-quality development. If these infrastructural urbanists' theories were to be categorized according to their attitudes and positions, then Stan Allen is essentially still implementing the promise of architecture's modernist view on material practices by looking at spaces from an ecological and tectonic perspective, in the process construing a new topography, and De Solà-Morales extends the Marxist theory of "alienation" to the study of space, exploring the transformation between legitimate and illegitimate forms. And from the perspective of the political economy of space, Keller Easterling identifies organizational agreements that transcend the aesthetic and the symbolic and explores infrastructure "beyond the reach of state" that cuts across administrative boundaries; Graham and Marvin understand the failure of modernism as a continuous disintegration of infrastructure from one entity into unbundled systems and base their hopes for a renaissance of urban life on the reorganization of the multiple forms of infrastructure. Dana Cuff, on the other hand, draws from American pragmatism, emphasizing the function of infrastructure in reconfiguring public life, using the example of urban catalysts to explore the possibilities of architectural interventions in the city. Set within the context of the failure of modernism and the subjectivity of infrastructure, all of these studies re-establish an urban architecture anchored to the site and the public sphere through a critique of the detachment of architecture from urban concerns in the late modernist and postmodernist periods. At the same time, all these theories draw a clear separation from postmodernism, including deconstructivism, by treating architecture's course of mediatization and symbolization as a fleeting interlude, aiming to redeem modernism's promises of public life, technological progress, and individual freedom.

"Infrastructure" and its progeny "infrastructural urbanism" were once alien issues to Chinese architecture and urban planning scholars. These were concepts that had emerged in the West, after reflecting on the failures of the neo-liberal political and economic strategies of the Reagan-Thatcher era; from resistance against the tendency for symbolistic architecture; from questioning the meaning of a post-modernist modernity; from the urgent need to reintegrate architecture, urban planning, and landscape architecture; and especially, from the criticism of the architect's receding position as a leading sculptor of urban space. At the same time, the focus on infrastructure in architecture closely relates to the continued study of modernity, as its efficiency is considered an important indicator in the research.

Infrastructure's changing status within modern architecture marks the evolution of modernist architectural thinking, with the current crisis of infrastructure being a major setback to the development of modernist architecture. Therefore, the study of urban architecture based on infrastructure is both instrumental and anti-symbolic, aligning it with the ideals of modernism. The innate affinity between infrastructure and public policy also makes it an important opportunity for architectural intervention in urban public life.

Precisely because infrastructural urbanism was once an exotic issue to Chinese architecture, it initially entered the country only as a spin-off discussion of landscape urbanism. In many cases, it appeared in the guise of design strategies—like the landscaping of infrastructure, or the renewal and revitalization of industrial heritage and transit-oriented urban development—often relegated to some operational routine, unable to penetrate into the central discourse of architecture critics and architectural theorists. Due to the differences in the speed of economic development, as well as in the planning and construction of systems in China and the West, the Chinese architectural community was for a long time unable to share the pain of Western architecture's erosion from the public sphere. Due to the need for spatial production during a period of high-speed urbanization, the local architecture circle has long been clinging to a safe haven formed by the inertia of its own development, while remaining deaf to impending dangers. However, under the so-called "new normal" of economic development and the gradual slowdown in large-scale construction activity led by the public sector, a large amount of architecture-related work is likely to be taken over by existing land development plans, big data and AI-assisted design, EPC contracts, and the design departments of consumer brands, causing Chinese architects to also feel some loss from being left out from the public sphere. Yet the process of modernization has not been halted by the temporary absence of architecture, as only its integration with capital, technology, and media has changed. Meanwhile, there exists a lack of awareness and action within architecture circles. The close collaboration and transferals of knowledge between various areas required for contemporary construction activities lie beyond the ability of professional architects. In a future with even higher divisions of labor, construction activities will be organized in a more decentralized, progressive, and refined way, and architecture will have to work closely with all kinds of construction subjects, while the architecture system will need to embrace various social and technological operating mechanisms. In order to influence the quality of public spaces and the built environment more profoundly, architects have started to not only adopt the latest methodologies from other disciplines, such as sociology, material sciences, environmental studies, and information technologies, but to also reflect on the place of architecture in the general discussion of modernity.

As a constant topic in the history of architecture theories, modernity can also benefit from new approaches and perspectives brought by infrastructure. Since the late twentieth century, modernity has emerged in multiple forms, with different cultures and regions experiencing modernity in different ways. Multiple modernities can thus characterize the modernization processes of different cultures backed by a strong modernist narrative. However, in the post-structuralist and post-colonial contexts, a consensus on the relationship between diversity and universality in the experience of modernity has yet to be found, even though the various modernization narratives emerging in the "Third World" each claim to be the "alternative" to the universal modernist discourse; in reality, a meaningful dialogue between these culturally diverse regional paradigms to form a holistic entity is lacking. But since the functions of infrastructure are nearly universal in the context of multiple modernities, the study of the history of contemporary architecture centered on infrastructure may solve this dilemma. Infrastructure as a system that transcends departments, disciplines, and boundaries is the key to understanding the many variants of modernity. It can remove the ideological fog and the cultural differences that permeate the discussion of modernity and expose the social and technological agenda behind a blinding form language. Still, the basic criteria of modernity—mobility, health, accessibility, freedom, and so on—would remain the entry point for examining the interventions of a new infrastructure-based architecture in the public sphere.

Terminological Flux in Infrastructure Research

The research of infrastructure within architecture has developed a terminological system that draws on concepts from urban sociology on the one hand, and on tools and methods from other disciplines, such as environmental studies, geography, landscape design, and engineering, on the other. These terms comprise two categories: space and function.

One attempts to define a new type of space—such as Manuel Castells' "space of flows," Richard Sennett's "contested space," and Michel de Certeau and Marc Augé's concept of "non-place." The other and its terms within try to define the functions and behaviors of the above-mentioned spatial types—such as connectivity, accessibility, and flow. For example, Frampton's concept of "megaform" is the first universal tool to describe the contemporary phenomena of the built environment since Reyner Banham's "megastructure." It is a résumé of the new spatial types constituted by the combination of megabuildings and megascapes. Frampton finds that topography has replaced structure as an important field of spatial interventions among contemporary large volumes. Manuel de Solà-Morales' L'Illa Diagonal Shopping Center is a prime example of this mega topography. The building occupies several blocks and blends into the street environment, creating its own topographical appearance. According to Frampton, mega topography is characterized by the combination of different functions, continuous surfaces, and horizontal extensions. These features encapsulate the functions and behaviors of the mega topography and separate it from the older concept of megastructures.

Contemporary infrastructure research must develop a new terminological system that encompasses the environmental, technical, and spatial phenomena of classic modern architecture, as well as the unique instances of regional modern architectural research. While examining the relationship between these aspects, the terminological system should also consolidate interdisciplinary knowledge. Furthermore, this terminology must be centered around the public values and efficiency criteria of the modernity discourse, so that infrastructure research can gain the disciplinary legitimacy of architecture.

Borrowing concepts from other disciplines involved in the research of the built environment is a viable shortcut for infrastructure studies to establish its own terminology and discourse. While scholarly attention to the history of the built environment has lagged behind, there does exist a global trend that has gradually shifted the attention from the research of architecture to the broader built environment. These studies attempt to reshape the entire landscape of human settlements with their multitude of built objects and systems, and even include the topographic, climatic, ecological, and media environments they influence. Because infrastructure covers such a wide area of the built environment, it is important to conduct thorough research into the origins of key terms in order to clarify their conceptual heritage, evolution, and relation to each other. Taking "topography," "boundary," "panorama," and "catalyst" as examples of spatial categories commonly used in infrastructure research, this essay has discussed the evolution of their research scope and their contributions to the discipline of architecture. These terms also reflect the diverse manifestations of infrastructure in the urban environment and the motives behind their creation.

Conclusion

Despite the fact that infrastructure is inextricably linked to the entire history of modernization and the discourse of modernity, we still need to recognize the specific context of its emergence, as this will facilitate our understanding of its framework and significance. The rise of infrastructure-led urban studies in the United States and its emergence as a new line of thought in American urban studies, following new urbanism and landscape urbanism, occurred within two interrelated contexts: the first is the collapse of the neoliberal economy pioneered during the Reagan-Thatcher era. The second—corroborating this collapse at a spatial level—is the aging of infrastructure and the fragmentation and alienation of urban communities throughout the United States. Architecture should, therefore, lay down the basic approaches and methodologies to integrate the accumulating knowledge on infrastructure into an academic discipline.

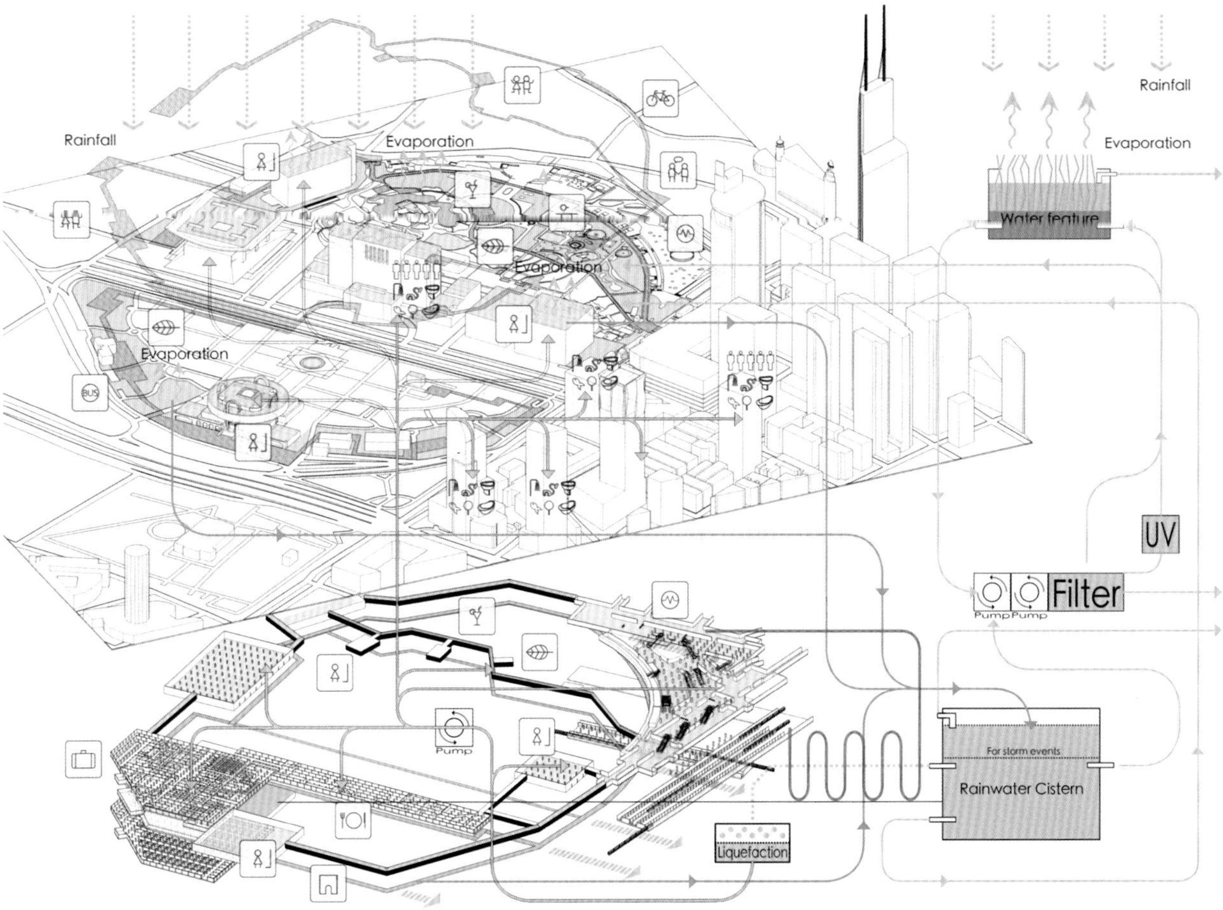

A reconstruction of Shanghai People's Square based on infrastructural facilities
© Design Studio "Architecture as Infrastructure" led by Tan Zheng and Yung Ho Chang

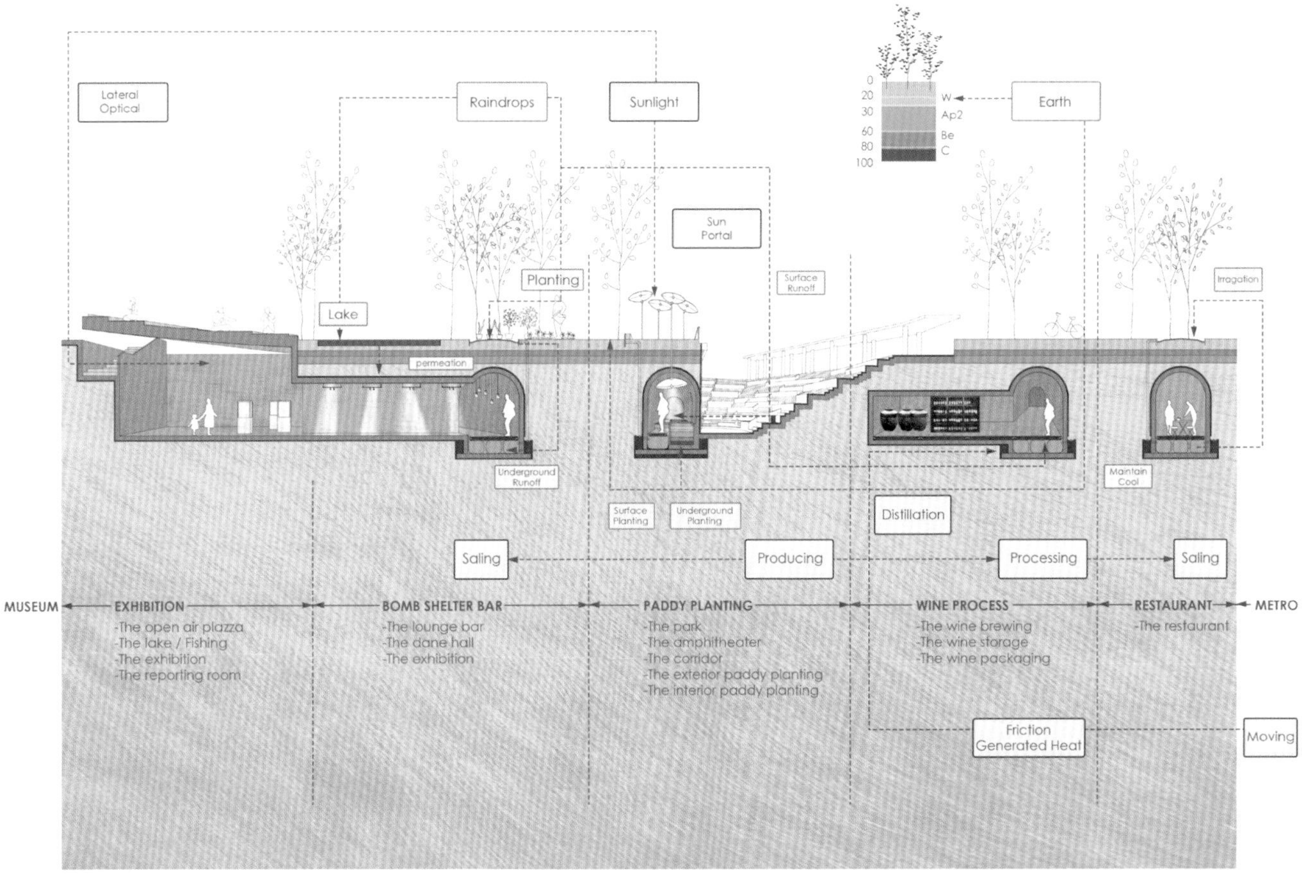

Section of a proposed underground recycle system of Shanghai People's Square based on infrastructural facilities
© Design Studio "Architecture as Infrastructure" led by Tan Zheng and Yung Ho Chang

ARCHITECTURE
CHINA

Infrastructure and Buildings for the 11th Horticultural Exposition of Jiangsu Province

Main Pavillon and Hotel

Land-Based Rationalism Design & Research Center

Architect: Land-Based Rationalism Design & Research Center, China Architecture Design & Research Group
Principal architect: Cui Kai, Guan Fei, Dong Yuanzheng
Design team: Fu Yifei, Liu Yadong, Bi Maoyang, Wang Deling, Zhang Jiashu, Guo Yiming, Dou Qiang, Liu Jianing, Guan Hui, Deng Xiaohuan, Zheng Bifang, Shi Hong, Song Minfei, Wei Jiayin
Landscape design: View Unlimited Landscape Architecture Studio, China Urban Construction Design & Research Institute Co. Ltd
Area: 52,374 square meters
Completion: In progress
Photography: Tian Fangfang

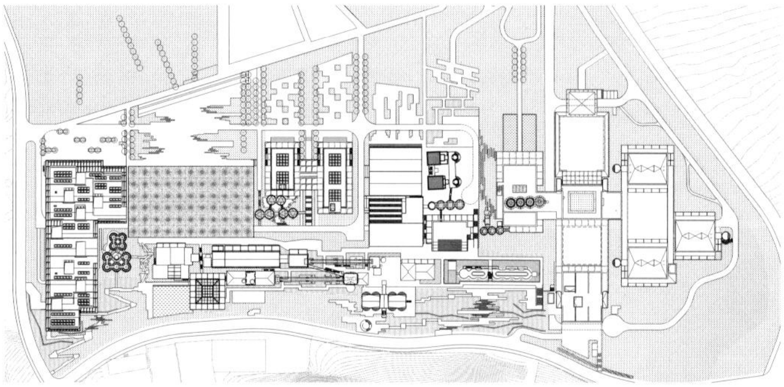

Site plan

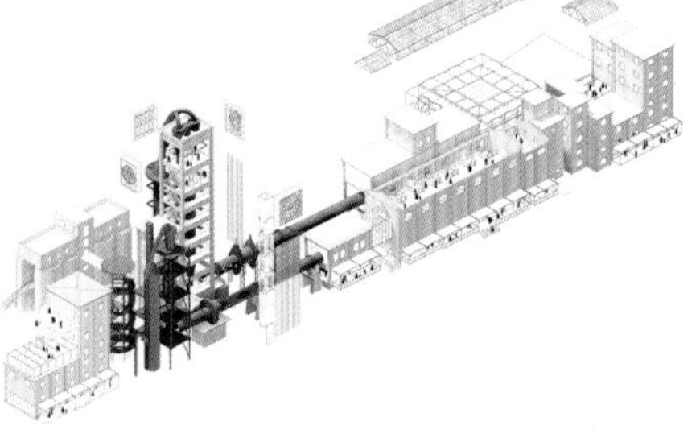

The site of the main exhibition hall is unique as it is built on the ruins of a cement factory from the 1970s. This is the main attribute that guides the design intention to restore the ecology, supplement it with urban functions, and to create a new type of green public space while also respecting its heritage.

Through a design strategy of light interventions, we were able to rejuvenate the dilapidated industrial ruins into a modern horticultural exhibition hall with lush greenery, providing an experiential and ecological public building—an ever-blooming Nanjing Garden—for the city's residents.

The light interventions are reflected through a light structure—using a prefabricated steel structure system to achieve an environmentally friendly, quickly assembled construction; a light image—the combination of slender structural components and vertical greenery to create a light architectural image, which contrasts with the coarse and heavy industrial buildings; and a light attitude—the borderless green garden pervades the industrial ruins, dissolving the buildings' own image, causing it to vanish into nature.

The light intervention strategy also increases the buildings' flexibility, so that they can be adapted to multiple functional and spatial requirements, and also allow for post-exhibition renovations and reuse.

Aerial view of main exhibition hall construction site

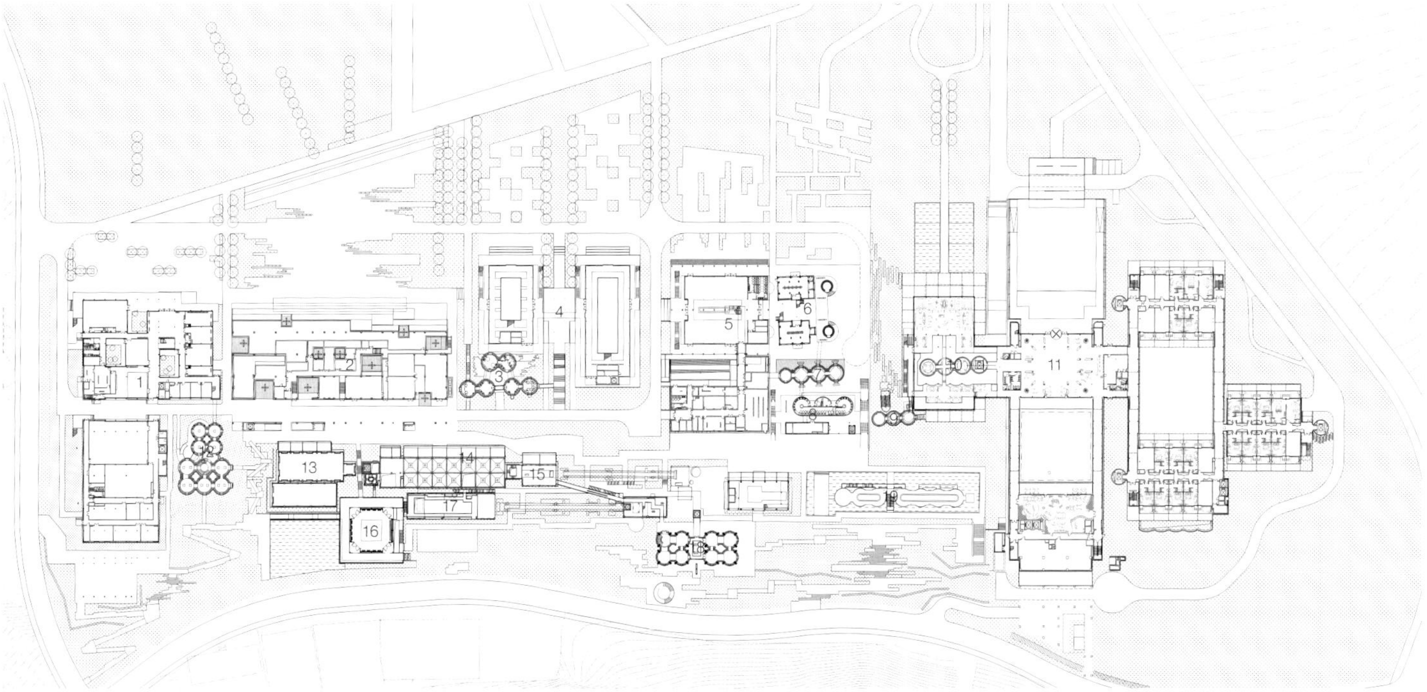

First-floor plan of main exhibition hall

1. Office area A
2. Exhibition plaza in area B
3. Restrooms
4. C area exhibition hall
5. D area dining area
6. Bar
7. Common rest area
8. F area business service area
9. Silo G
10. Hotel experience exhibition hall
11. Hotel
12. Office reading room
13. Outdoor exhibition 1
14. Outdoor exhibition 2
15. Outdoor exhibition 3
16. E area exhibition hall
17. Outdoor exhibition 4
18. Café
19. Silo C

View of Silo E construction site

Silo C

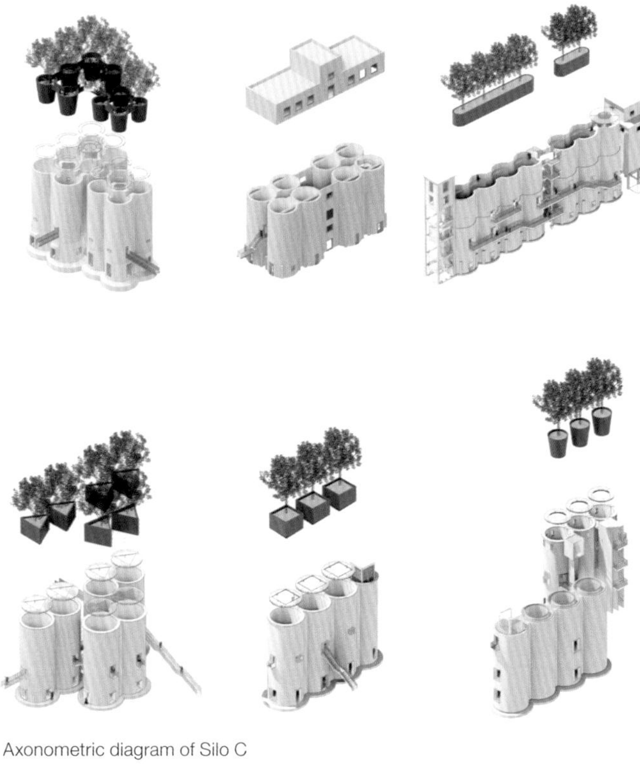

Axonometric diagram of Silo C

View of main entrance to exhibition plaza construction site

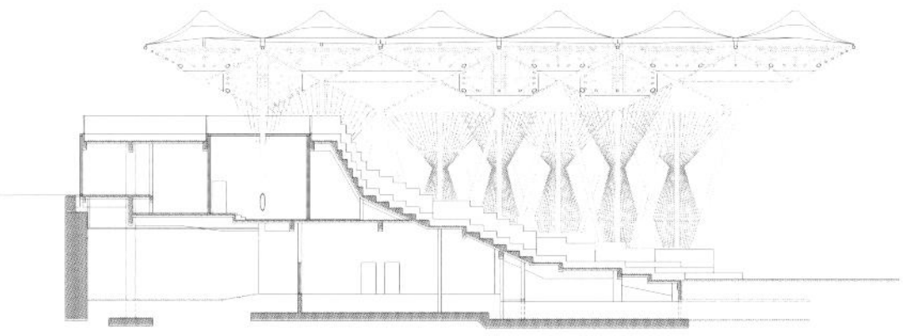

Section of the entrance structure

1. Terrace
2. Café
3. Visitor center

Exterior view of main entrance to exhibition plaza

Exterior view of C area exhibition hall

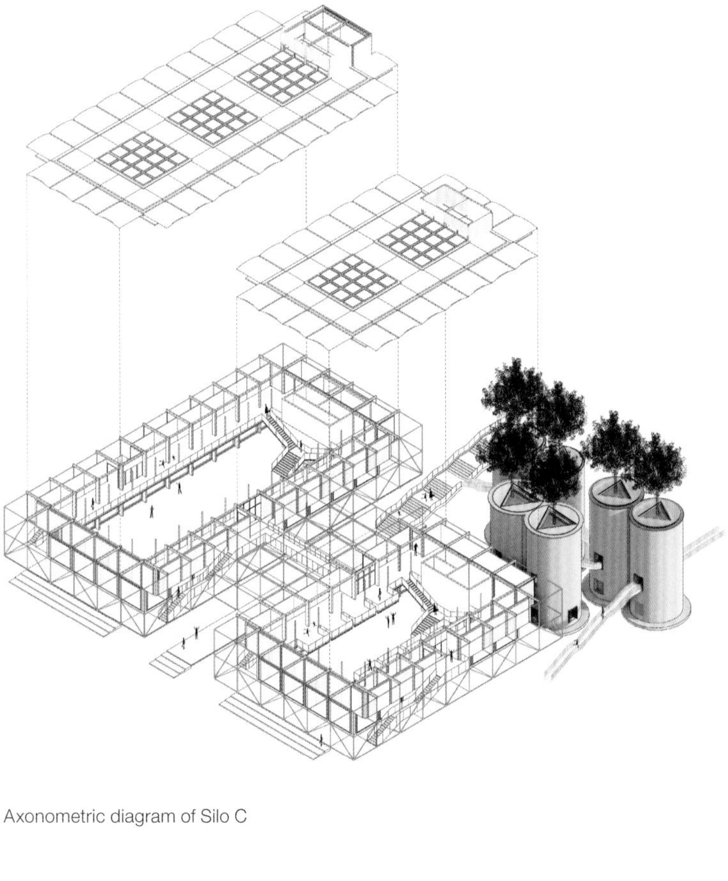

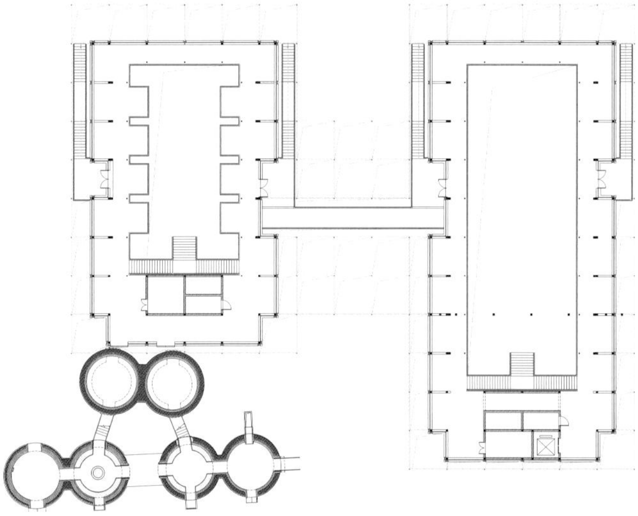

Second-floor plan

Axonometric diagram of Silo C

View from hallway of C area exhibition hall

First-floor plan of restaurant area

1. Restaurant
2. Restroom
3. Strong and weak electricity room
4. Air-conditioned room
5. Range hood room
6. Garbage disposal
7. Dishwashing room
8. Pantry
9. Grease trap
10. Main and non-staple food warehouse
11. Cold meat kitchen
12. Cargo channel inspection area
13. Inspection office
14. Rough food processing
15. Cold storage
16. Freezer
17. Fresh air engine room
18. Chinese food kitchen area
19. Bar
20. Rest area
21. Warehouse

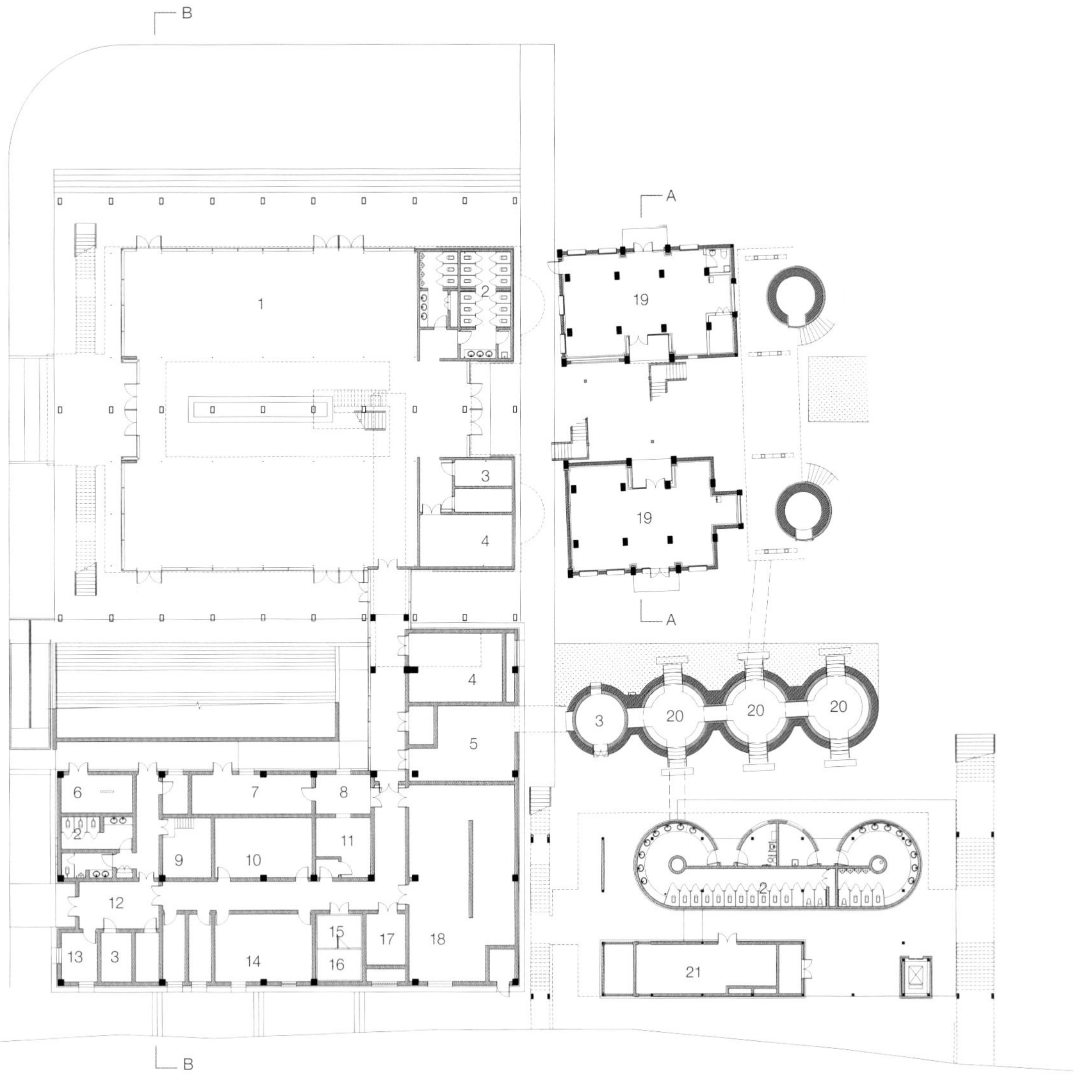

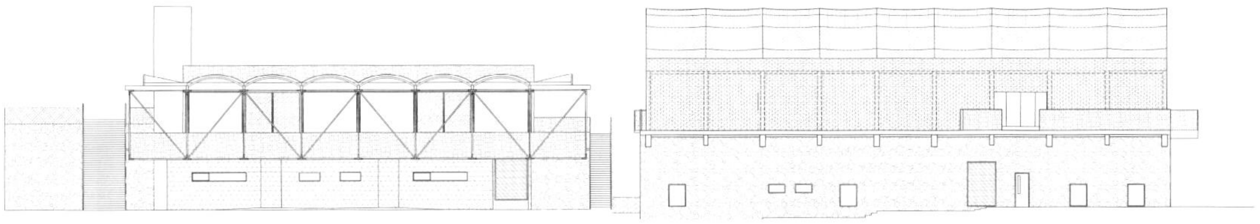

South elevation of restaurant area

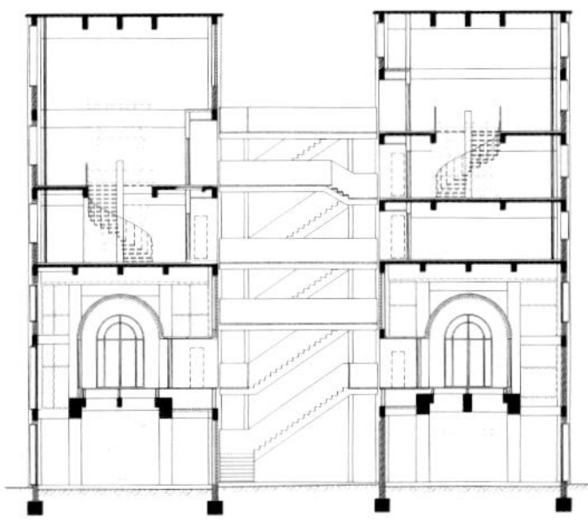

A-A section of restaurant area

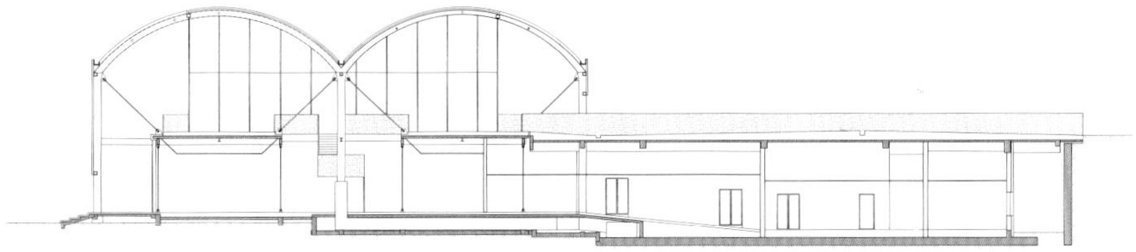

B-B section of restaurant area

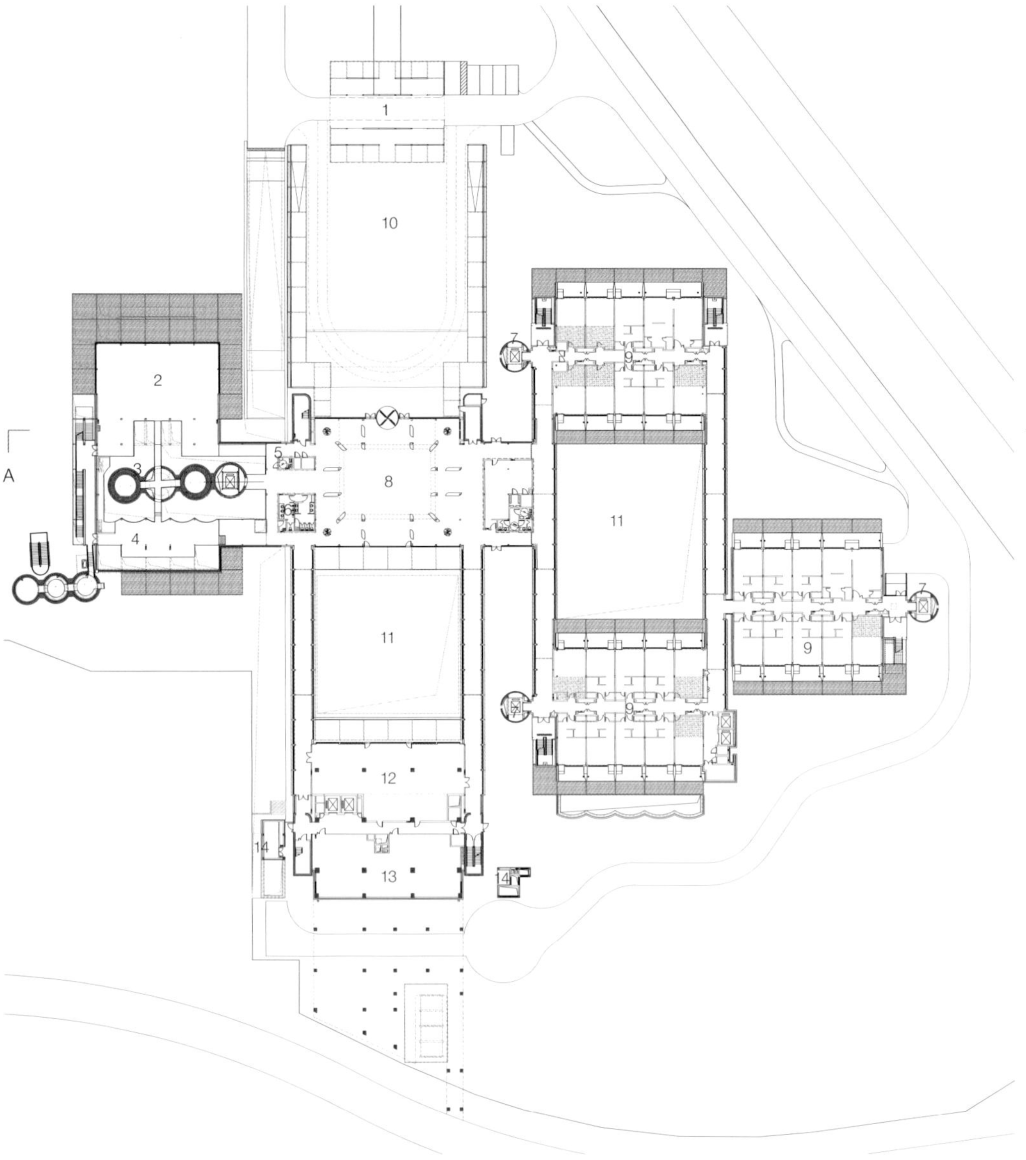

First-floor plan of hotel

1. Main entrance foyer
2. Lobby
3. Experience hall
4. Café
5. Strong and weak electric well
6. Restroom
7. Outdoor glass elevator
8. Lobby
9. Guestroom area
10. Main entrance courtyard
11. Sunken courtyard
12. All-day dining
13. Kitchen
14. Equipment room

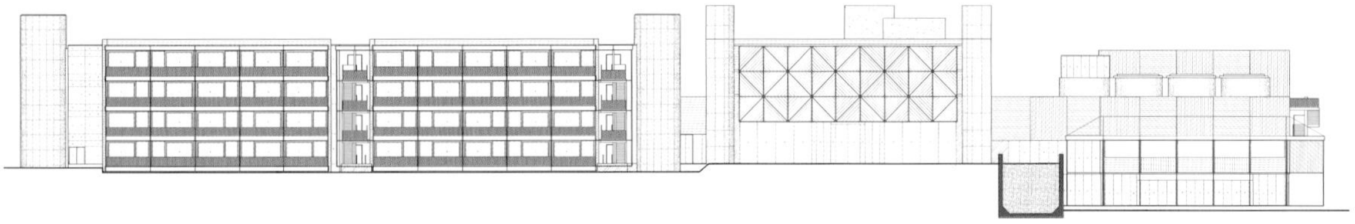

South elevation of hotel

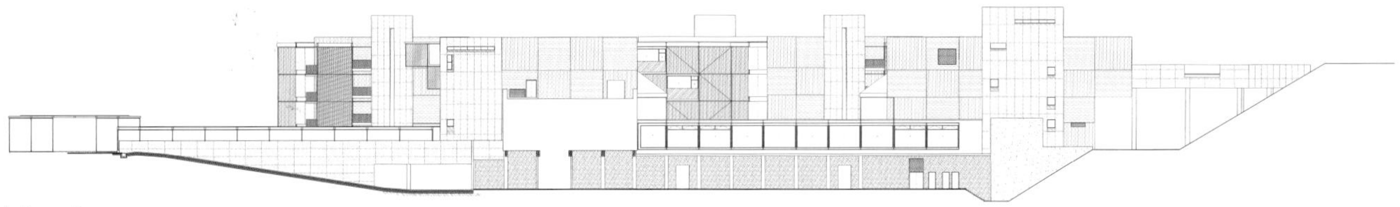

A-A section

View of hotel construction site

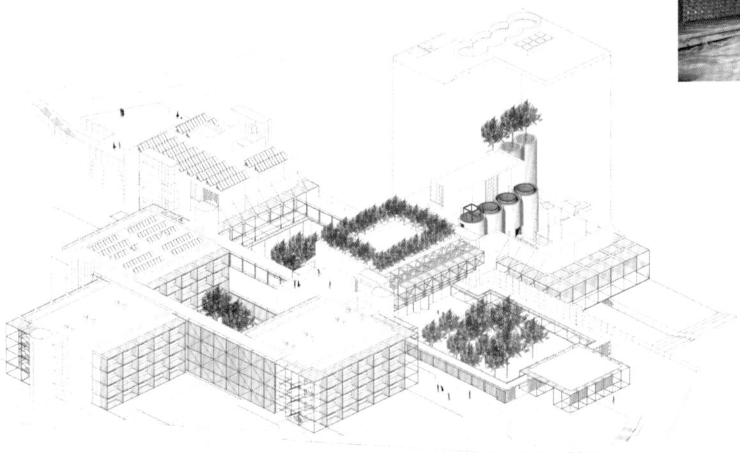

Axonometric diagram of hotel

Rendering of hotel's public area

The Future Garden

Land-Based Rationalism Design & Research Center

Architect: Land-Based Rationalism Design & Research Center, China Architecture Design & Research Group
Principal architect: Cui Kai, Guan Fei, Yang Lin
Design team: Jiang Xin, Zhou Yilin, Wang Jun, Zhao Chunlong, Li Meirong, Zhang Yu, Wang Ziang
Structural engineer: Wang Ji, Ye Yao, Wang Jianzhe, Wan Siyu
Electrical engineer: Wang Sixiang, Zhang Ya, Huo Danyang
Interior design: Zhang Zhejing
Landscape: Atelier DYJG
Area: 46,600 square meters
Completion: In progress
Photography: Tian Fangfang

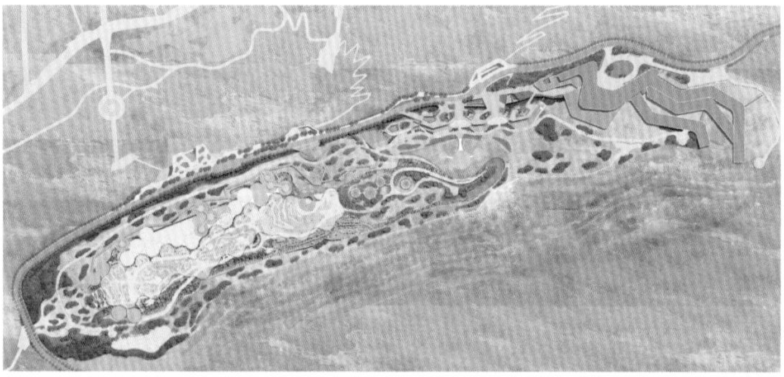

Site plan

Confronted with the enormous scale of the remnants of the Mount Kong mine pit, academician Cui Kai and his team decided to borrow the imagery of traditional Chinese landscape paintings, employing ecological restoration as a concept, technological innovation as a means, and artistic experience as a context, to create a magnificent garden of the future, which revives the abandoned mine pit into a landscape wonderland.

1. Mystic cloud pond
By integrating large mist generators in the unique environment, clouds are created at the bottom of the mine pit, which convey a rich humanistic atmosphere and landscape poetry. Similar to a traditional ink painting, the clouds and mist gradually fill the pit, hiding the majestic cliff wall and the water pond, thus forming a cloud pond.

2. Time and space tunnel
The design provides a unique experience to visitors entering the Future Garden by transforming an existing mining tunnel and its vertical shaft. Visitors pass through a 140-meter-long horizontal tunnel equipped with multisensory sound and light installations to reach a 30-meter-deep shaft with a diameter of about 14 meters. From there, they can ascend to the Underwater botanical garden via elevator.

3. Underwater botanical garden
The botanical garden stands at the bottom of the site's deepest pit, presenting a dreamy and futuristic atmosphere along the concept of a shimmering botanical garden. A 20,000-square-meter roof surface consisting of nearly 16,000 square meters of umbrella-shaped pergolas and 6,000 square meters of roof area for commercial spaces is evenly covered with recyclable water, with an overall water depth of 10 centimeters, and 35 centimeters in specific plant cultivation areas. The roof is level with the side of the pit, reflecting the towering cliff walls to the south like a mirror, enhancing the visual effects of dusk, dawn, rain, and fog. Inspired by lotus leaves, the structure is composed of 42 umbrella-shaped units with a diameter of 21 meters, while the overall form resembles an artificial tree. The main reticulated shell structure is made of stainless steel with a reflective finishing applied to the surface of the columns in order to make them appear as slim as possible. They also reflect the surrounding environment and blend in with the existing plants. The water roof employs acrylic for the bottom of the pool, as well as a secondary structure, making the overall roof surface more transparent.

Aerial view of botanical garden

View of botanical garden construction site

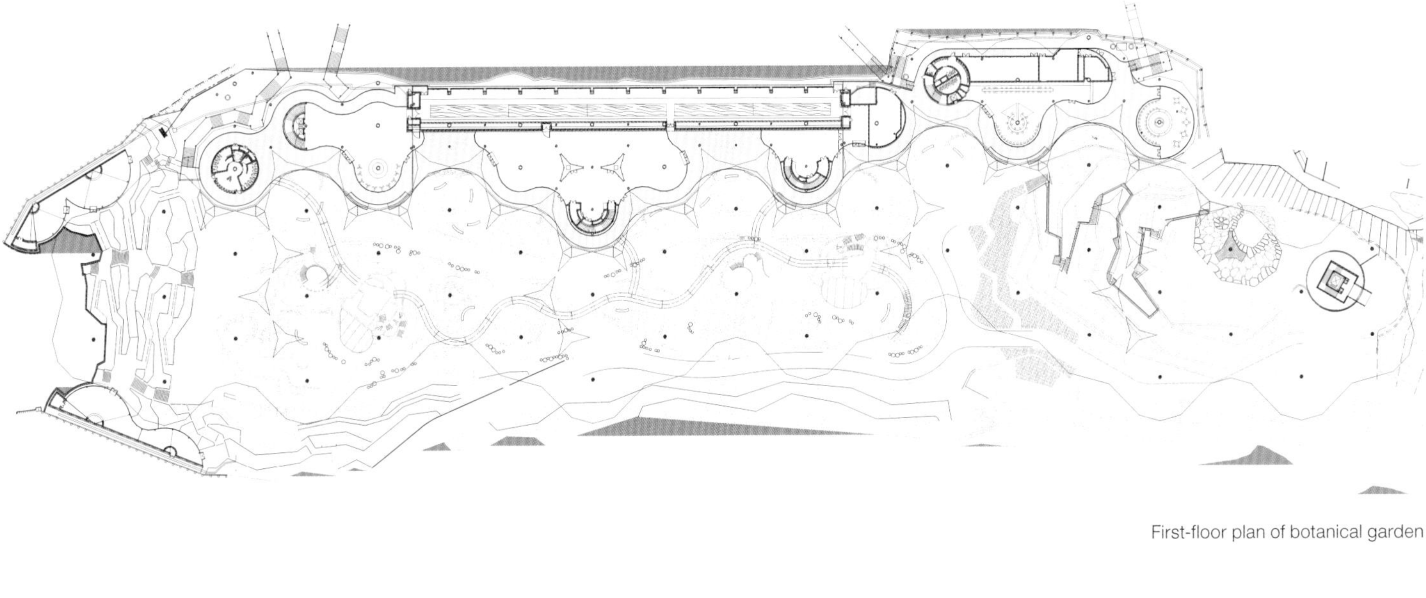

First-floor plan of botanical garden

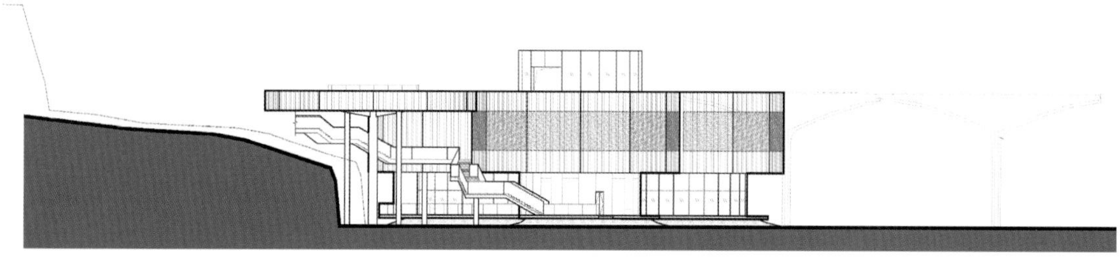

Elevation of botanical garden

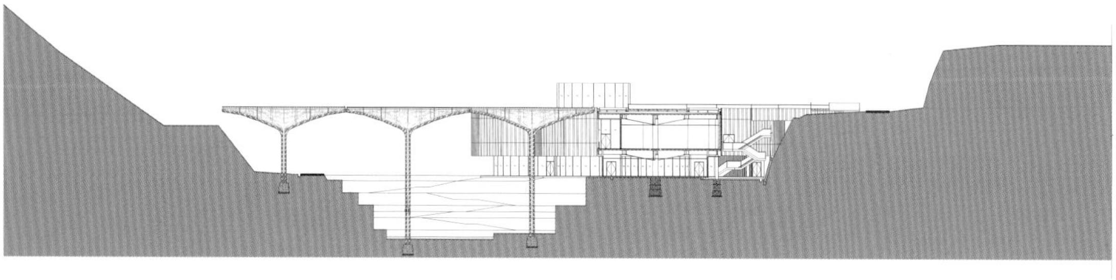

Section of botanical garden

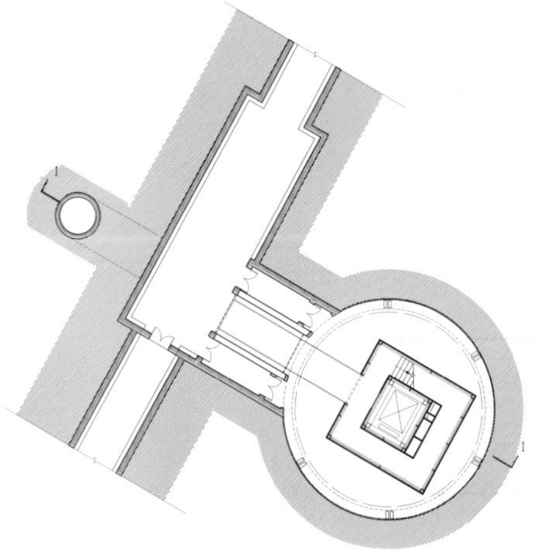

Plan of mine pit elevator

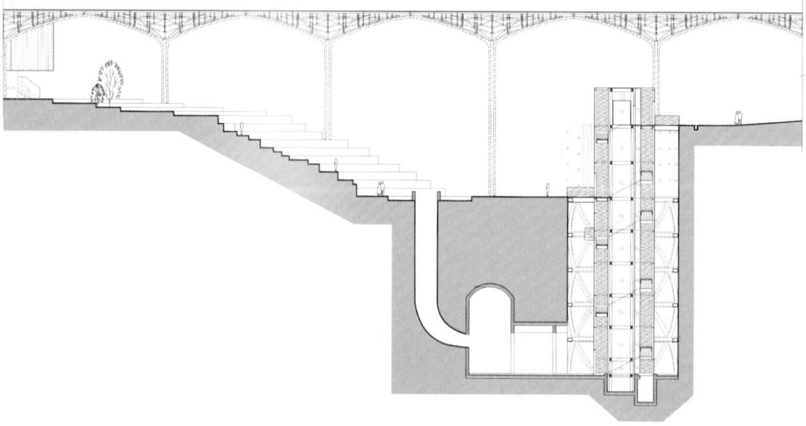

Section of mine pit elevator

4. Cliff theater

The 1.2-kilometer-long, 200-meter-high slope of the mine pit is magnificent, appearing like an enormous landscape painting during the day, and transforming at night into a backdrop for an elaborate light show that is projected onto the cliff. Featuring indoor and outdoor platforms, as well as private rooms, staggered grandstands are located opposite the cliff wall, specifically designed for viewing the light show. In total, they can accommodate around 2,500 spectators. A huge stage in front of the cliff appears as if its floating on a body of water; the reflections of the mountains and the lighting of the water create another stunning scene and present the stage as a performance venue to be viewed from the grandstands.

5. Banyan Tree Future Garden Hotel

Located on the easternmost side of the site, the building is elevated above the mine pit, connecting its northern and southern sides like a bridge. Inspired by an unfinished stele at the Yangshan Quarry, the overall shape of the building extends along the pit, but is elevated to separate the new building from the mine. This allows for the preservation of the original cliff and existing topography, while maximizing the unique character of the Banyan Tree Hotel. The elevated structure reminds visitors of the original layout of the pit and further reflects on its nature as a park built in a former mine. By carving holes into the structure, 115 guestrooms are created, creating a simulation for guests to experience the lives of cave dwellers. The public areas of the hotel are designed to be a single block of stone, which mutually complements the cliff to reach an overall spatial climax.

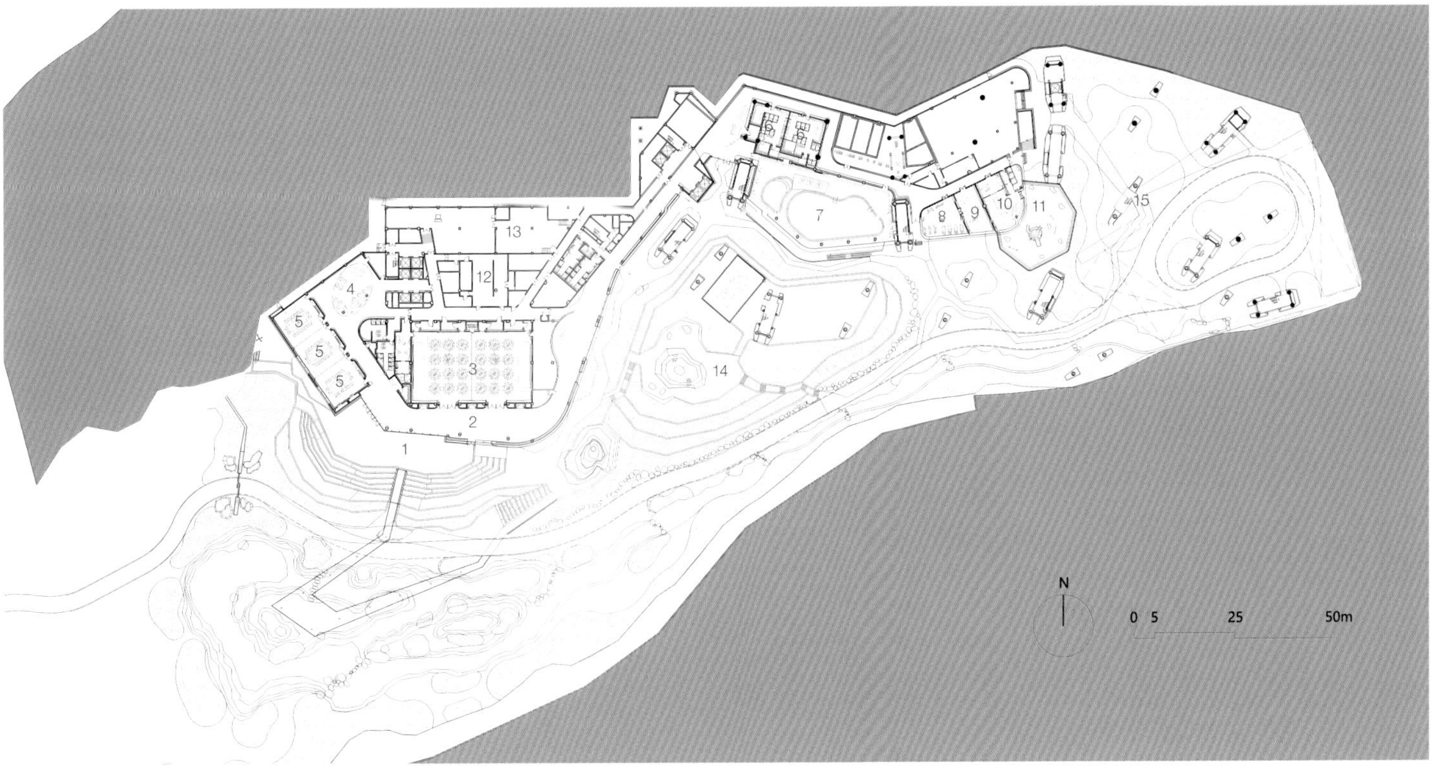

First-floor plan of Banyan Tree Hotel

1. Entrance of banquet hall
2. Foyer of banquet hall
3. Banquet hall
4. Tea break area
5. Conference room
6. Fitting room
7. Swimming pool
8. Gym
9. Yoga room
10. Children's room
11. Children's outdoor playground
12. Kitchen
13. Equipment room
14. Exterior platform

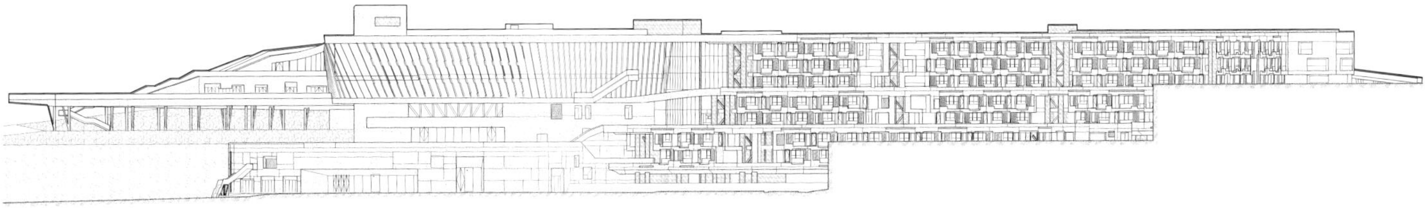

Elevation of Banyan Tree Hotel

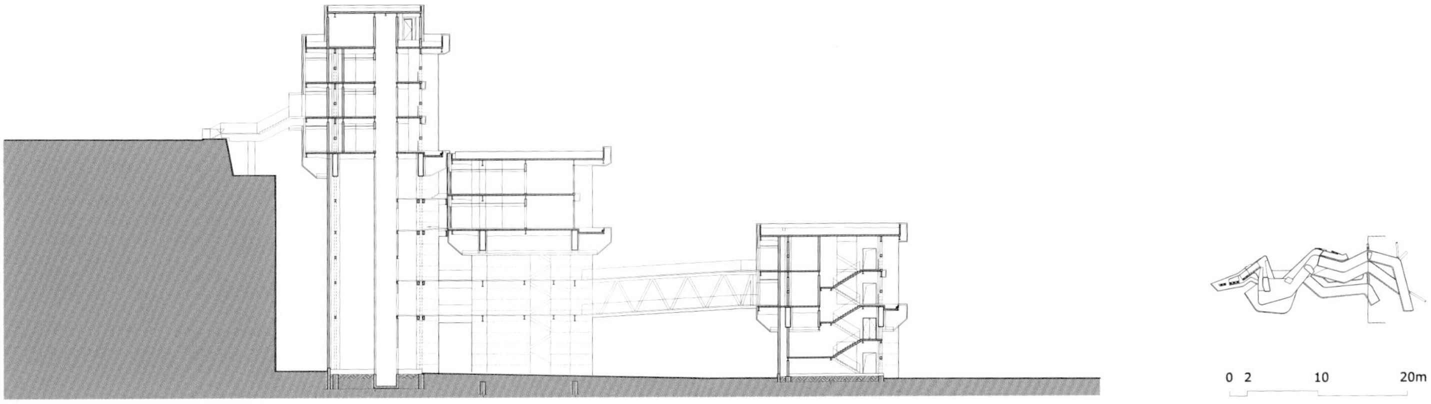

Section of Banyan Tree Hotel

Exterior rendering of Banyan Tree Hotel

View of Banyan Tree Hotel construction site

View of cliff theater construction site

Exterior rendering of cliff theater and stage

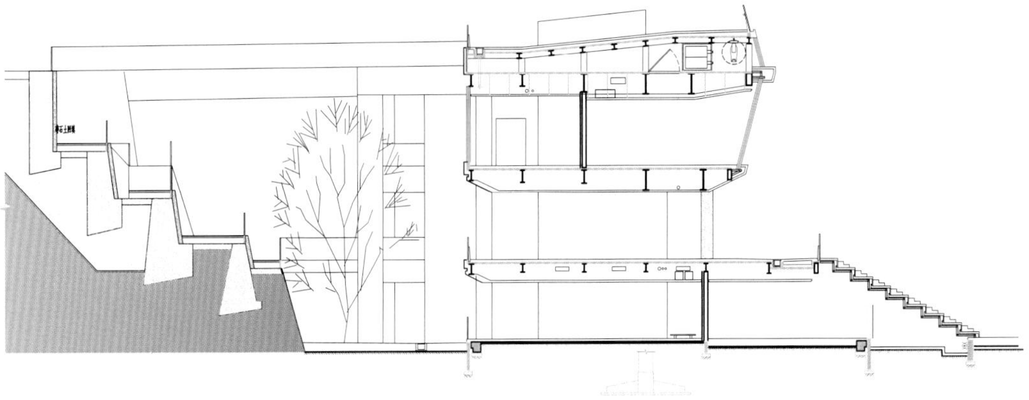

A-A section of cliff theater

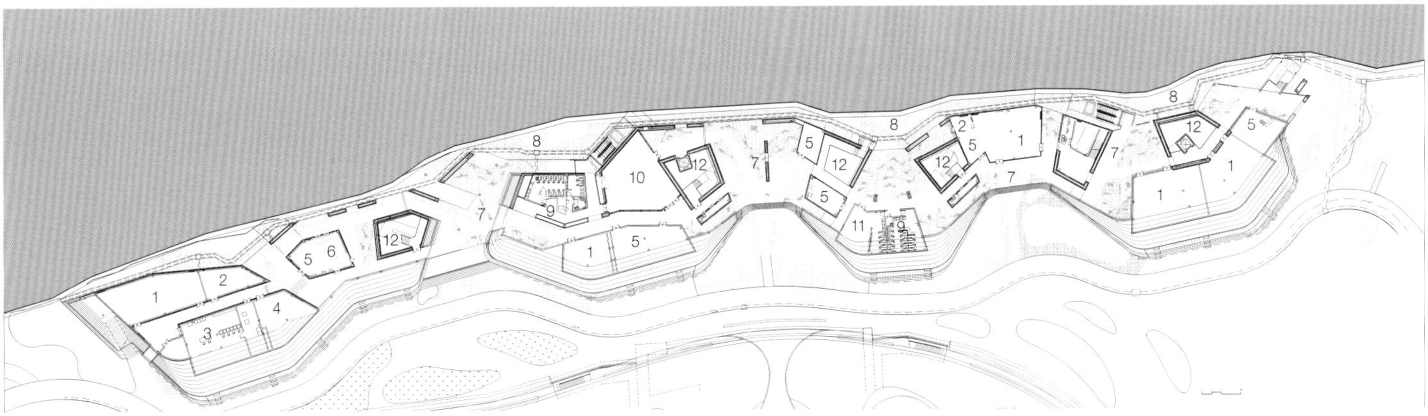

First-floor plan of cliff theater

1. Electricity room
2. Office
3. Fire and security control room
4. Water mist control room
5. Air-conditioning equipment room
6. Landscape garden
7. Cliff garden
8. Restroom
9. Preparation room
10. Shops
11. Garden

The Westin Hotel

Wang Jianguo, Shan Feng

Principal architect: Wang Jianguo, Shan Feng
Design team: Wang Jianguo, Shan Feng, Liu Huiyu, Hou Yanpu, Yao Xinyue, Tang Weiwei, Wang Jifei, Shen Yuchi
Structural engineer: Yang Bo, Zhou Chenkai, Li Liang
Electrical engineer: Ye Fei
Area: 43,294 square meters
Completion: In progress
Photography: Tian Fangfang, Wang Jianguo, Yao Xinyue, Sun Xiaoqian, Shi Fei

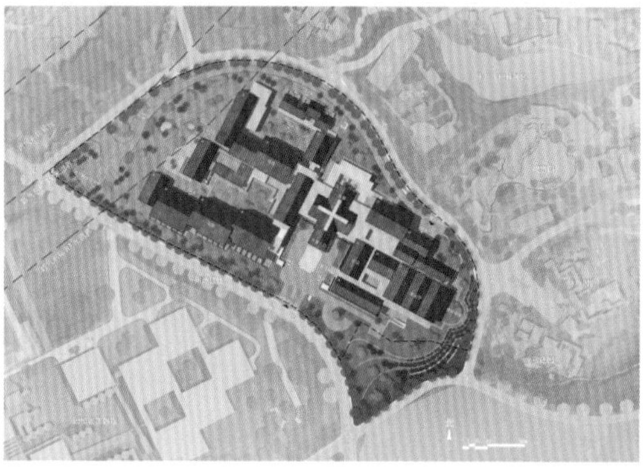
Site plan

The Westin Hotel of the Horticultural Expo, Tangshan is located to the east of the main exhibition hall for the Horticultural Exhibition of Jiangsu Province and right next to the City Exhibition Park. The total land area of the project is 45,115 square meters, with a total construction area of 43,294 square meters, including 32,009 square meters aboveground and 11,285 square meters underground.

The design borrows from traditional Chinese landscape imagery and comprehensively includes the interaction and visual relationship with the surrounding natural landscape and the themed city gardens in its considerations. It echoes their shape and topography to create an elegant and natural architectural image.

The building follows the site's terrain, which is elevated in the northwest and lower in the southeast. The relatively large public areas are concentrated in the south side, while the guestroom complexes with their courtyards and changing building heights are placed in the north. Between them lies the central lobby, which forms a visual corridor that leads from the roadside toward the natural garden landscape, while also enabling an effective organization of the visitor flow. Breaking up the entire space into parts, which creates gradual drops in the height of the building volumes, and the treatment of the sloping roofs, makes the structure appear like a stacked village when viewed from the direction of the themed city gardens, the two together forming an integrated scenery. The design also carefully avoids the West-East Gas Pipeline, which passes the site to the northwest, taking advantage of the required building distance to create a relaxing atmosphere with outdoor hot spring pools near the indoor swimming pool and spa area.

As an international five-star resort hotel, the Westin Hotel of the Horticultural Expo hosts 260 rooms set against the backdrop of nature, including 80 rooms with private hot springs, providing an ideal space for high-level exhibitions and forums in Nanjing's Jiangning district. As it creates a comfortable and livable resort for guests, it also expands the range of hotels serving Mount Tang.

View of Westin Hotel construction site

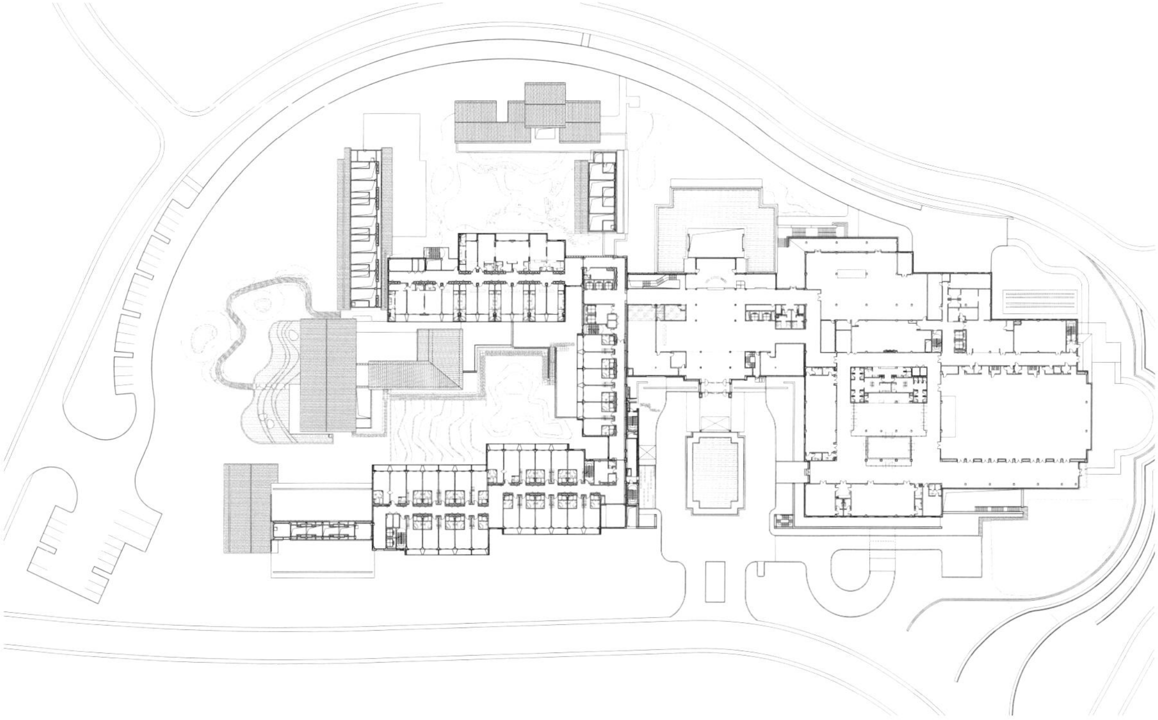

74.5-m-level floor plan

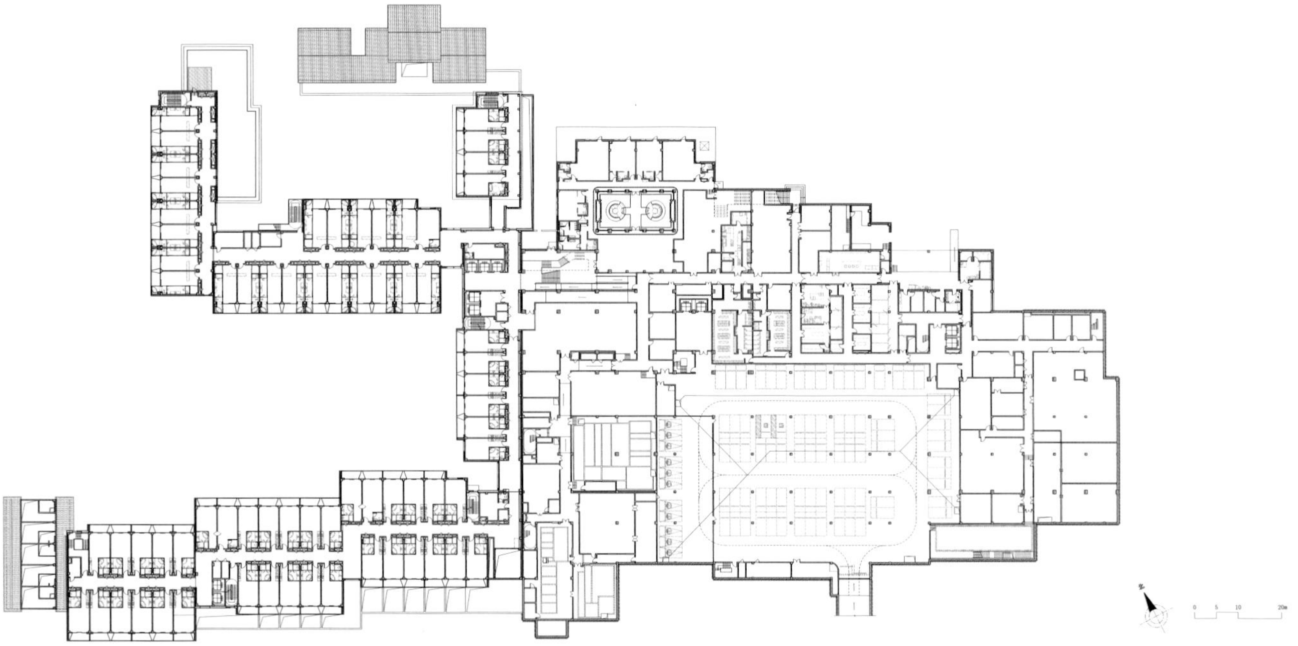

70.8-m-level floor plan

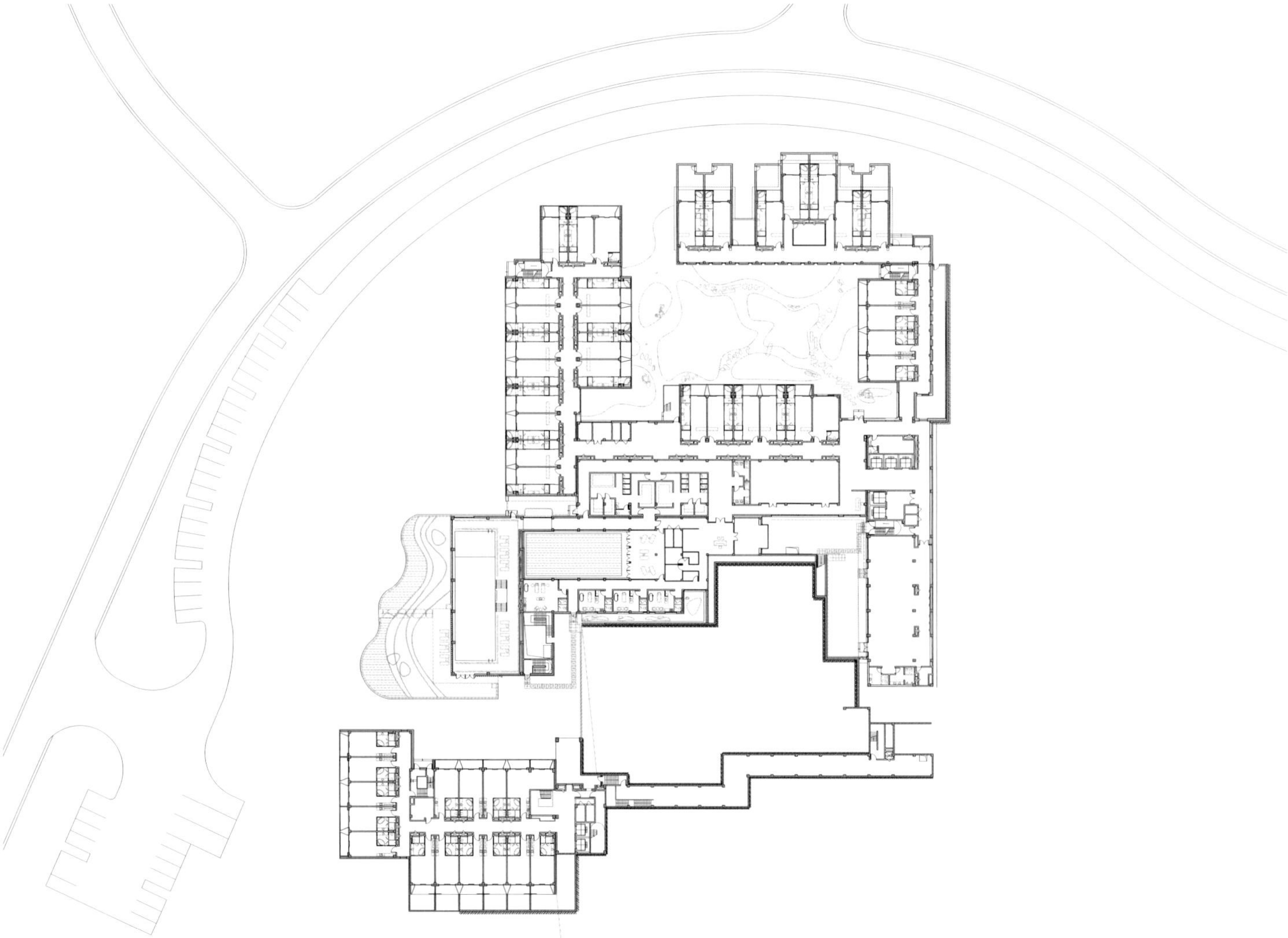

64.3-m-level floor plan

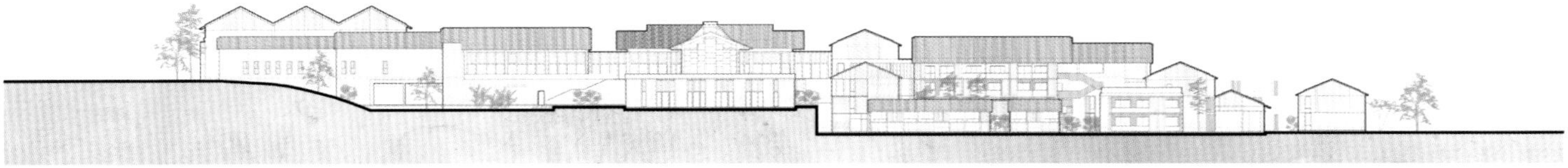

South-west evelation (elevation of main entrance)

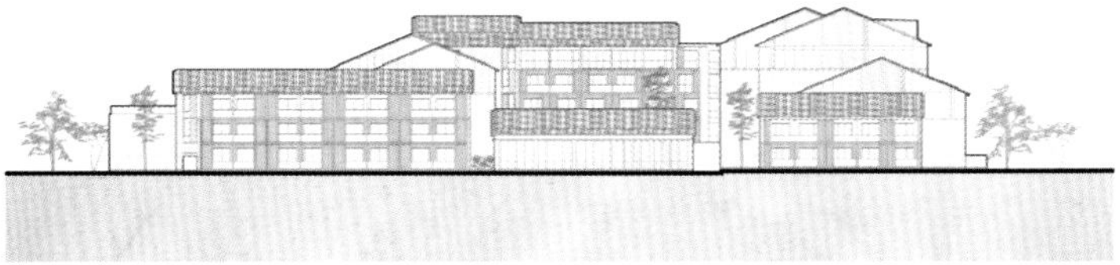

North-west elevation

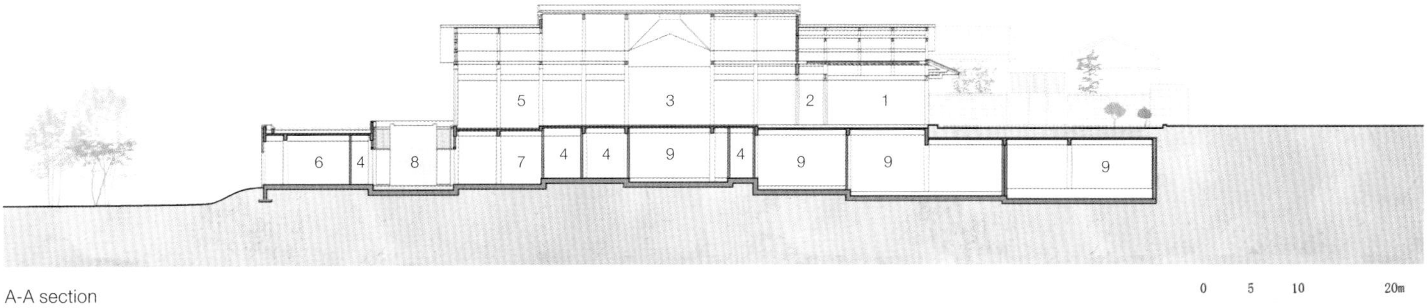

A-A section

1. Entrance porch
2. Hallway
3. Lobby
4. Corridor
5. Lobby bar
6. Private room
7. Chinese dining hall
8. Garden
9. Equipment room

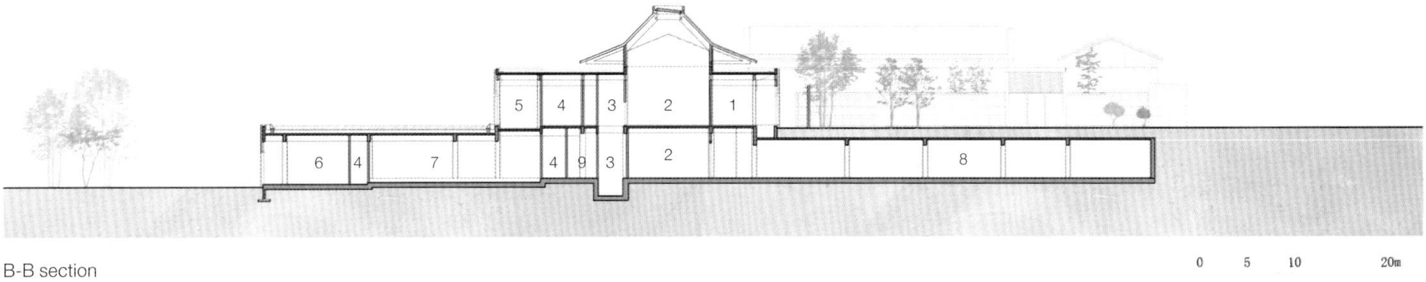

B-B section

1. Business center
2. Elevator hall
3. Elevator shaft
4. Corridor
5. Lobby bar
6. Private room
7. Chinese cuisine kitchen
8. Parking lot
9. Equipment room

View of main entrance

1 | 2
3 | 4

1-2. Exterior view of Westin Hotel
3-4. Construction site view of Westin Hotel

Westin Hotel and surrounding scenery

Aerial view of Westin Hotel

The First Entrance Building and Visitor Center

AZL Architects

Architect: AZL Architects
Principal architect: Zhang Lei
Design team: Jin Haibo, Hong Siyao
Construction period: In progress
Photography: Tian Fangfang, Zhang Lei

Site plan

The visitor center of the 11th Horticultural Exposition of Jiangsu Province sits to the west of the main entrance of the exposition park, with a section of steps that face the plaza. The continuous steps and resting platforms form a vertical connection between the plaza and its roof, outlining a design that creates a delightful space while emphasizing a spatial symbol. The nature of "new organic architecture" is to eliminate the boundary between architectural form and the actual functional space; the form itself composes an open and welcoming public space, which users are willing to experience and interact with. New organic architecture helps redefine the expanding distance between architectural spaces and people, with the hope of bringing the human intervention of construction—which has been grossly invading the natural environment for a long time—back to its basics as a platform for human life. The wide steps of the building facing the entrance plaza create a rich sense of "ritual" as they are ascended, making the spatial experience in that moment unique. People can experience the flow of time and a different aspect of nature through the space. The richness in the spatial creation also contributes to establishing a living space that produces a sense of ritual and belonging—a unique bond between people, architecture, and the outside world is thus formed. Ritualistic places arise from tradition and point toward a new civilization, thus representing symbols and landmarks in themselves.

New organic architecture respects and promotes not only the use of traditional architectural craftsmanship, but also the research and application of appropriate local materials and construction methods to evoke the physical and spiritual nature of the site itself. For example, the façade of the visitor center is clad in gabion walls with stones gathered from a quarry near the entrance of the expo park. The concept of "building with nature" not only emphasizes regional materials and construction methods, but more importantly, respects the fundamental human desire to return to nature in the process. New organic architecture also creates an ecosystem: the roof of the visitor center leaves plenty of space for natural plant growth, which catalyzes the merging of the physical space with the natural environment.

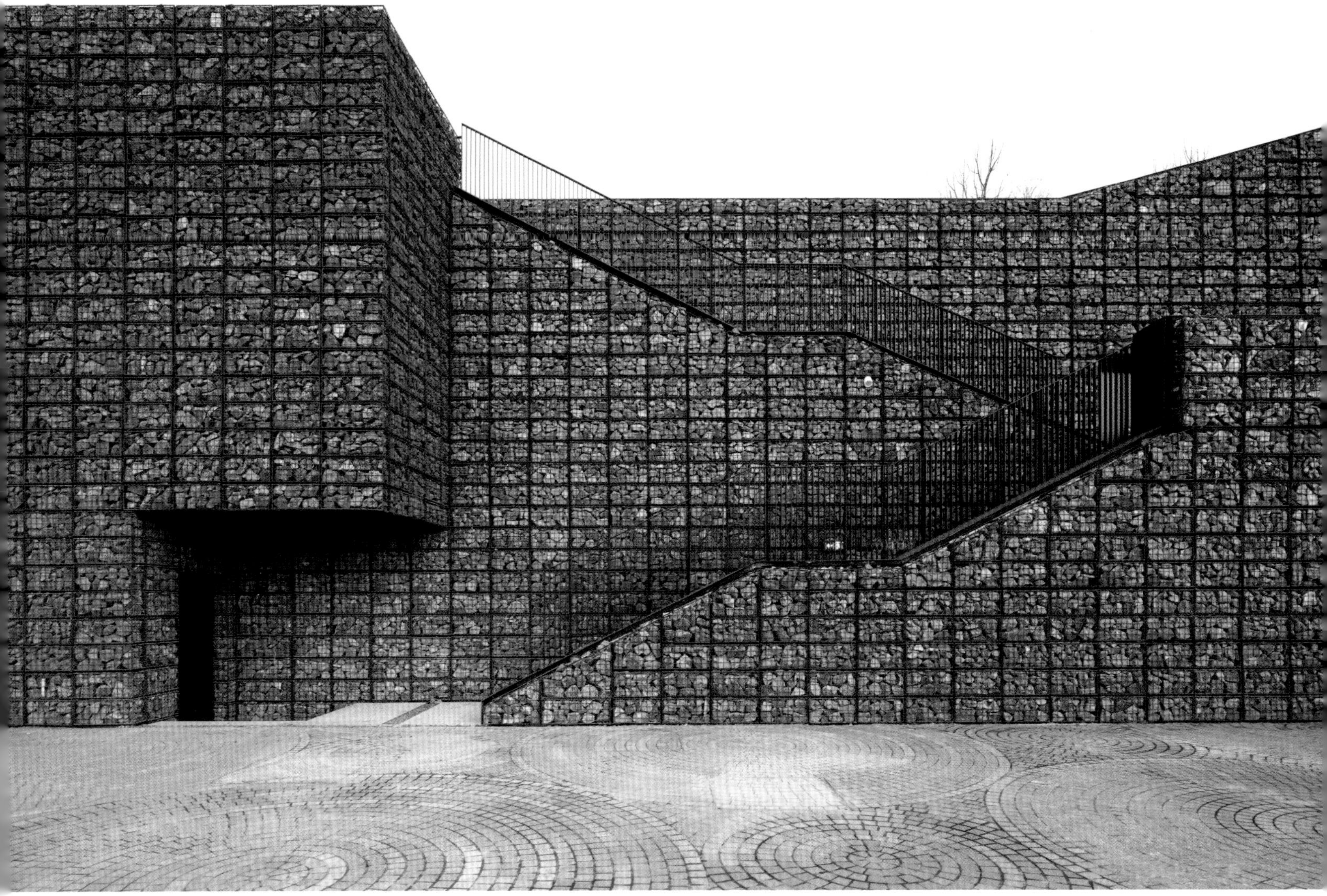

View of the first entrance building and visitor center construction site

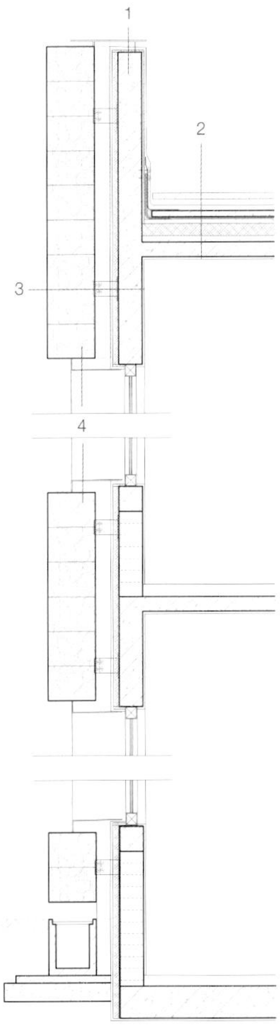

1. 1 cm rusty steel plate top
   Steel keel
   Substrate walls
2. 30 mm reddish-brown precast concrete slab
   60 mm C30 fine stone waterproof concrete
   10 mm 1:4 lime mortar
   3 mm self-adhesive polyurethane polymer
   Modified asphalt waterproofing membrane
   30 mm C20 fine stone concrete leveling layer
   65 mm extruded polystyrene sheet
   15 mm 1:2 cement mortar leveling layer
   30 mm foam concrete slope finding layer
   Cast-in-place reinforced-concrete roof panels
3. Φ8 steel cage reddish-brown fluorocarbon coating (filled with local stone)
   Hot diffusion galvanized steel keel
   3 mm flexible water-resistant putty layered leveling
   6 mm polymeric waterproofing and anti-cracking mortar
   40 mm cotton rock slabs
   15 mm 1:3 waterproof mortar leveling layer
   Substrate walls
4. Rusted steel plate window coverings
   Steel cage wall

1. 30 mm reddish-brown precast concrete slab
   50 mm 1:2 cement mortar bonding layer with embedded light strip
   20 mm C20 fine stone concrete leveling layer
   C30 waterproof fine stone concrete treads same as roofing structure
2. Fagopyrum
   Planting soil
   Fine stone concrete leveling layer
   C30 waterproof fine stone concrete treads same as roofing structure

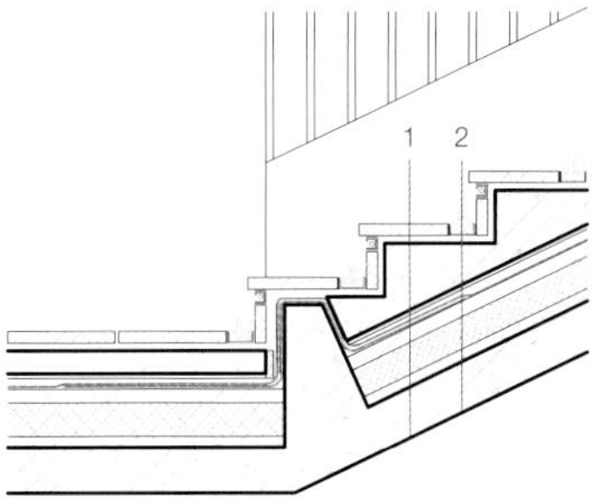

1. Fine leaf manzanita
   Planting soil
   Gravel filter layer with 20–50 grain size
   Geotextile
   Root-puncture-resistant waterproofing membrane
   30 mm drainage tabs with bumps up
   C30 waterproof fine stone concrete flower pond
   10 mm 1:4 lime mortar
   3 mm C20 fine stone concrete leveling layer
   65 mm extruded polystyrene board
   15 mm 1:2 cement mortar leveling layer
   30 mm foam concrete slope layer
   Cast-in-place waterproof reinforced-concrete roof panel

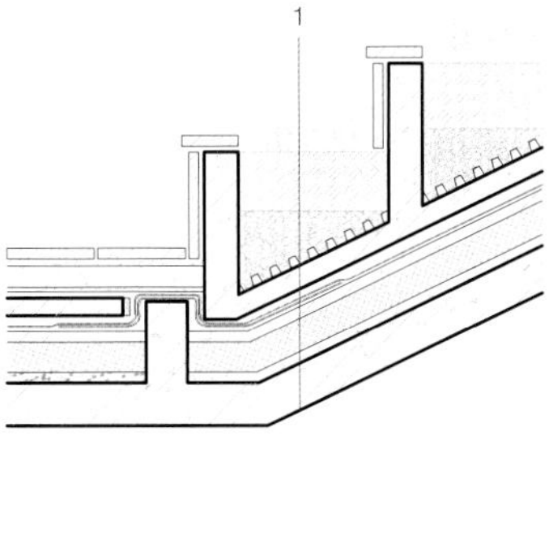

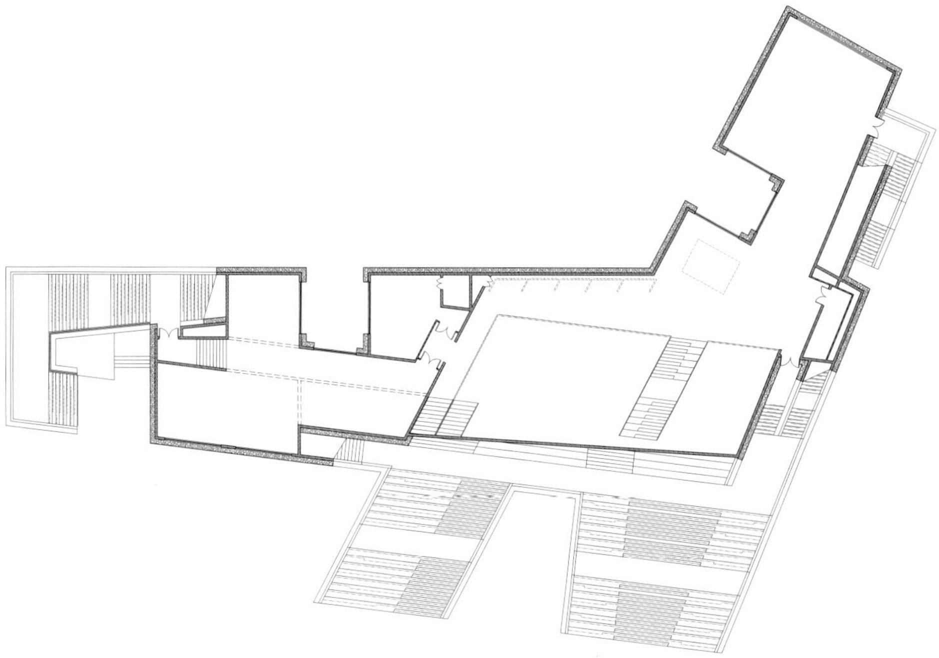

Second-floor plan of visitor center

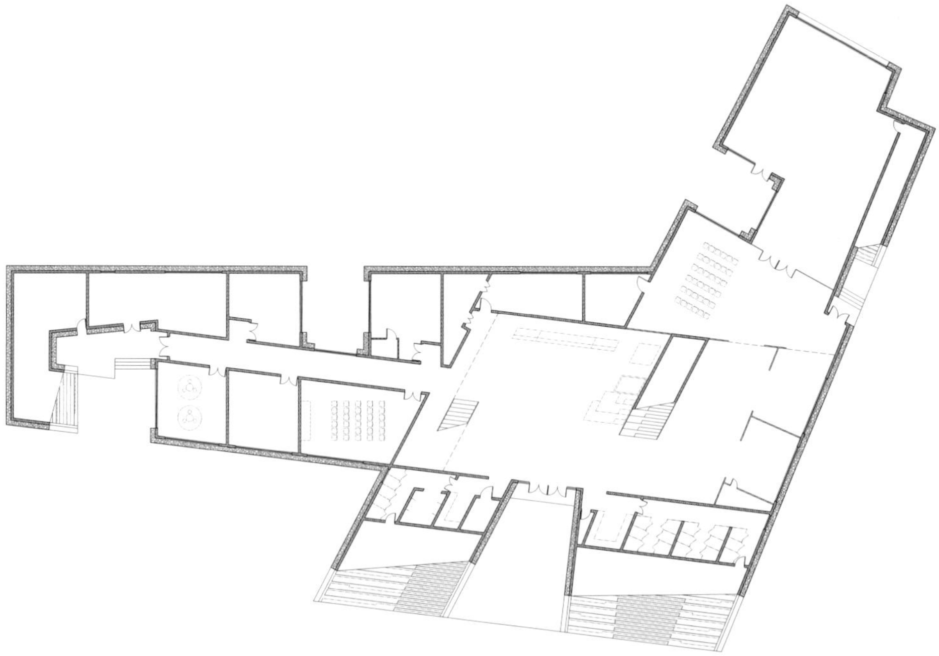

First-floor plan of visitor center

Elevation of visitor center

Exterior view of visitor center construction site

Interior view of visitor center construction site

Model of the first entrance building and visitor center

Rendering of the first entrance building and visitor center

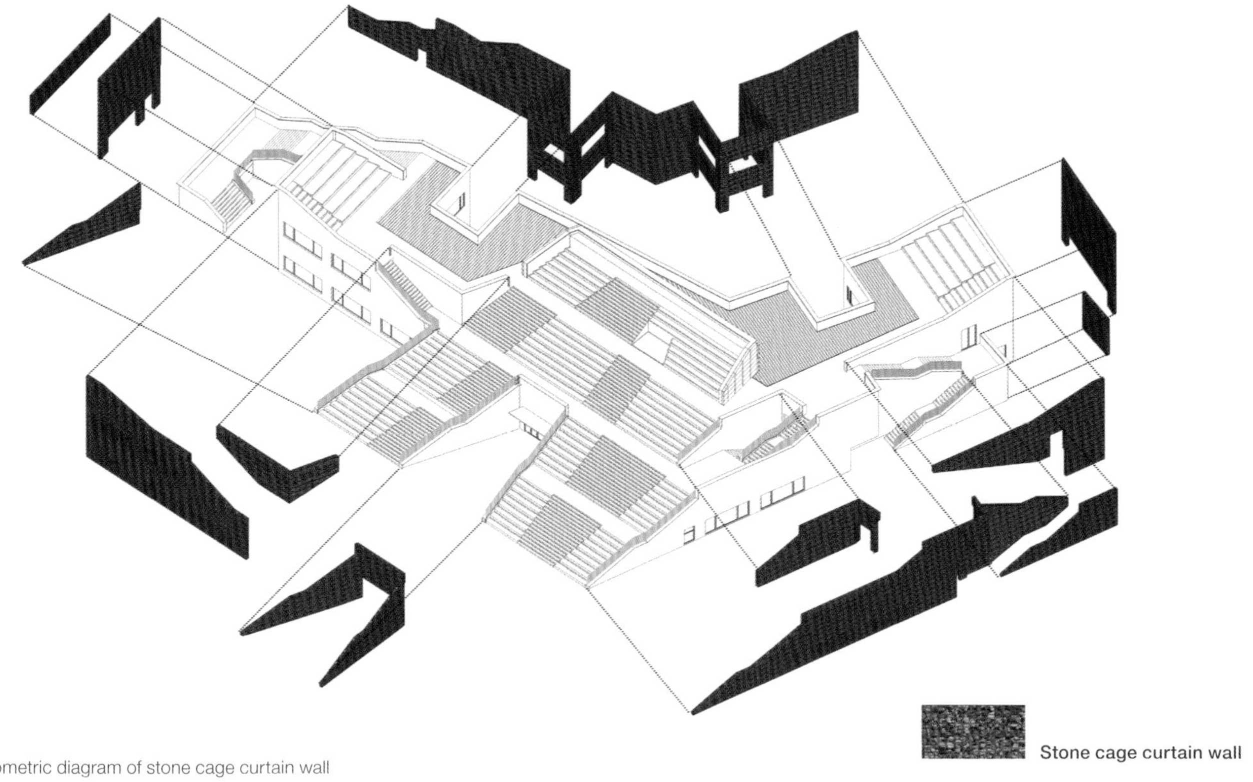

Axonometric diagram of stone cage curtain wall

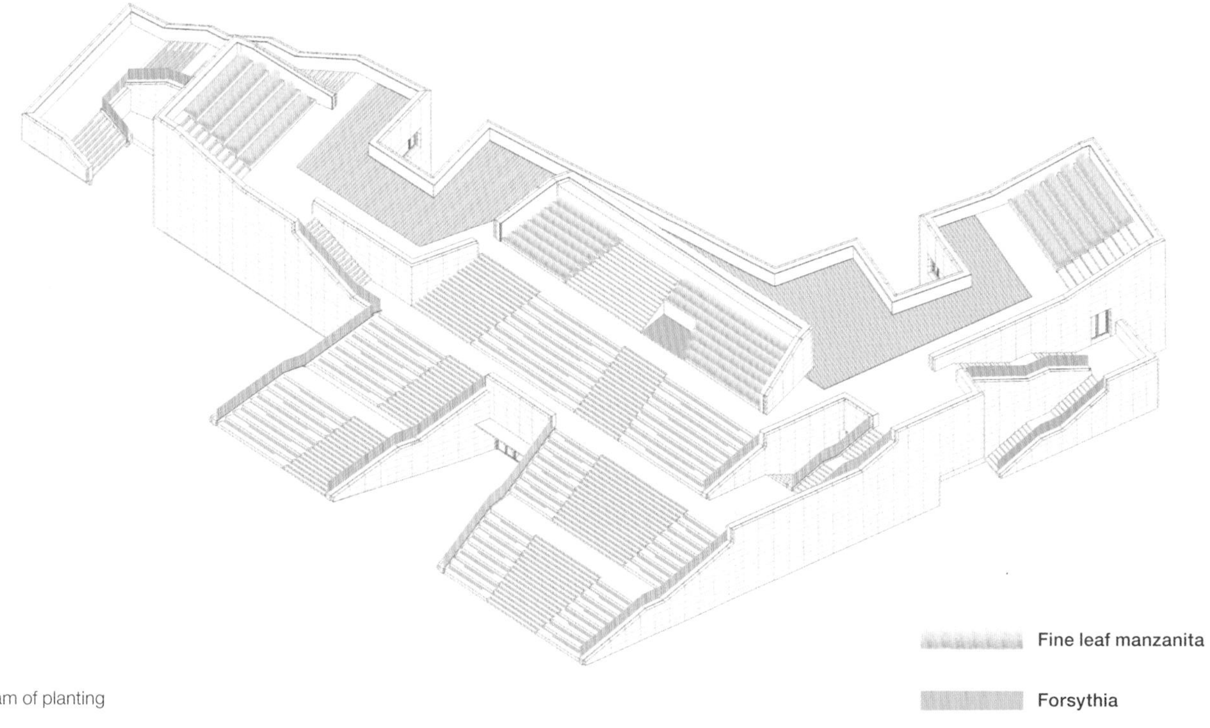

Diagram of planting

Exterior view of visitor center construction site

View of detail construction site

View of stone cage construction site

Geology Museum

Atelier Deshaus

Architect: Atelier Deshaus
Principal architect: Liu Yichun
Project architects: Chan Xiongai, Shen Wen, Chen Yu, Wang Yi, Zhang Xiaoqi, Chen Yuwei, Chen Xu, Chen Chih-han
Collaborator: Nanjing Yangtze River Urban Architectural Design Co., Ltd.
Site area: 37,497 square meters
Floor area: 12,856 square meters
Completion: In progress
Photography: Tian Fangfang

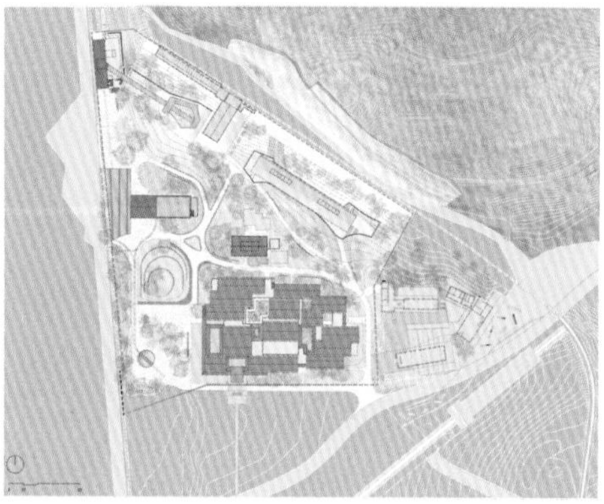

Site plan

Dedicated to the popularization of geological science and related culture during the horticultural exhibition, the Geology Museum also cleverly incorporates the North Gate Station of the park train and a range of comprehensive services offered to visitors at the expo park's northern entrance. In this way, the approach becomes an effective answer to the sustainability concerns of the project. Furthermore, the design fully integrates the geological features and ecological environment of the site, preserving the existing large trees, characteristic vegetation, and natural topography to the greatest extent, while also retaining the invaluable industrial remnants on the site. The natural and human histories, as well as the contemporary culture of the site are interconnected and interwoven into a new organic whole by implanting new contemporary buildings derived from the analysis and extraction of the architectural vocabulary of the existing industrial heritage. This approach also enhances the overall cultural image of the northern entrance area of the expo park.

According to the preliminary investigation of the site, the northeast side of the construction area neighbors the geological profile of Bangchui Mountain. The Geology Museum, hence needs to fully take into consideration the organic relationship between the future indoor display and the geological profile. The site is also an important part of the former China Cement Factory, which was established in September 1921 and identified as one of the earliest cement plants in the nation, following the Qixin Cement Factory, which was first invested in by Japan. From the point of view of industrial heritage, it is essential to fully explore the historical and cultural value of the cement factory in the design of the project. Adding to these characteristics, the site is also heavily covered in a distinctly distributed forest, which creates a pleasant atmosphere and a strong sense of history. The entire 60,000-square-meter site—including the 5,000 square meters of the four Huase Station plots—and its surrounding environment, as well as its rich historical, cultural, and geological elements have been comprehensively considered in the planning and design process.

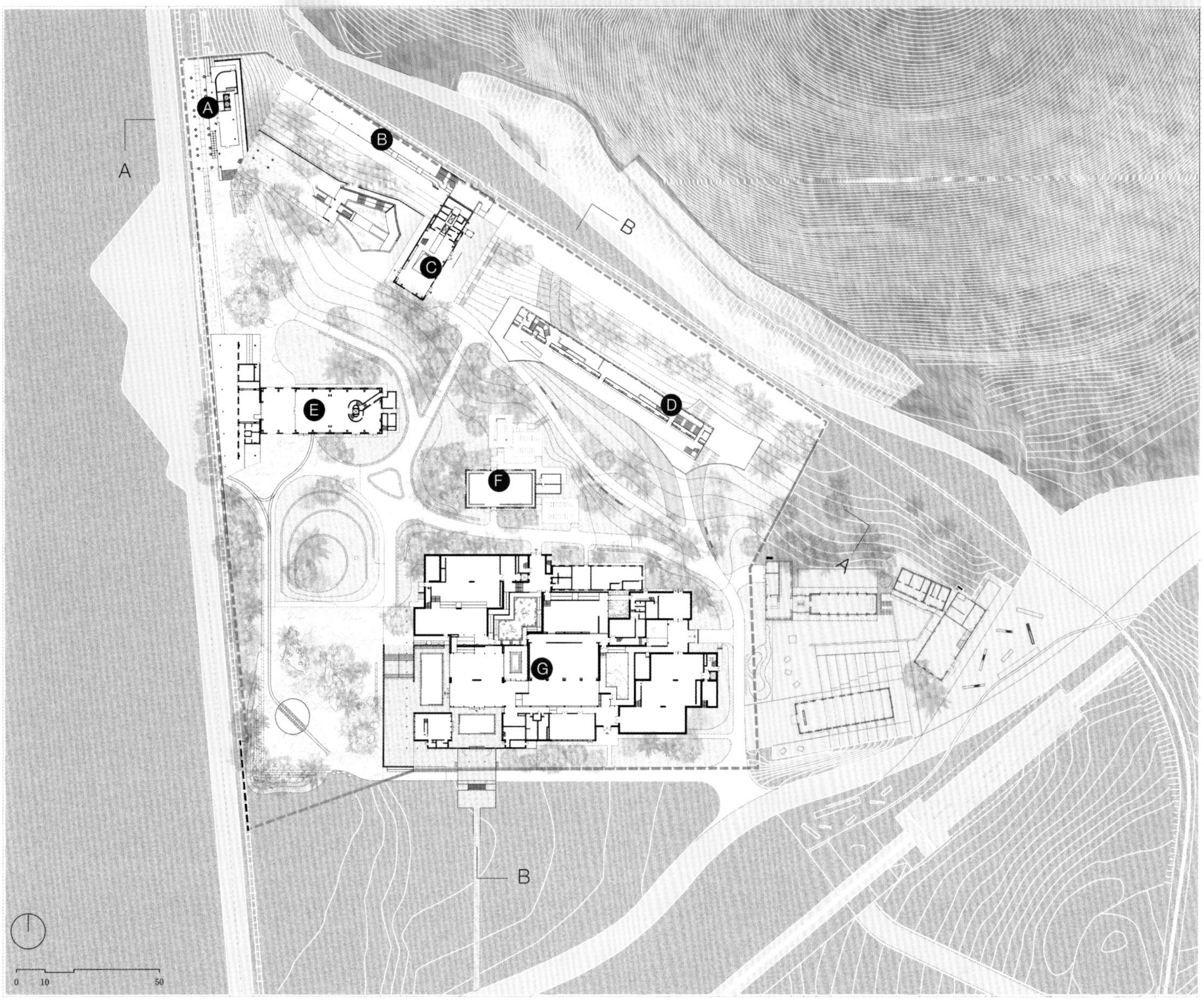

First-floor plan of Geology Museum

A. Café and restaurant
B. Railway station
C. Transition space
D. Culture Museum
E. Railway station and Visitor Center
F. Multifuction hall
G. Exhibition center

Exterior view of café and restaurant area

1 | 3
2

1. Interior view of transition space construction site
2. Interior view of multifunction hall construction site
3. Exterior view of café and restaurant area

1. Exterior view of railway station construction site
2. Interior view of railway station construction site
3. Interior view of exhibition center construction site

Detail of Culture Museum section

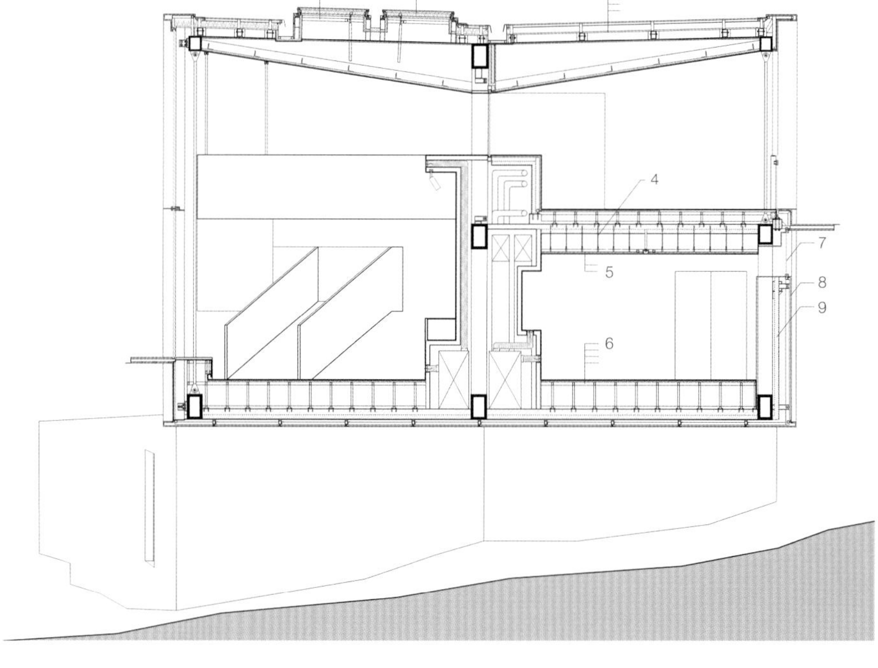

1. 3 mm fluorocarbon-sprayed aluminum veneer
   Aluminum alloy panel
   Aluminum alloy frame
   60x60x4 rectangular steel tube
2. 130 mm class A thermal insusation rockwool
   Electric window openning putter
3. 1.0 mm Al-Mg-Mn upright seaming board
   Waterproof membrane
   Sound-absorbing layer: 25 mm glass wool, 24 kg/m^3
   0.8 mm galvanized profiled steel sheet
4. F8 rod: M8 expansion bolt fixed
   50 mm main keel: 50x15x1.5
   50 mm secondary keel: 50x20x0.6
   300x600 arrayed light steel keel ceiling
5. 12 mm flame retardant board
   Double 9.5 mm gypsum board
6. Fireproof floor
   Soundproof and moisture-proof mat
   Double 12 mm flame retardant board
   40x60x4 mm galvanized square steel tube
7. Hollow tempered ultra-white glass
   6 mm ag+12 mm ar+6 mm ag
8. 20 mm anodized aluminum honeycomb panel
   1mm aluminum veneer+18 mm aluminum honeycomb
   +1 mm aluminum panel
9. Insulation layer, waterproof layer

Exterior view of Culture Museum

1. Interior view of Culture Museum
2-3. Exterior view of Culture Museum construction site

Exterior view of Visitor Center

A-A section

Exterior rendering of exhibition center

Interior rendering of exhibition center

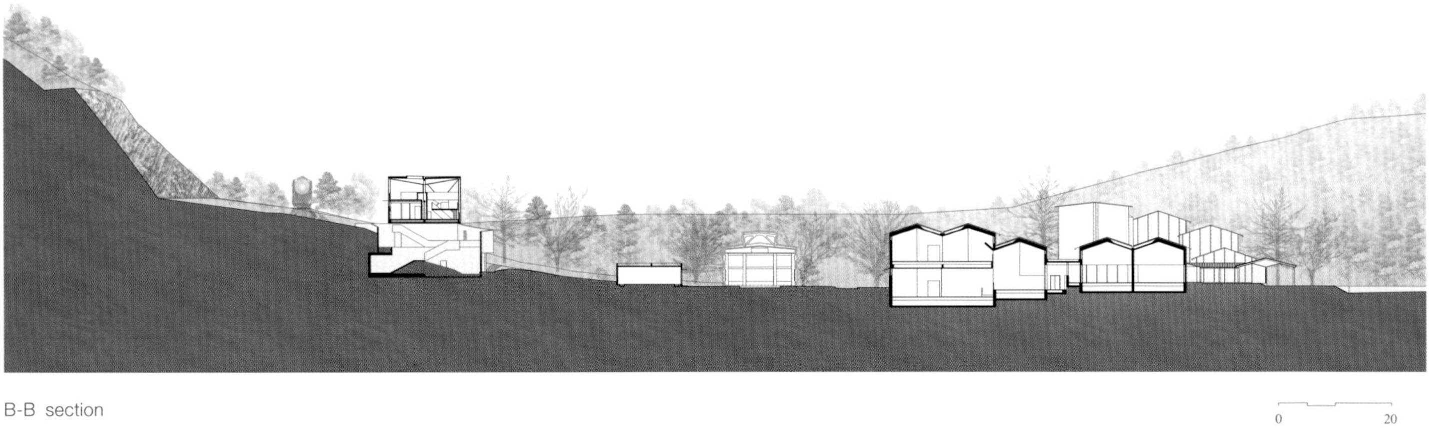

B-B section

Interior rendering of exhibition center

Interior rendering of exhibition center

Rendering of exhibition center courtyard

Radisson Blu Hotel

Archi-Union Architects

Architect: Archi-Union Architecture Design Co., Ltd.
Principal architect: Philip F. Yuan
Design team: Jie Gao, Weizhe Gao, Xiangping Kong, Yiyun Zhao, Teng Long
Site area: 24,577 square meters
Floor area: 34,646 square meters
Completion: In progress
Photography: Tian Fangfang

Site plan

Through geometric topological changes, the Boutique Garden Hotel located on the east side of the expo park aims for a harmonious symbiosis of the hotel's mass with the surrounding mountains, forests, and lakes. Continuity, randomness, and spontaneity play crucial roles in the creation of the space's form and site, thus remodeling the soul of the place. The integrated parameterization of geometry, structural performance, and construction robotics materialize a space of new technology.

The overall layout of the hotel is based on the existing geometric language of the earth, with a 15-meter height difference shaping the winding landscape of the site. The natural terrain is, therefore, adapted and its original geometric logic is used as a starting point for the simulation of a self-organizing multi-agent-particle algorithm. In the simulated space, the original topographic information of the site and the trajectory of people moving through the hotel becomes input to influence the movement of the particles. Driven by these parameters, the trajectories and directions of the particles spontaneously create a coherent, visible, and unified pattern of integrated paths and movements. Through the architect's subsequent optimization and integration, a semi-autonomous and spontaneous intelligent architectural form is generated. The emerging morphology divides the building into two functional areas—north and south—and five different shifts in elevation, which host interrelated and isomorphic functions such as guestrooms, lobby and reception area, wellness and spa area, as well as catering and entertainment facilities. With the nonlinear circular path of the garden expo connecting all of these facilities, the building forms its own system. It dovetails with the texture of the cliff and echoes the earth and open field to maintain a continuous association with the surrounding environment, which in turn results in a rich, interesting, and multi-directional spatial experience. The heteromorphic structural columns in the lobby and swimming pool areas are designed through digital methods that take both topological geometry and structural performance into account. This creates a dualistic balance of form and function, as well as beauty and reason, to form a comprehensive load relation with the wooden roof structure. The high-dimensional geometric aesthetic and structural rationality achieve unity in the lobby area, which is suffused with a sense of divinity.

The hotel is designed to comply with a five-star standard and features 153 guestrooms in total, in addition to a full range of hotel amenities like lobby, bar, all-day dining, Chinese restaurants, banquet halls, a conference center, a swimming pool, a gym, and hot springs, and spa facilities. The aboveground portion of the hotel is

Aerial view of hotel construction site

divided into a North Building and a South Building, connected by two covered bridges. The North Building hotel lobby on the central axis divides the space into a public and private area in the east and west wings, respectively. The east wing hosts specialty restaurants, an all-day eatery and kitchen, banquet halls, and a conference center, along with corresponding facilities. The west wing is primarily occupied by sixty-two guestrooms. The underground section of the North Building is mainly used for the hotel's logistics storage, machinery, and as storage rooms and an underground parking garage with eighty automated parking spaces.

The aboveground portion of the South Building mainly consists of guestrooms and the hotel's wellness facilities. The wellness area is concentrated in the northeast corner of the South Building. Distributed from the first to the third floor, these include indoor and outdoor spas, a gym, a heated swimming pool, and supporting technical facilities. The guestrooms are concentrated in the east, south, and west wings of the South Building, with ninety-one guestrooms in total.

Built with digital construction methods and traditional materials such as brick, concrete, wood, and shale tiles, the long, gray structure extends unhurriedly across the open field. Characterized by a strong sense of ritual, the lobby space carries the rhythm of light, while the free-flowing geometric roof displays a sense of continuity and strength, depicting an aesthetic interest in traditional cultural symbols. This seems to place the building on the long axis of time and culture, showcasing the tranquility and natural atmosphere of residential architecture. Altogether, these elements create a spiritual place with local characteristics.

Models of hotel

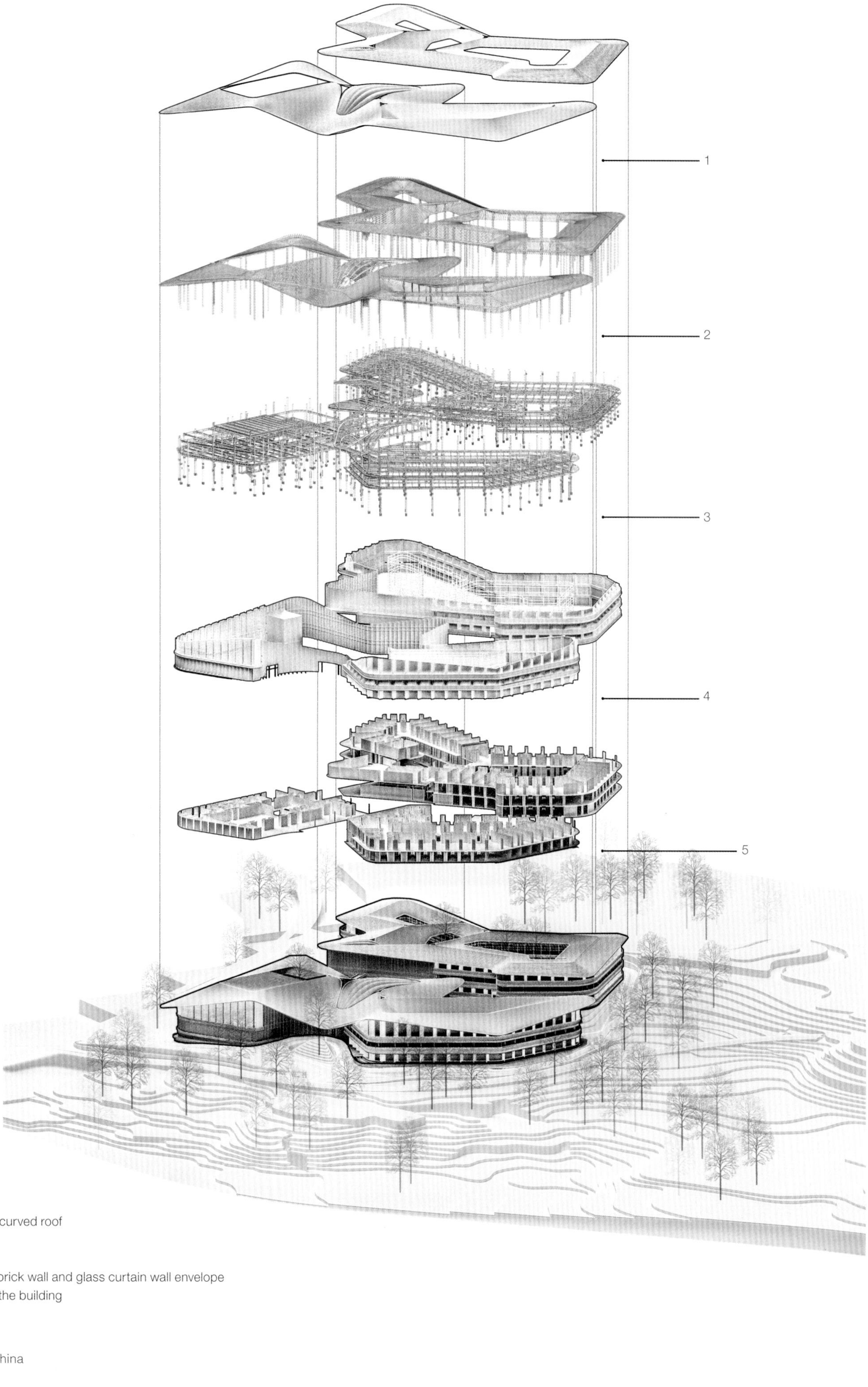

Axonometric diagram

1. Waterproof tiles for curved roof
2. Timber frame
3. Steel frame
4. Digitally fabricated brick wall and glass curtain wall envelope
5. Internal partition of the building

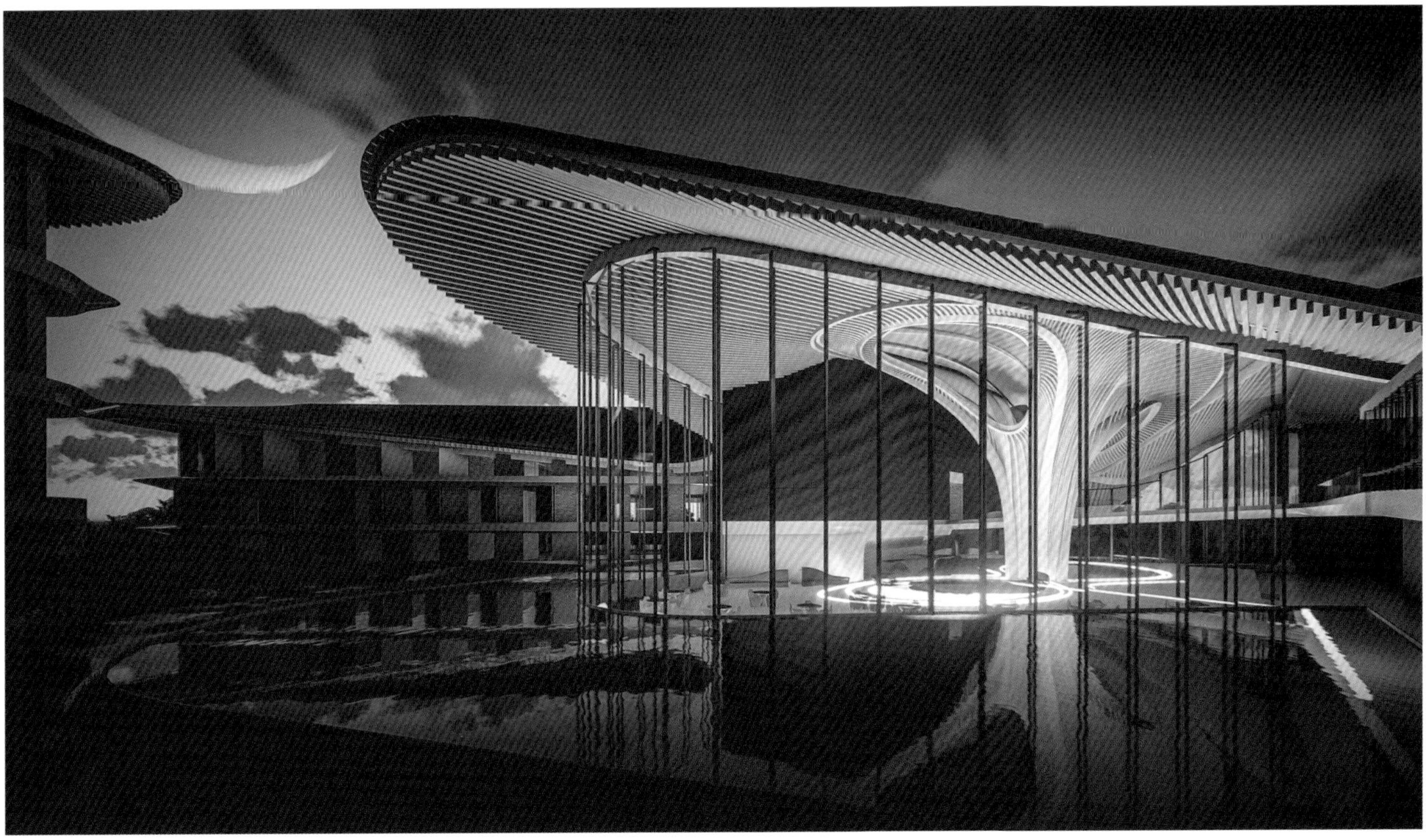

Exterior rendering of hotel from courtyard

View of digital design construction site

First-floor plan of hotel

View of digital design construction site

North elevation

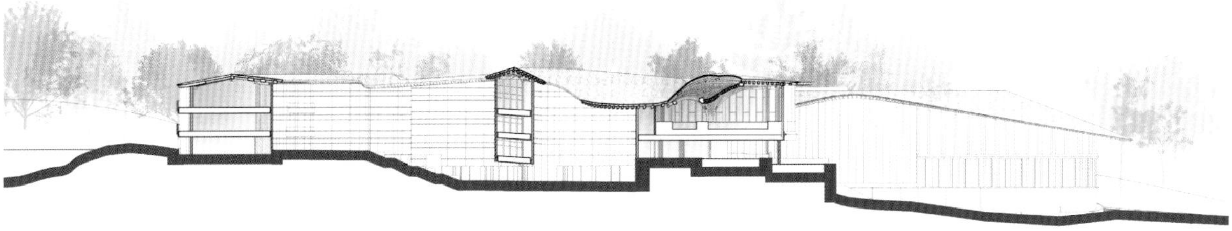

A-A section

Huanghua'an Inn

Rurban Studio

Architect: Rurban Studio
Principal architect: Li Li
Design team: Huang Yuqing, Liu Chang, Hao Jing
Site area: 8,844 square meters
Floor area: 6,243 square meters
Completion: In progress
Photography: Tian Fangfang

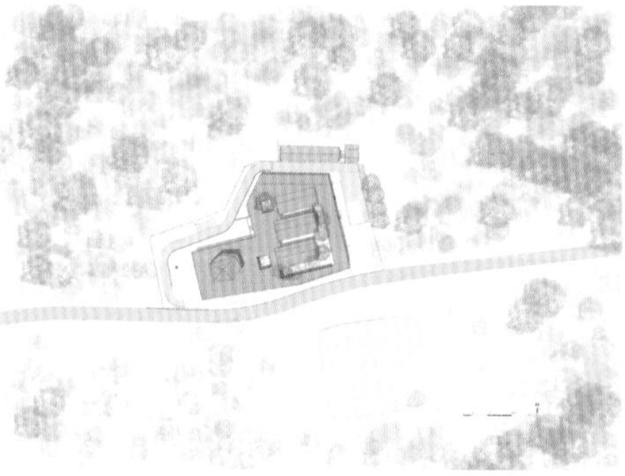

Site plan

With a total area of about 5,600 square meters, Huanghua'an Inn is a medium-sized boutique resort hotel. It is located in the woodland west of the third entrance to the expo park for the 2021 Horticultural Exposition of Jiangsu Province. To the north, the project site is backed by the Huanghua'an geological section of Bangchui Mountain, and to the south across the valley, it faces a mountain cliff.

The original site lies on a gentle slope at the southern foot of the Bangchui Mountain, with a height difference of nearly 12 meters between the northern and southern end of the construction area. It hosts a natural path connecting the main road of the expo park to a hiking trail leading toward the geological section. Apart from dozens of Chinese parasol trees growing on the slope, a red brick building with a single corridor stands on the north side of the site. Formerly used as a field trip dormitory by a geological institute in Nanjing, its style is elegant, and form in good condition.

The architects chose to respond to the site's cultural and natural conditions in a positive way, developing its potential to the fullest while preserving its original characteristics. On the one hand, the overall form of the new building follows the profile of the hillside, with staggered units planted in response to the terrain and a roof surface that is opened up in some areas to allow space for the Chinese parasol trees. On the other, the old dormitory of the geological institute was renovated, so that the project's old and new elements could complement each other. The building's highest point, a rock-shaped observation deck on the west side, breaks through the building's gentle, low-key skyline and forms a harmonious proportional relation with the horizontal width of the roof. Here, visitors can view the surrounding panoramic landscape, including the mountain cliffs, geological fault lines, and entering visitors. The hiking trail toward the geological features of the Huanghua'an section has also been improved upon, enabling visitors to climb the mountain and experience the wonders of nature. In addition, the building hosts a pipeline bringing in water from the nearby hot springs of Mount Tangshan. After their tour of the expo park and the mountain, guests will not only be able to relax in the cascading hot spring pools on the east side of the inn, but also have the opportunity to experience this same comfort with their own private baths.

Exterior rendering of Huanghua'an Inn

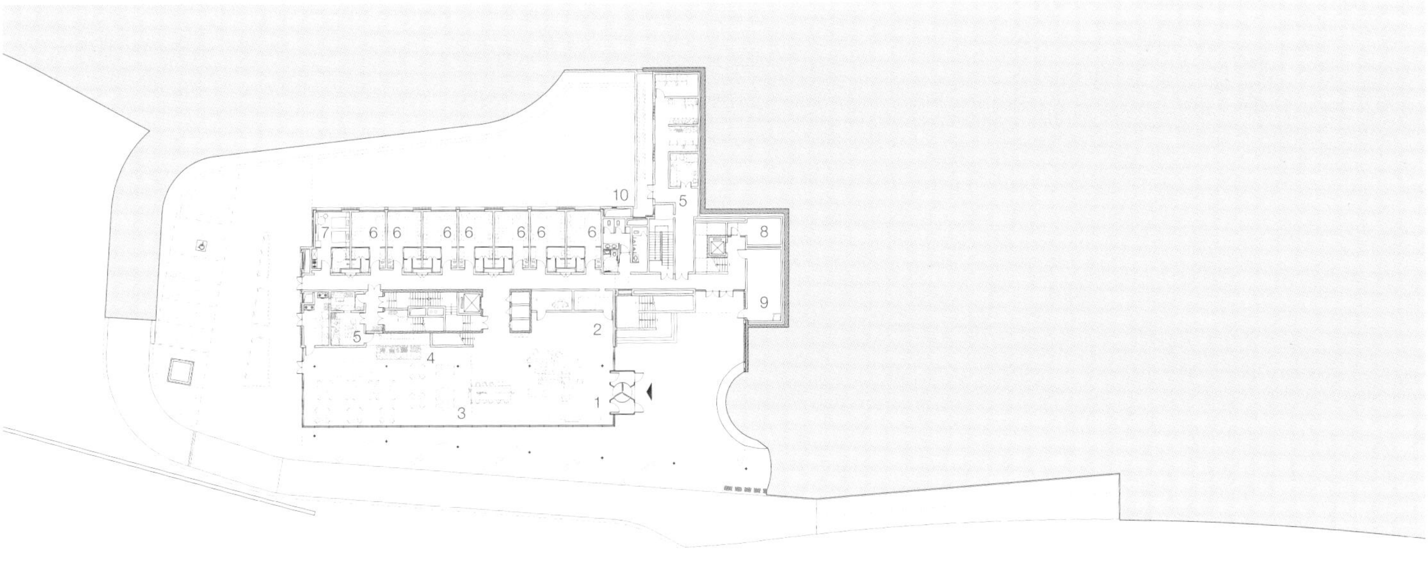

First-floor plan of Inn

1. Service hall
2. Reception
3. Waiting area
4. Restaurant
5. Kitchen
6. Guestroom
7. Accessible rooms
8. Laundry
9. Fire control room
10. Courtyard

View of construction site

Aerial view of construction site

West elevation of Huanghua'an Inn

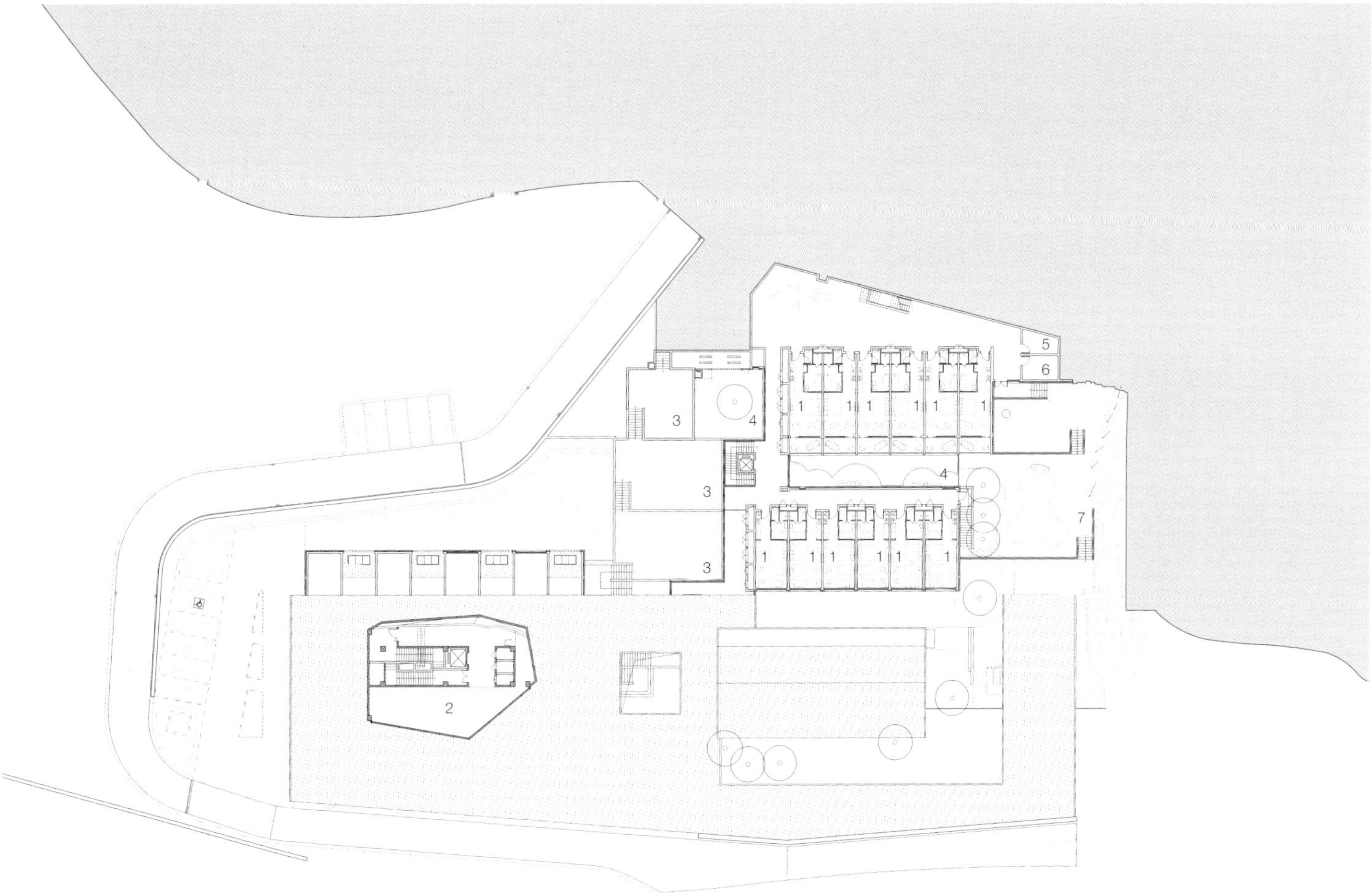

Third-floor plan

1. Guestroom
2. Recreation area
3. Hiking trail
4. Courtyard
5. Disinfection room
6. Smoke exhaust room
7. Pool area

Rendering of rockery and waterfall

Rendering of inner courtyard

Huanghua'an Inn and the surrounding scenery

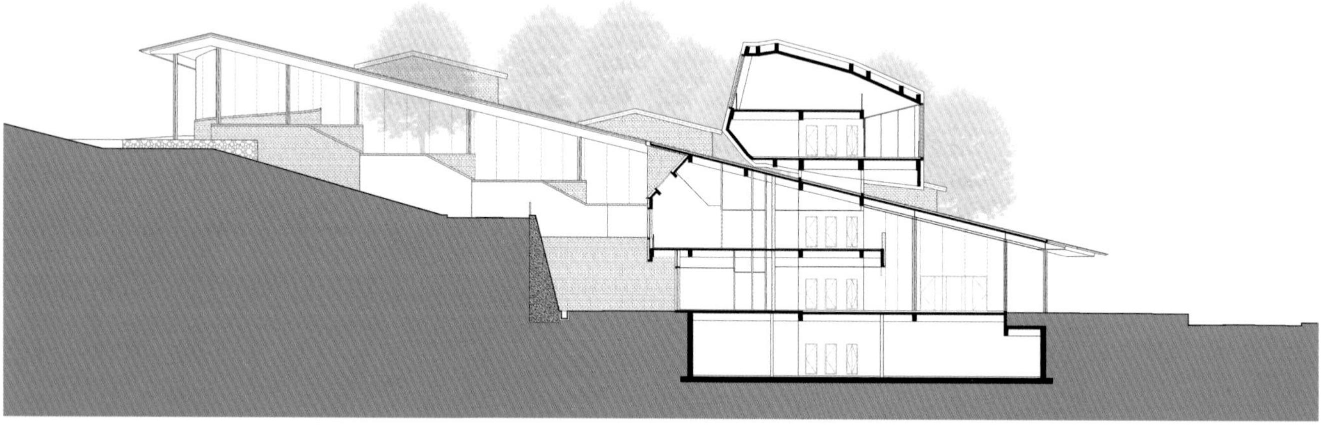

A-A section

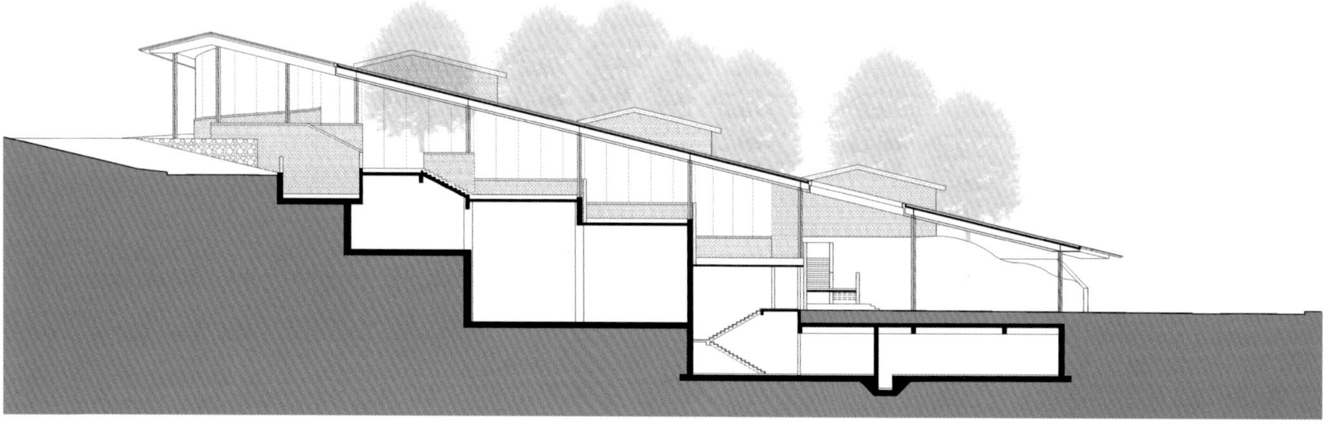

B-B section

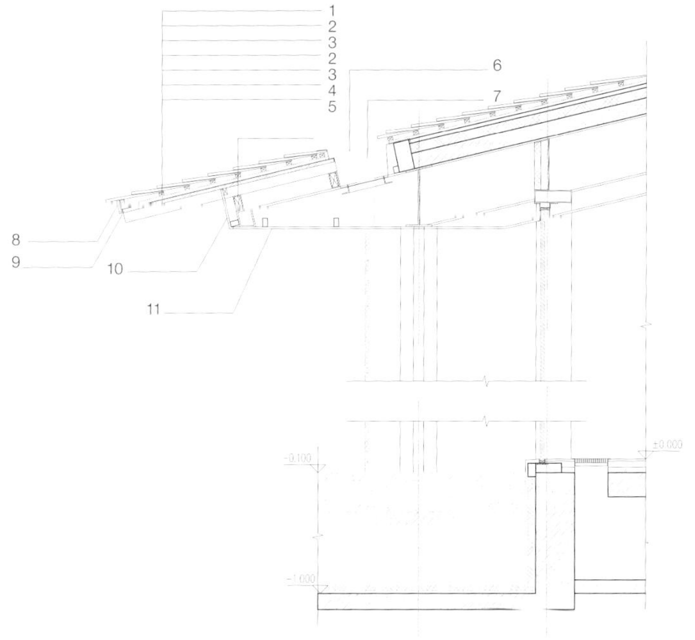

Detail of section

1. 20 mm anti-corrosion wood panel finish
2. 30x30 anti-corrosion wood hanging shingle bar
3. 2 mm self-adhesive membrane waterproofing
4. 20-mm-thick wood plastic board
5. 75x75x4 steel rafters
6. Same color and size of finished PVC rainwater grate plate with anti-corrosion wood
7. 2 mm galvanized steel sheet, coated with polyurethane waterproofing material inside
8. 20 mm wood eaves sealing board
9. Metal water bar
10. Dark-gray aluminum eaves sealing
11. Wood veneer honeycomb panel

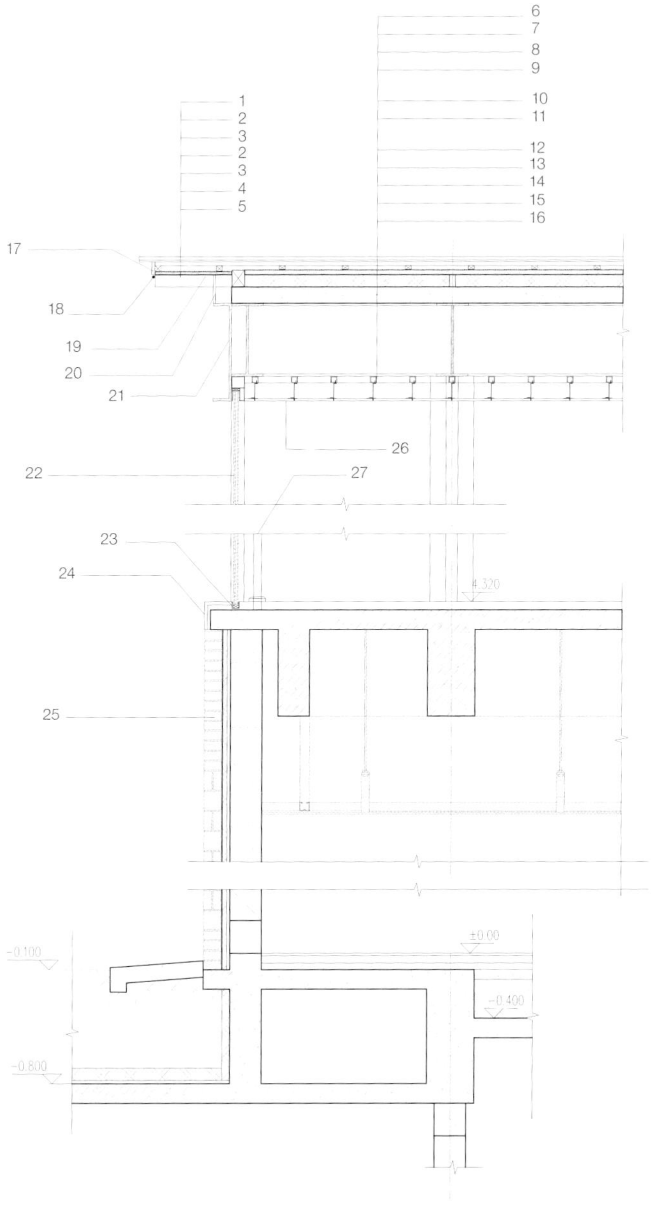

Detail of section

1. 20 mm anti-corrosion wood panel finish
2. 30x30 anti-corrosion wood hanging shingle bar
3. 2 mm self-adhesive membrane water proofing
4. 20 mm wood roof board
5. 75x75x4 steel rafters
6. 20 mm anti-corrosion wood panel finish
7. 30X30 anti-corrosion wood hanging shingle bar
8. 2 mm self-adhesive membrane water proofing
9. 30x30 anti-corrosion counter batten
10. 30 mm C20 fine stone concrete
11. 2 mm self-adhesive membrane waterproofing
12. 75 mm XPS extruded plastic sheet
13. 1.5 mm JS waterproof coating
14. 1000 mm cast-in-place reinforced-concrete
15. Steel beam
16. Light steel keel imitation wood grain honeycomb panel finish
17. 20 mm wood eaves sealing board
18. Metal water bar
19. 20 mm wood roof board
20. Dark-gray aluminum eaves sealing
21. Dark-gray channel steel eaves sealing
22. Glass curtain wall
23. Polyurethane caulking
24. 20 mm brick finish
25. Red brick
26. Light steel keel honeycomb aluminum panel
27. Window guard railing

Huayu Station

NATURALBUILD

Architect: NATURALBUILD
Principal architect: Shui Yanfei, Su Yichi
Design team: Zhou Xiaoyan, Yang Yuwei, Tan Jiaqi, Lv Yuan, Wang Haocheng, Chen Kun, LiuHeng, Liu Wenhao, Zhou Jian, Ding Xiang
Area: 2,518 square meters
Completion: In progress
Photography: Zhou Guyang

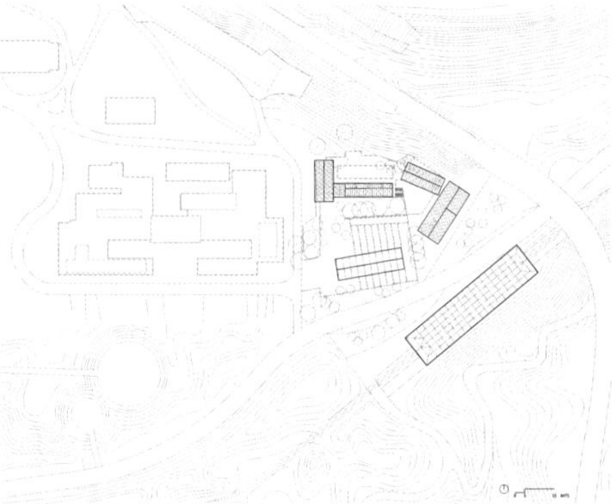

Site plan

Huayu Station of the Nanjing Horticulture Expo, adjacent to the north entrance plaza is is an important node connecting the future garden area and the Geology Museum. It takes on the functions of the service center near the square, seeing to reception inquiries, catering, cultural innovation and multifunctional exhibitions. This project consists of the renovation of the existing buildings and the design of a small train stop.

The predecessor, a cement factory, was used for equipment storage and processing. The original buildings were constructed decades ago and showcase the universal design of that time. However, through minor adjustments in the overall visage of the constructions, a sense of age could be elaborated. The factory buildings on the site are not the oldest buildings in the plant area, being only supporting buildings, hence, if the traces of history were to be enlarged in microscopic methods, they would need the support of conditions.

The factory has been on the site for almost two to three decades, even through the ultra high-speed development of China's social environment. Although this time frame does not constitute as historical time and is not long enough for the building to be listed, it did make allowances for it to occupy a more permanent position in history, resulting in not a single building, but a group of buildings remaining on the original site. As the current condition of the original plant was good, it was transformed and reused.

Given the consideration of the times and the conditions of the place, the situation proved advantageous to retain the original sense

Huayu Station construction site

View of central stage construction site

of architecture and its place in history. In terms of location strategy, a time sense of the period is clearly presented—by retaining the buildings of the past and clearly showing the new buildings at the same time. In terms of functions, the smooth transition and use, during expo and post-expo, where it can face a more public life in the future are considered. Based on these intentions, the layout of the site forms several squares with different elevations by taking advantage of the enclosure formed by the original buildings, combing the height difference and retaining trees through the architectural design. The original building retains and reinforces the original stone façade and displaces it into the steel structure to support the new aluminum roof. The new train station is designed to support the light and transparent roof through a simple large-span structure, using new materials and construction to respond to the historical elements of industrial materials. Both the new buildings and the reconstructed buildings are presented in different postures, and the buildings themselves and the site are constantly in dialogue and evolution.

In the future, the buildings in this area can cooperate with the north entrance square as an open venue to serve the surrounding citizens and gradually integrate as a part of public lifestyle.

Aerial rendering of station

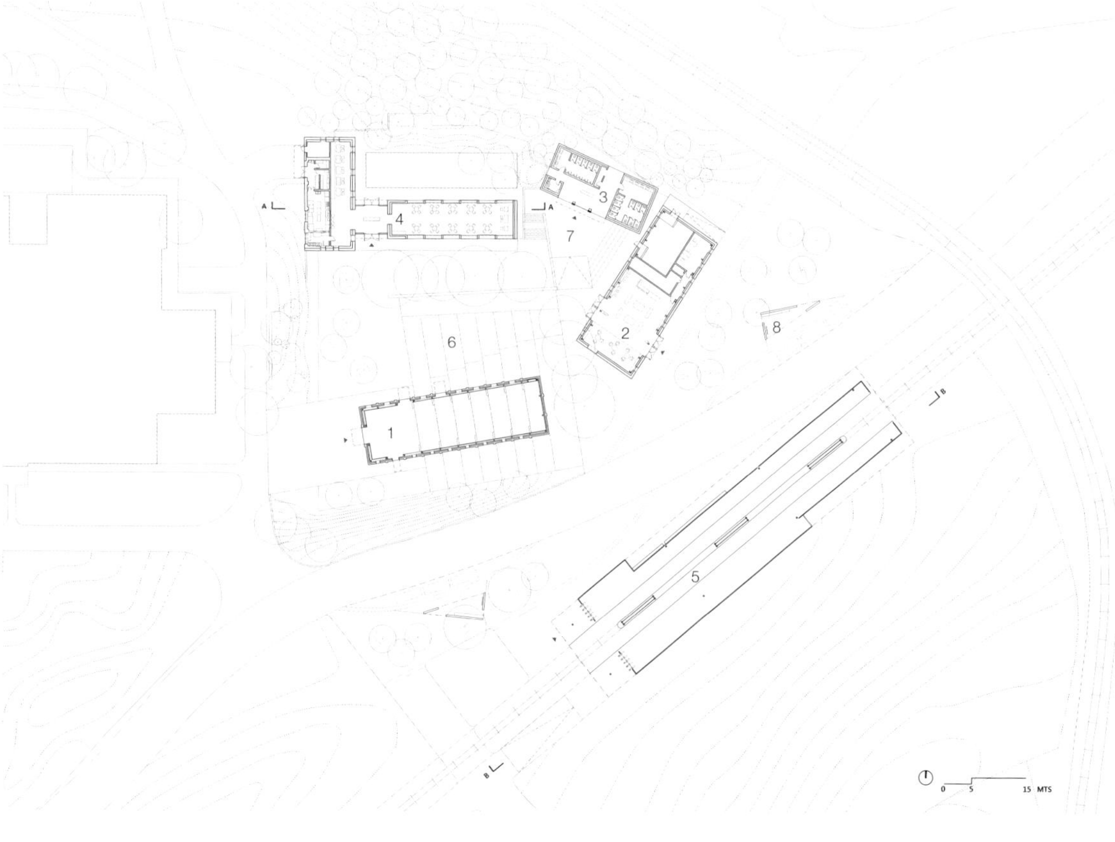

Ground-floor plan of station

1. Exhibition hall
2. Information centre
3. Restroom
4. Restaurant
5. Train station
6. Central stage
7. Sunken courtyard
8. Bus-stop

Night view of Huayu Station construction site

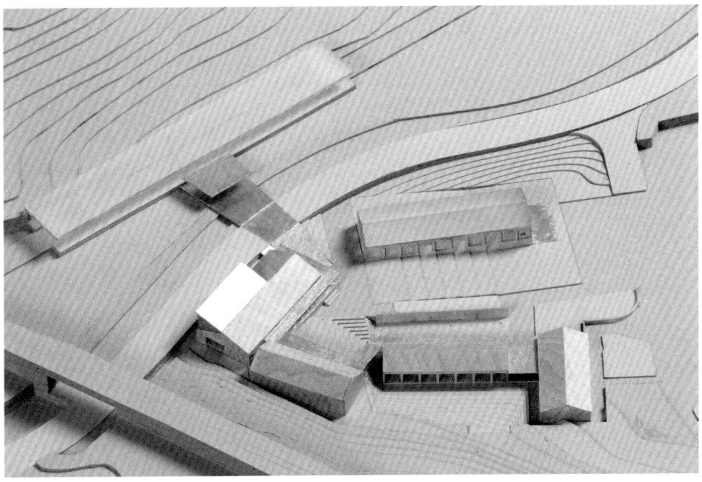

1 | 2
  | 3

1. Conceptual model
2. Site analysis
3. Original site

Night view rendering of Huayu Station

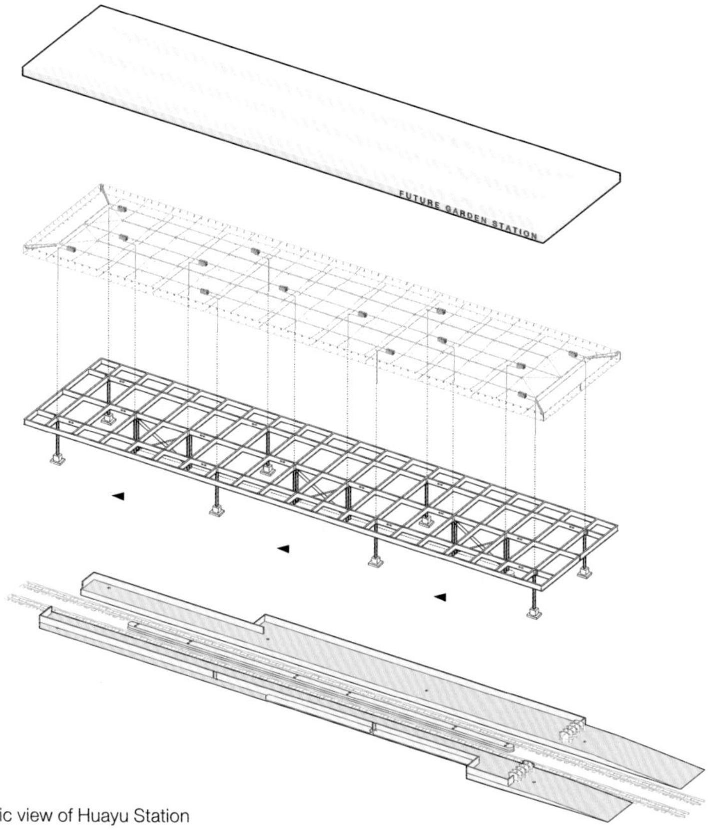

Axonometric view of Huayu Station

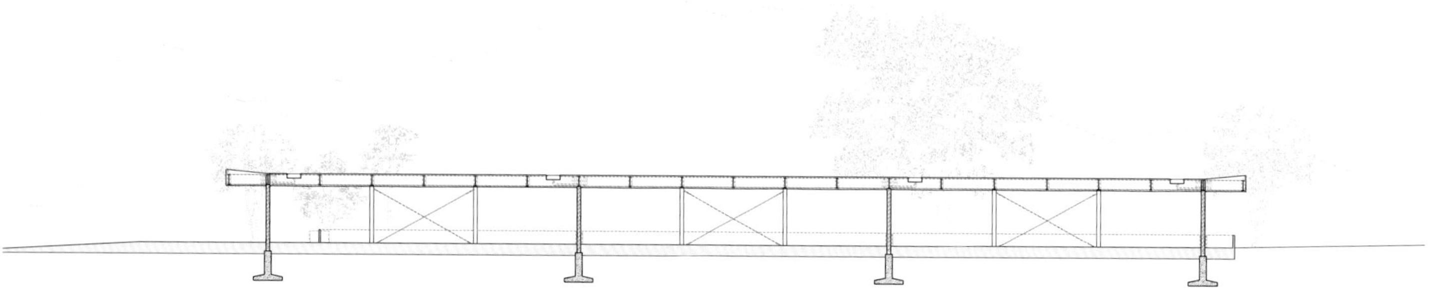

Longitudinal section of Huayu Station

View of Huayu Station construction site

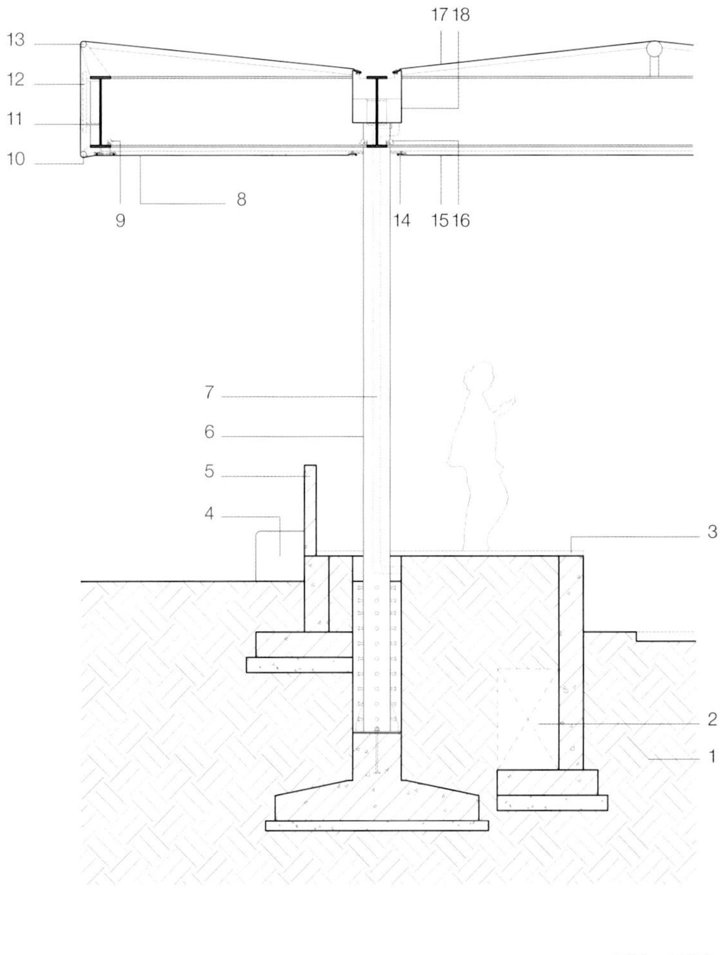

Detail of polytetrafluoroethylene and steel structure

1. Mountain rock
2. Municiple culvert
3. Polished concrete finishing
4. Cast-in concrete bench
5. Wood-grained cast-in concrete barrier
6. 273 mm diameter steel hollow column
7. Pre-embeded PVC downpipe
8. PTFE membrane FGT250M
9. LED strip lights
10. 60 mm steel pipe
11. 700x200 mm steel I-Beam
12. LED light box VI system
13. 60 mm steel pipe
14. Zinc coat binder plate
15. PTFE membrane FGT250M
16. LED strip lights
17. PTFE membrane FGT600
18. Zinc coat gutter

Floral Pavilion

genarchitects

Architect: genarchitects
Principal architect: Xue Zhe, Fan Beilei, Kong Rui
Design team: Liu Yang, Li Lanruo, Zang Min, Tao Shuting, Wang Shiyu, Chen Xi, Liu Jinghuan, Sun Haonan, Liu Weinan, Yang Tianyu
Area: 2,050 square meters
Completion: In progress
Photography: Tian Fangfang

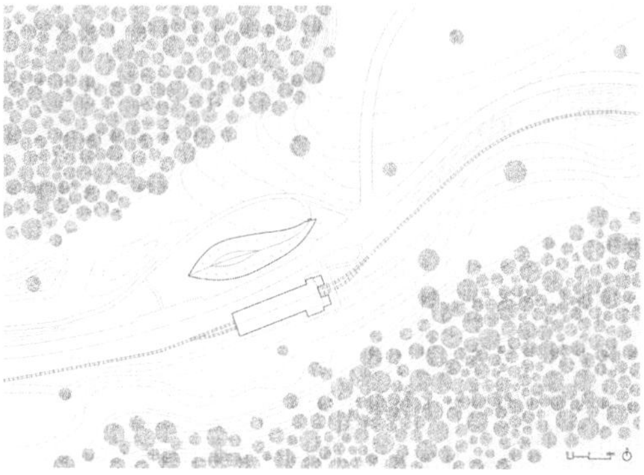
Site plan

Nestled in a valley surrounded by rolling hills to the north and south, this pavilion serves as a plant-themed exhibition hall and café for the Horticultural Expo. From the outset, equal importance was assigned to not only looking outward from the space to the surrounding natural scenery, but also inward at the ornamental plants. As visitors enter from the external scenery, they would need a space shielded from the sunlight and noise where they can unload their luggage, sit in silence, have drink or chat, and appreciate the landscape. Swivel bar stools allow them to face different directions to catch a glimpse of the flowers in the center of the hall that extend to the left and right, against a backdrop of lush hills. As visitors walk through the space, they can admire the plants that fill the flowerbed and experience the changing topography of the site. In the master plan, the pavilion looks like a boat sailing through the hills. To that effect, gazing westward along the unfolding terrain, one feels as if they're standing at the prow and looking out.

The building employs a steel-wood structure with prefabricated components. In order to create an uninterrupted view of the landscape, the structural components are placed on the periphery, with the spindle-shaped wooden pillars surrounding the flowerbed bearing most of the roof's load. Like an inverted umbrella, the roof's radially-arrayed wooden beams are centrally connected at the top by tie rods.

To maintain the roof's balance, additional steel tie rods, with a diameter of four centimeters, are arranged spaced four meters apart along the outside of the exhibition hall. These bars match the dimensions of the façade's glass panels, causing the roof to appear as if it's floating in the air.

Inside the hall, dark tones are applied to instil a sense of calm and create a theater-like backdrop for the glowing flowerbed in the center and the bright scenery outside.

Interior view of pavilion construction site

Exterior view of pavilion construction site

Interior view of pavilion

Exterior view of pavilion construction site

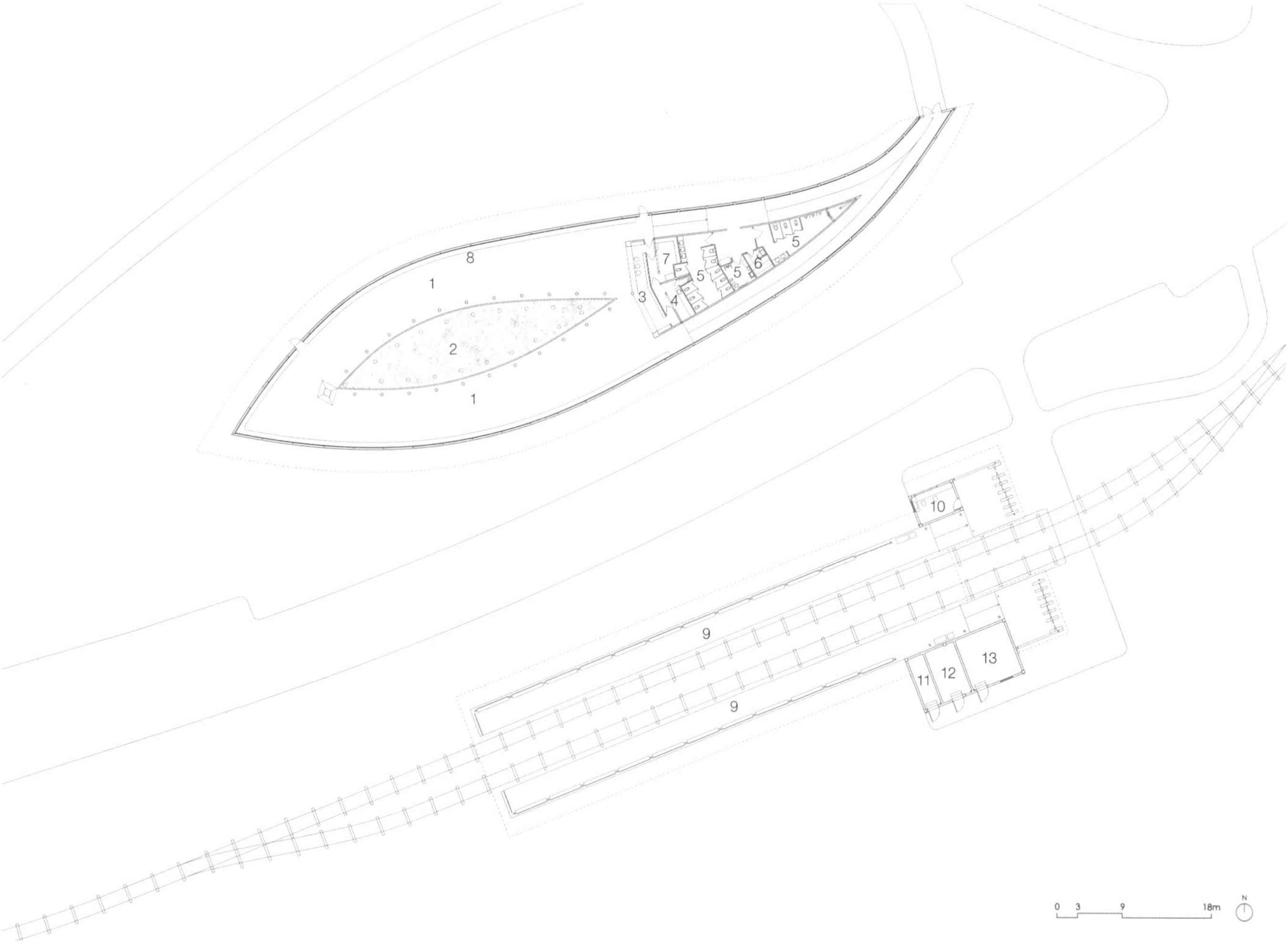

First-floor plan

1. Exhibition area
2. Parterre
3. Information and bar
4. Pantry
5. Restroom
6. Staff room
7. Manager's room
8. Bar table
9. Platform
10. Ticket office
11. Fire control room
12. Electrical room
13. Mechanical room

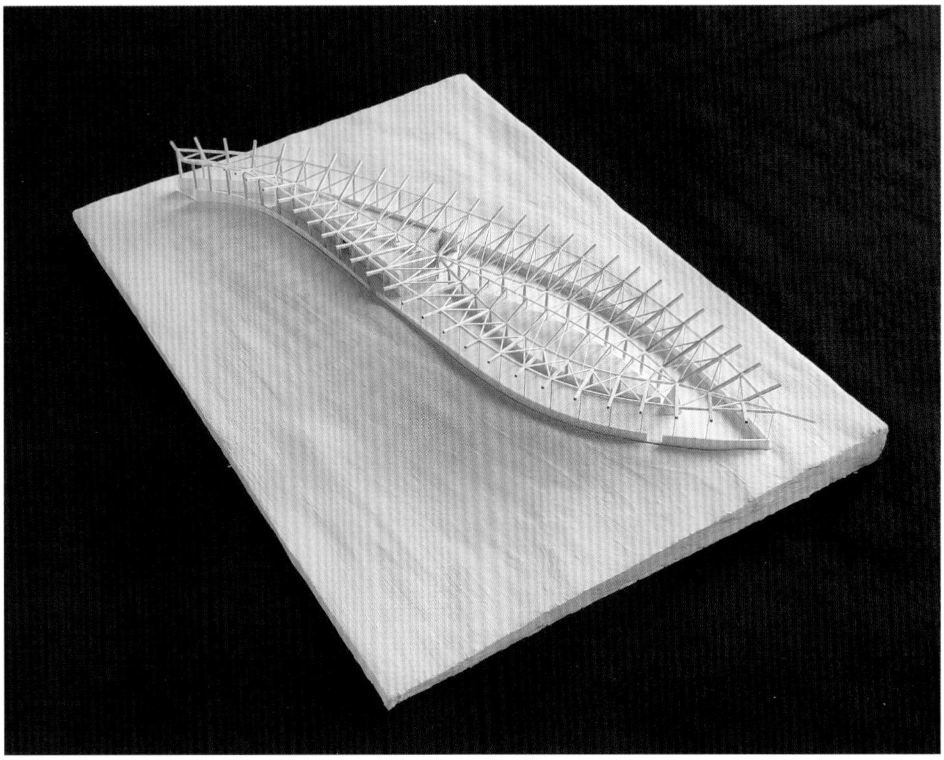

Model of pavilion

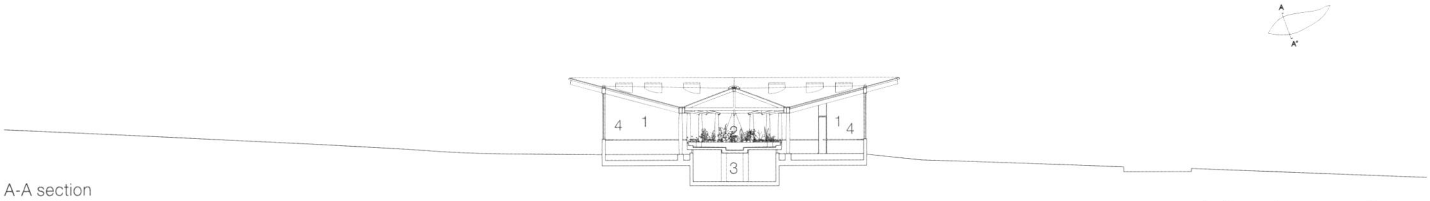

A-A section

0 3 9 18m

1. Exhibition hall
2. Parterre
3. Mechanical area
4. Bar table

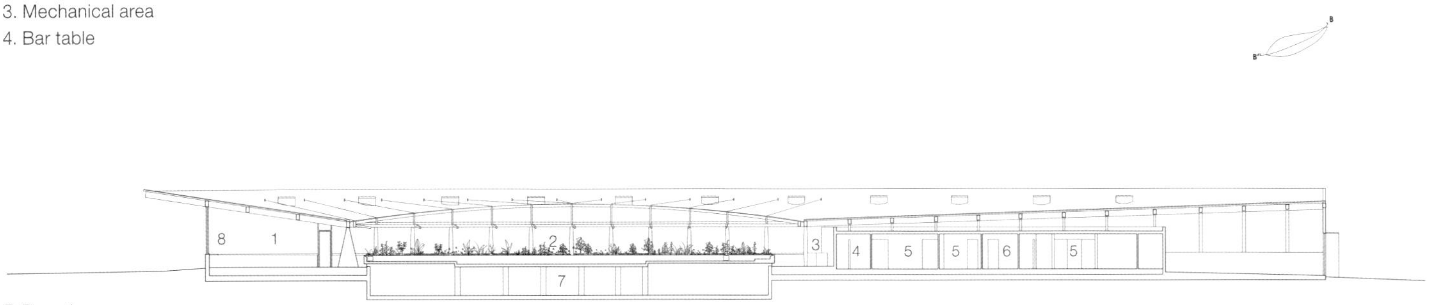

B-B section

0 3 9 18m

1. Exhibition hall
2. Parterre
3. Information and bar
4. Pantry
5. Restroom
6. Staff room
7. Mechanical area
8. Bar table

View of train station construction site

Construction detail of train station

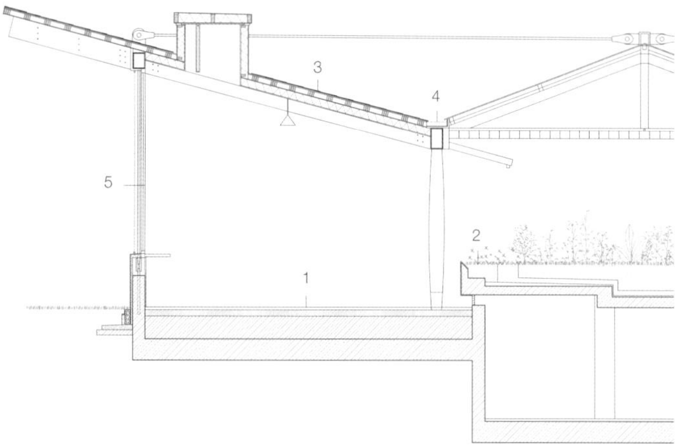

1. Black cast-in-place terrazzo anti-slip and wear-resistant flooring layer
   Fine stone concrete protective layer
   Cement mortar
   Concrete bedding layer
   Crushed stone or crushed brick compacted
   Compacted plain soil
2. Planting soil mulch layer
   Geotextile filter layer
   Plastic sheet drainage layer
   Cement mortar protection layer
   SBS modified bitumen waterproofing membrane (root-puncture-resistant)
   Modified asphalt waterproofing coating membrane
   Cement mortar leveling bonding layer
   Reinforced-concrete structural slab
3. Asphalt shingle special steel, nail-fixed
   EPDM rubber waterproofing membrane
   OSB board
   Structural grating (inner sky composite rockwool fireproof insulation board)
   PE film
   Fireproof gypsum board
   Glue-laminated wood beam
4. Perforated aluminium sheets
   Metal guttering
   Metal drop rods
5. Glass
   Steel tie rods
   Metal decorative mesh

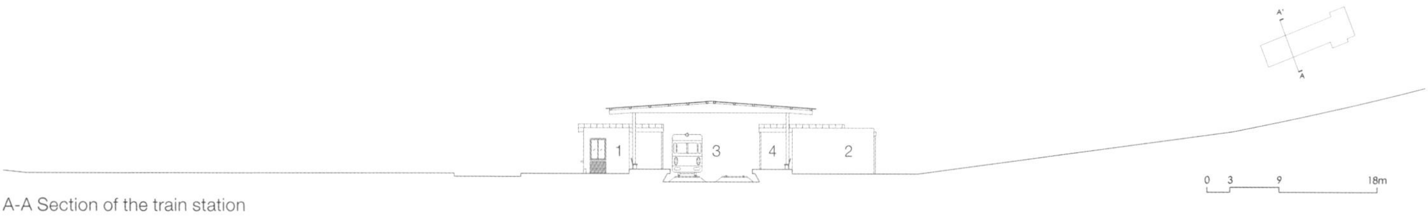

A-A Section of the train station

1. Mechanical room 2. Ticket office 3. Railroad 4. Platform

Huase Station

TAOA

Architect: TAOA
Principal architect: Tao Lei
Design team: Wang Wenzhi, Chen Zhen, Sun Lang, Duan Zhenqiang, Tao Ye
Area: 1,175 square meters
Completion: In progress
Photography: Tao Lei, Tian Fangfang

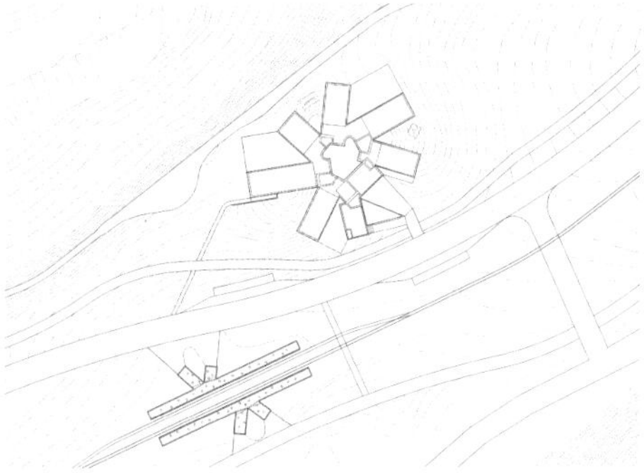

Site plan

Huase Station lies on a sloping hillside with a height difference of 4 meters between the northwestern and southeastern corners. By combining eight spatial volumes that encompass different functions, the building designs a shared central water courtyard and a horizontal space that extends from the slope. As a viewing space and service node on the central axis of the expo park, the design aims to provide visitors who are passing through or stopping to rest with a landscape interface that is continuous throughout the interior and exterior of the space.

The form of the building adapts well to the sloping terrain and the soothing surrounding landscape, with every two out of the eight volumes forming a group that semi-encloses the shared courtyard. In doing so, semi-private and partially-open spaces emerge to draw the view from the inside to the distant outside. Around the central water courtyard, each group of spatial volumes is slightly raised in line with the slope of the site. This reduces damage to the hill, while successfully integrating the building with the terrain, changing the height of the spaces accordingly. The emerging overlapping spaces collide with and squeeze against each other, giving rise to lighting towers that form brightly lit court spaces. They provide the flowing circular space with plenty of natural light and create a contrast with the water courtyard; they also form a cut between different spatial functions, introducing some tension into the space, which was not originally horizontal. Together with the central water courtyard, the lighting towers endow the building with a soul, creating a rich and multi-dimensional spatial rhythm. When moving around its interior, the building constantly interacts with human perception and establishes a sensitive connection with the original site and the external environment.

In order to match the natural environment of the surrounding site, the building is made of fair-faced concrete. Like stone, concrete originates from the earth and will exhibit natural traces over time. Returning to the directness and simplicity of nature, this building stands distinct from urban architecture.

The Huase Station aims to explore the relationship between architecture, man, and nature. Compared with the city, Huase Station is a building in nature, even becoming a part of nature itself. Its hard concrete shell is like a rock—quiet and eternal; it is a stone flower that blooms on this land.

Exterior view of station construction site

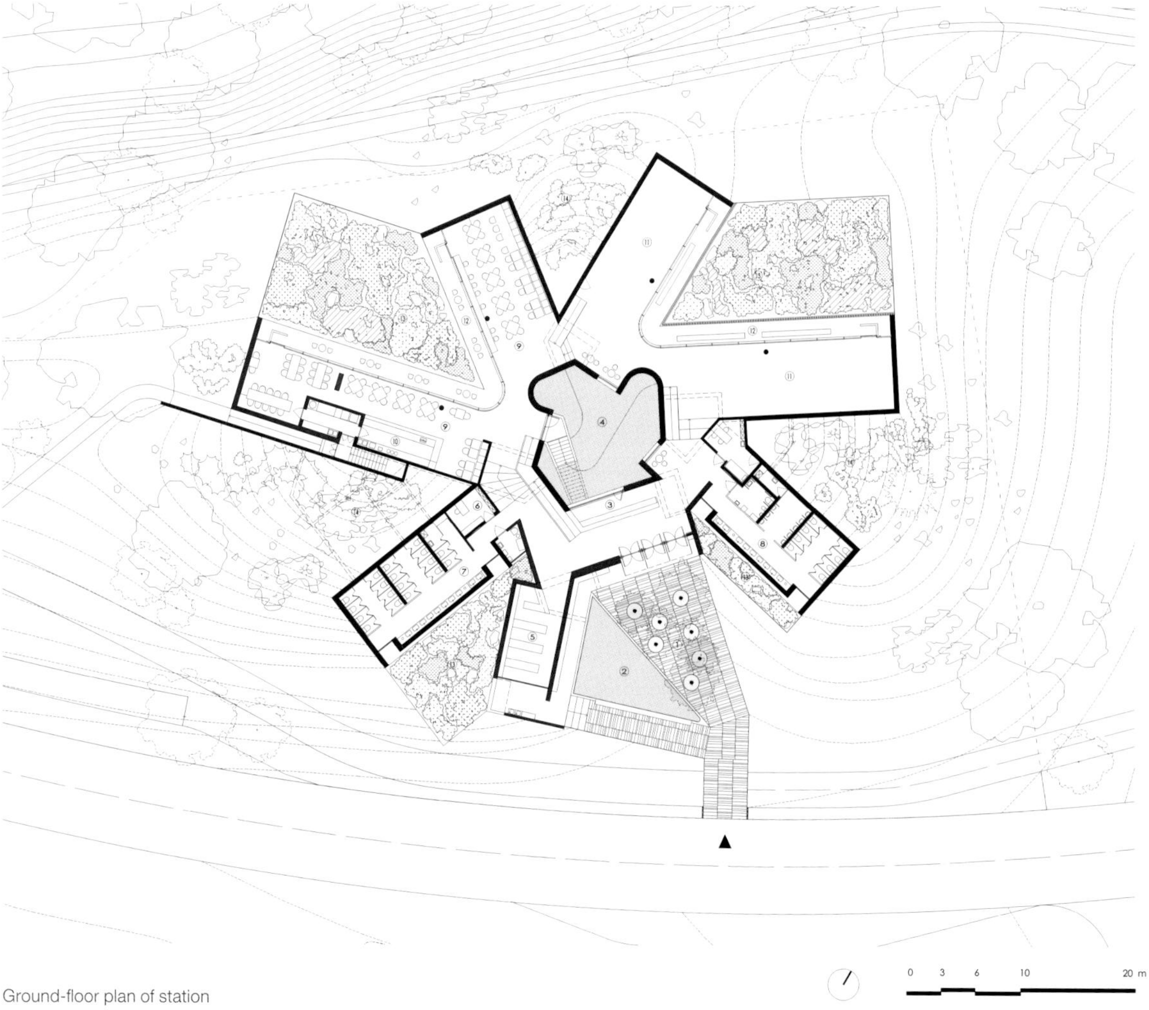

Ground-floor plan of station

Rendering of courtyard

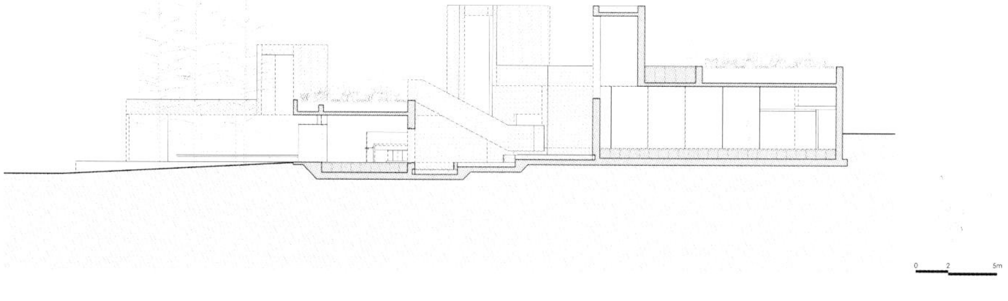

A-A section

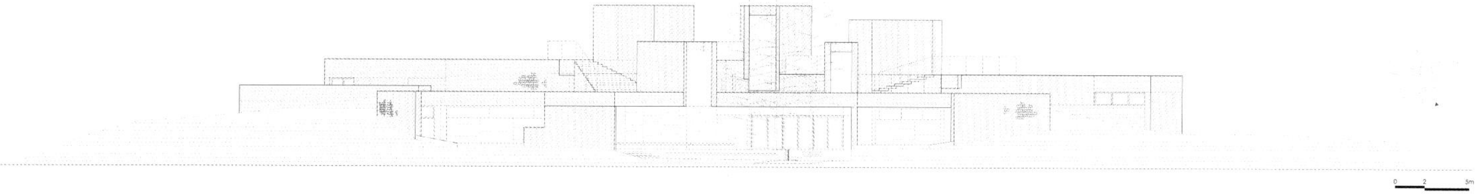

B-B section

Interior renderings of station

View of courtyard construction site

Interior view of station construction site

Exterior rendering of station

Night view of station construction site

Huaxiang Station

Zhou Ling

Principal architect: Zhou Ling
Design team: Zhou Ling, Dai Lulu, Sun Xiaoyu, Tan Ming, Zhang Chunting, Yang Dan
Area: 1,095 square meters
Completion: In progress
Photography: Tao Lei, Tian Fangfang

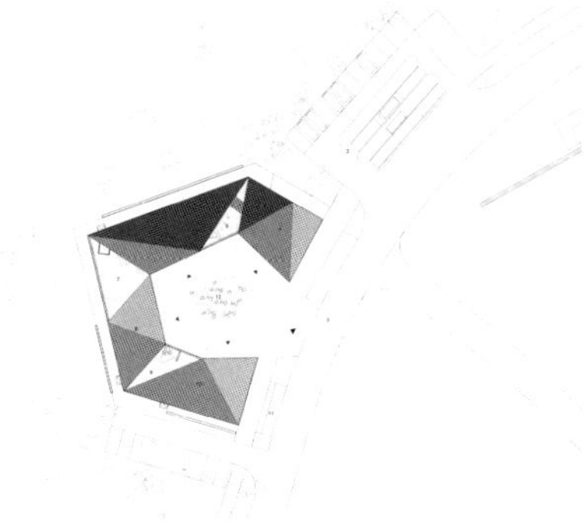

Site plan

Located north of the main road in the southwestern area of the expo park, the Huaxiang Station is a pavilion for the 11th Horticultural Exposition of Jiangsu Province in Nanjing. Surrounded by mountain ranges to the north and south, it's characterized by an undeniable sense of place. The design concept for the project was derived from the painting *Cloudy Ravine and Pine Shade* by Gong Xian, the most famous among eight Qing Dynasty painters from Nanjing. As there were plenty of rocks at the site, the project was accordingly named Rocky Ravine and Pine Shade. The building adopts the form and structure of traditional courtyard dwellings of the region south of the Yangtze River, adjusting it to suit, such as a sloped roof that transforms the angular shape of the original design. The complex appears to be protruding out of the foot of the mountain like a rock, embodying the spirit of famous Ming Dynasty steles in the area. Multiple service functions are assembled around a central "pine shade" courtyard, combining the functions of a highway service area and an airport terminal. The circular layout also enables visitors to reach specific functional areas in the shortest time, and is also distinct and easily recognizable.

This project has three main features: the optimized, streamlined walking distances, instant recognizability, and compounded flexible functions. It also embodies three combinations: the combination of morphed boulders and residential space, of natural terrain and artificial landscape, and of its use during and after the Horticultural Exposition.

The station's four volumes correspond to its four main functions as a shop, a restaurant, an exhibition area, and a public place, respectively. The plane is strictly controlled by a network of columns, all converging on specific grid points, which benefits the stability of the structural system. The entrance of each volume is concave, creating transitional spaces. The two sides of each entrance thus form a niche that can be used as an equipment or administrative room, as it at the same time helps to maintain the integrity of the inner space.

Three smaller courtyards—Listening to the Rain, Viewing the Mountains, and Appreciating the Bamboo are designed along techniques used in traditional Chinese garden design. Through the combination of pavement, bonsai plants, tables, water pools, and other elements, they recreate the artistic concepts of "drinking tea and listening to the rain," "climbing the mountain and watching the pines," and "having a feast and appreciating bamboo." The three courtyards are also indirectly connected through large windows that provide visitors with everchanging views when walking through the station—a phenomenon often experienced in Chinese gardens.

View of station's courtyard

View of wall and material

The beauty of the courtyards is enhanced by the layered stone blocks of the courtyard walls that highlight the intimate sceneries that they frame. Terrazzo floors contrasting the brawny exterior are applied inside the station; the rest of the walls and the roof are made of fine and smooth wood. The two complement each other to create a distinct spatial experience. Echoing the main body of the building, the bar is also made of stacked rocks, while the furniture arrangement reflects Ming Dynasty culture, with a series of Ming-style elements decorating the space.

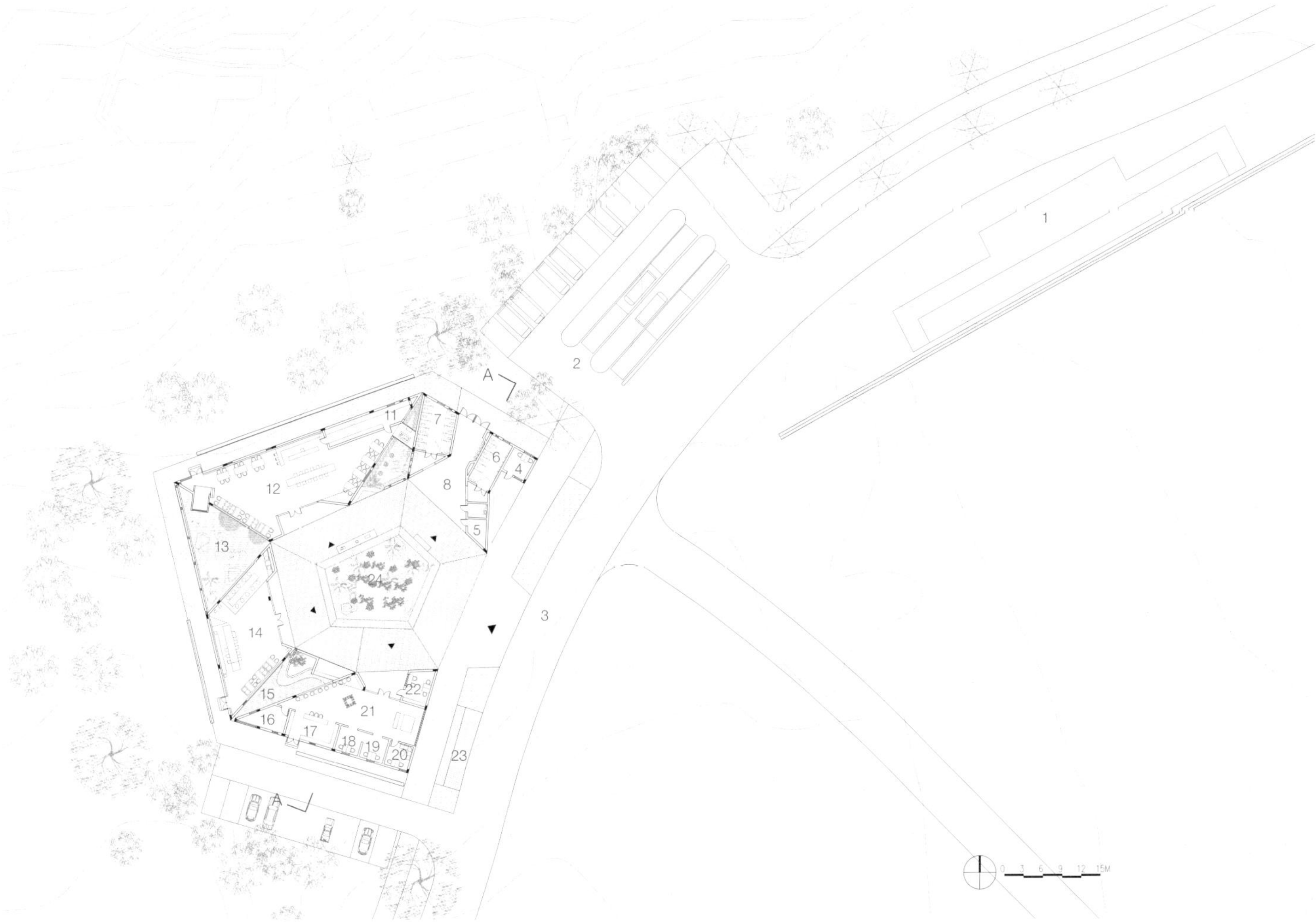

Ground-floor plan of station

1. Raiway station
2. Battery station
3. Main road
4. Ticketing
5. Electrical room
6. Men's restroom
7. Women's restroom
8. Front office
9. Water garden
10. Tearoom
11. Processing room
12. Restaurant
13. Mountain garden
14. Café
15. Bamboo garden
16. Office
17. Small supermarket
18. Infirmary
19. Lost and found office
20. Station for lost children
21. Enquires
22. Ticketing
23. Bicycle island
24. Center garden

Interior rendering of station

Interior view of station

Exterior rendering of station

Elevation of station

A-A Section

Exterior rendering of station

Interior rendering of station

Design model of station

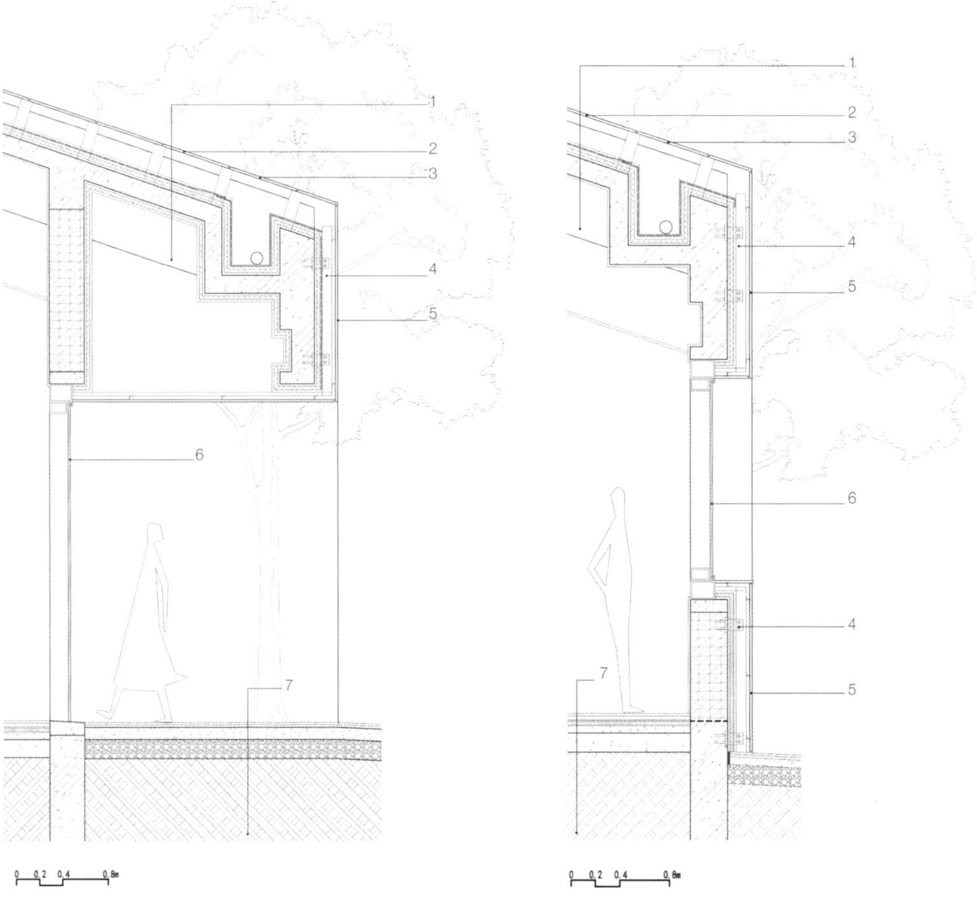

Detail of walls

1. Stone slab elevated roof
   20 mm 1:2.5 or M15 cement mortar protective layer, surface-smoothing and calendering
   3 mm foamed polyethylene film isolation layer
   1.2 mm self-adhesive polymer modified asphalt
   Waterproofing roll-roofing material
   1 mm synthetic polymer waterproofing coating film
   35 mm C20 fine stone concrete leveling layer
   75 mm extruded polystyrene sheet
   Reinforced-concrete floor panel
2. Stone cover elevated roof
3. Gable stone cover plate
4. Stone curtain wall main keel
5. Exterior stone wall panel
6. Low-e hollow transparent glass
7. Insulation material

Banshan Hotel

HKS Architects

Architect: HKS Architects
Principal architect: Zhang Jian
Design team: Wang Huaichang, Shao Yi, Li Haoyuan, Xia Xin, Shi Sheng, Guo Kangjian, Shao Jingyi, Yu Yue, Zhong Yunsen
Area: 18,937 square meters
Completion: In progress

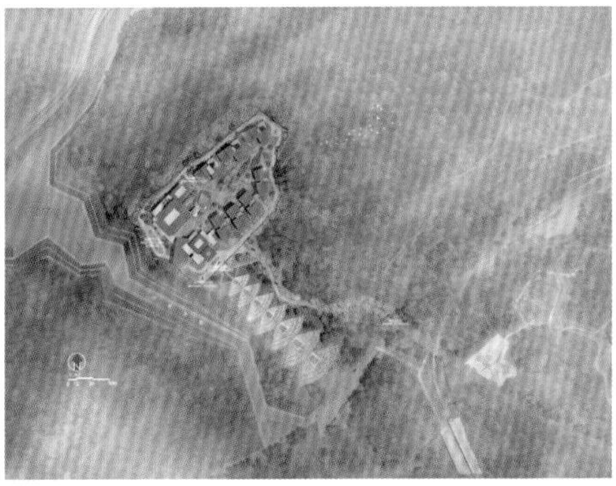

Site plan

The Banshan Hotel is located in the northwest of the expo park for the Horticultural Exhibition. Easily accessible from the city through the future Mengbei Station of Nanjing's Metro Line 4, it is part of the urban renewal master plan's garden area and lies close to the intersection of Third Ring Road and Mengbei Road. Located halfway up the mountain—the inspiration behind the name "banshan," meaning "mountain" in Chinese—and to the east of the natural chasm that marks Entrance No. 1 to the park, the hotel is surrounded by natural hills and forests; also facing the terraced Sea of Flowers to the south, it exhibits beautiful natural landscape in its vicinity.

The project has a total land area of 24,136 square meters, a total floor area of approximately 18,937 square meters, and fulfills the standards of a five-star boutique hotel. With eighty-five rooms, the design aims to limit the buildings' construction height in an effort to preserve the mountain's contour in the background.
The design concept is based on the idea of an urban paradise. People who have lived in the city for a long time always yearn to live in a natural paradise. While it may be hard to achieve that, escaping from the distractions and bustle of the city on a day off is comparatively easy. The design enables the tranquillity that people long for, allowing their bodies and minds to feel the power of nature.

The building volumes are broken down as much as possible to provide the best landscape views from the hotel's public areas and guestrooms, which include the large terraces of blooms of the Sea of Flowers to the south of the site. The hotel's buildings resemble a village growing organically from the uneven terrain. A long winding path presents the hotel drop-off point at the end; upon alighting, guests duck under a canopy that leads to the hotel lobby, which sits directly in front of a central waterscape. The hotel's all-day dining restaurant is cantilevered on the second floor like an overhanging rock, echoing the surrounding hillside. To meet the needs of guests, a multifunctional hall, a specialty restaurant, and a gym and swimming pool are arranged in the northwest of the site. Guestrooms on the south side are cantilevered off the ground, providing great views of the Sea of Flowers. The rooms on the north side are elevated higher than those to the south, and are connected by a water system. These rooms on the north side of the courtyard are mostly two stories high and lifted off the ground, with the rooms on the first floor having their own independent courtyards, while the rooms on the second and third floors hang over the water features. Guests can thus enjoy the hotel complex's internal water landscape and also take in the distant natural scenery through the raised elevation of their rooms.

Rendering of hotel courtyard

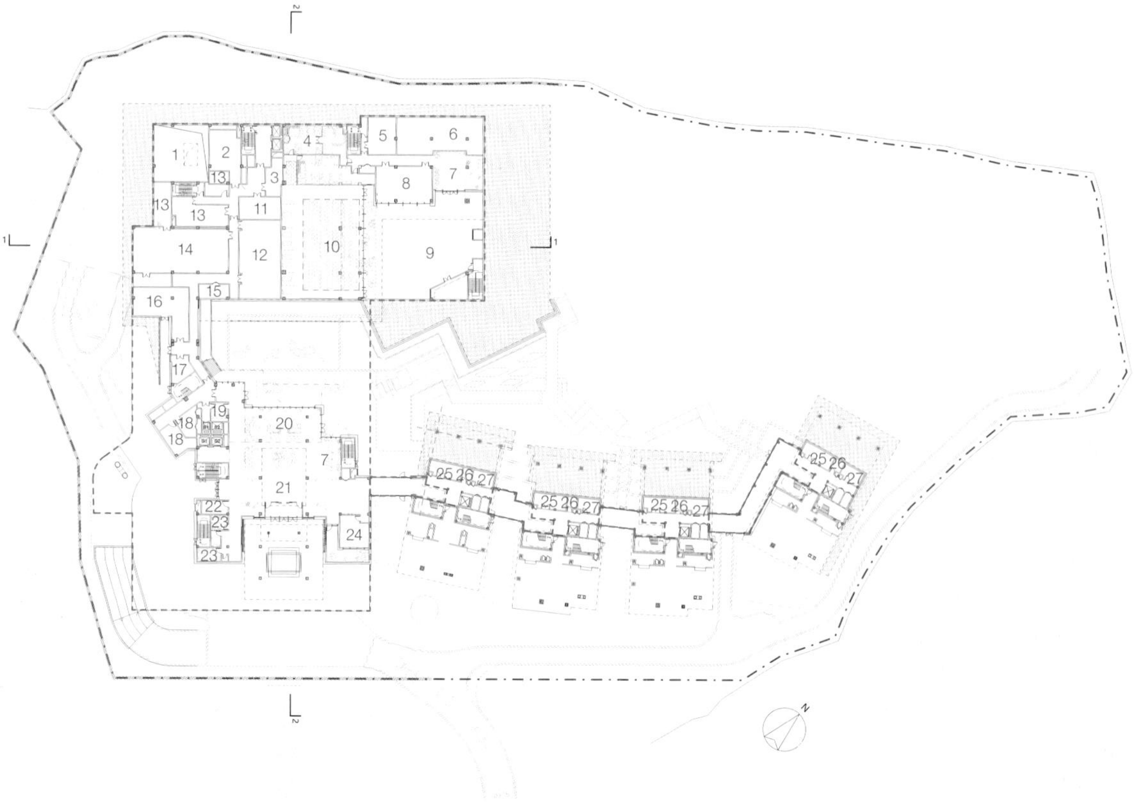

First-floor plan

1. MEP
2. MEP
3. MEP
4. Locker
5. MEP
6. MEP
7. Reception
8. Gym
9. Garden
10. Swimming pool
11. MEP
12. MEP
13. MEP
14. MEP
15. MEP
16. MEP
17. MEP
18. Staff lounge
19. Pantry
20. Lobby lounge
21. Lobby
22. Luggage
23. Restroom
24. Administration office
25. Fan

Aerial view of the hotel

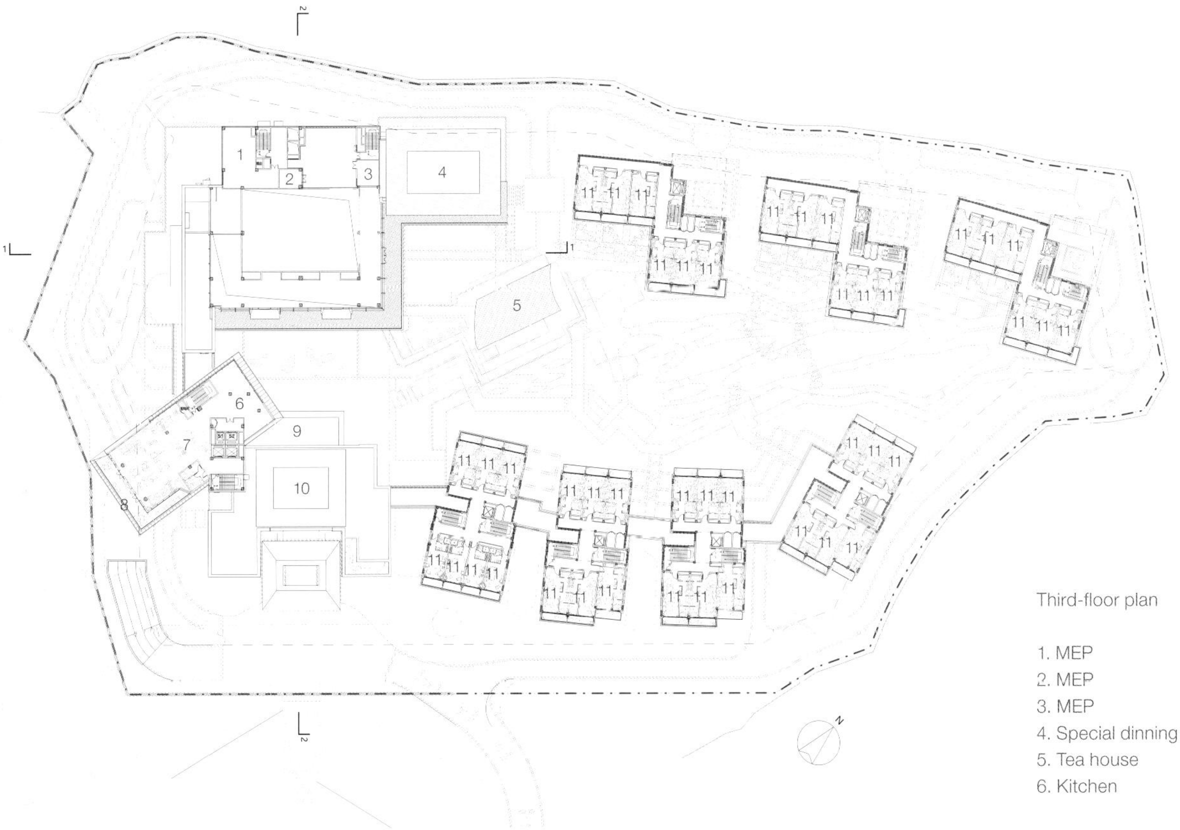

Third-floor plan

1. MEP
2. MEP
3. MEP
4. Special dinning
5. Tea house
6. Kitchen
7. All-day dinning
8. Balcony
9. Lobby lounge
10. Lobby
11. Guestroom

Rendering of hotel garden

East elevation

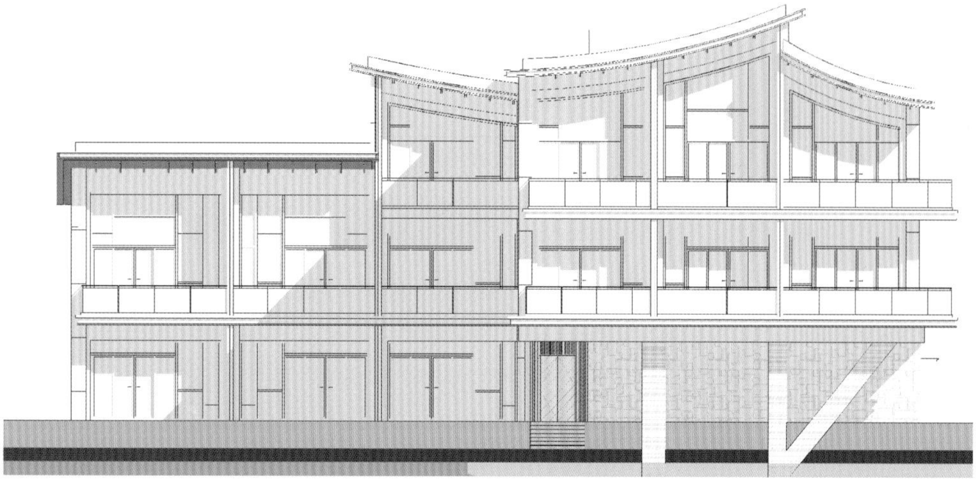

South elevation

Rendering of water courtyard

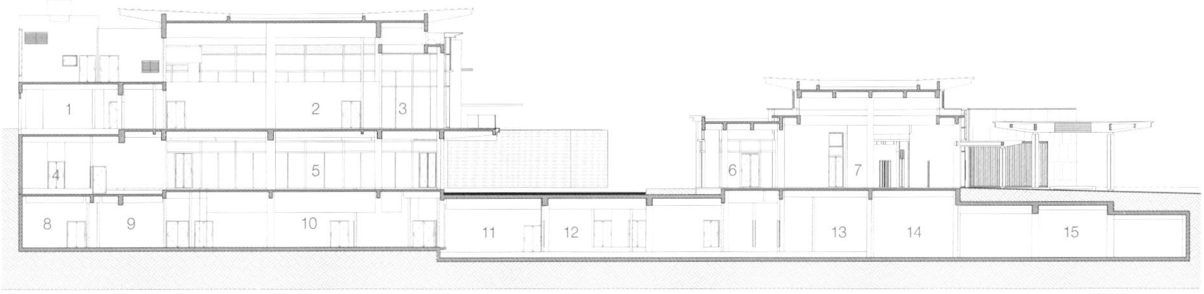

Section of lobby to multifunction building

1. Kitchen
2. Multifunction room
3. Pre-function room
4. Locker
5. Corridor
6. Lobby lounge
7. Lobby
8. MEP
9. MEP
10. Engineering room
11. Staff dinning
12. Staff kitchen
13. Storage
14. Parking
15. Parking

Section of multifunction building

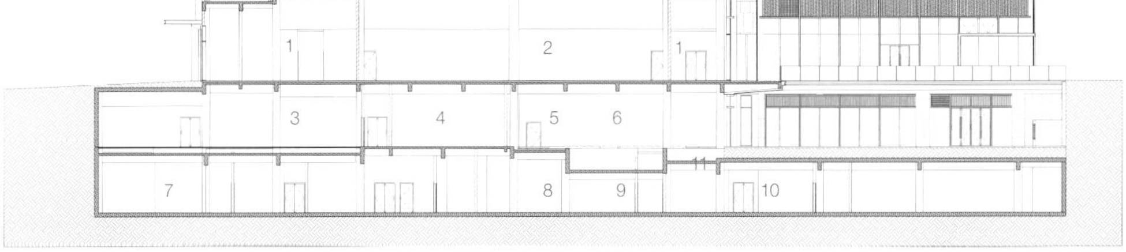

1. Pre-function room
2. Multifunction room
3. MEP
4. MEP
5. Corridor
6. Swimming pool
7. HR office
8. Engineering room
9. Storage
10. MEP
11. Administration office

Aerial rendering of Expo Village

Expo Village

A former farmland, the site of Pan Garden that serves the Expo Village is located naturally in the countryside and currently being developed as part of the Horticultural Exposition of Jiangsu Province. Through the establishment of a public space, which combines horticulture and nature, an interesting composition that includes mountains and water is formed.

Set in between a planned order and the wilderness, the Expo Village combines villages and residences, while providing exemplary residential spaces; it creates a living pattern characterized by houses, courtyards, and fields.

The space is based on the archetype of the courtyard and forms ninety-nine different courtyards, arranging the diversity of the Expo Village within one unified ambiance that recalls the atmosphere of the region south of the Yangtze River.

The architecture studios involved in the design of the Expo Village project are: Vector Architects, Ge Ming Studio and Scenic Architecture Office.

Aerial rendering of east section of village

Landscape planning concept of Expo Village

A. Hua Yuan (Flower Garden)
B. Tian Yuan (Field Garden)
C. Qu Yuan (Canal Garden)
D. Hu Yuan (Lake Garden)

Vector Architects

Architect: Vector Architects
Principal architect: Dong Gong
Design team: Liu Chen, Zhao Wei, Zhao Dan, Li Jiayi, Lin Cenhan, He Mengxian, Jin Weixi
Area: 6,150 square meters
Completion: In progress
Photography: Tian Fangfang

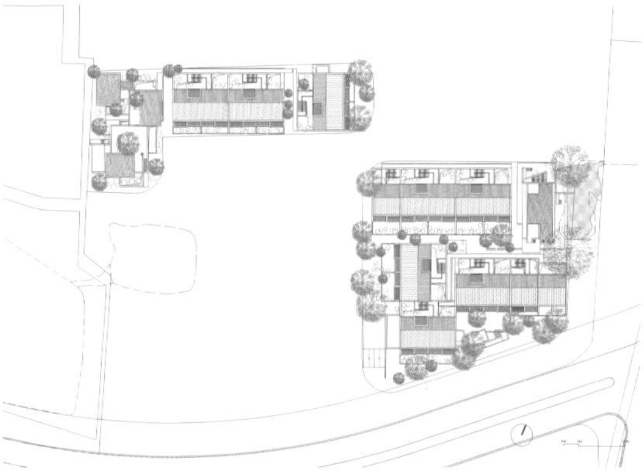

Site plan

Located to the north of Nanjing's Tangshan Mountain, the Expo Village occupies the northeastern side of the expo park. It distills the memories and culture of the local people and combines them with the Horticultural Expo and its surrounding landscape in the aim of creating a contemporary-life experience in the countryside. The spatial structure of the Expo Village has been designed based on the streets and courtyards typical to the residential textures of the Jiangnan region south of the Yangtze River.

The streets shape the public space, while the courtyards define the living spaces. This creates a multitude of spatial levels through the relationship of spatial boundaries. Juxtaposed courtyard groups scattered within the site are flanked by courtyard walls that help to shape an atmospheric, dense, and flowing public space that can be extended, narrowed, or enlarged as required, to serve as a resting area. Eaves extending from the courtyard walls form covered corridors connecting the public space and courtyard entrances. Walls surround the guestrooms in the courtyard and divide the semi-public space from the private space, providing solitude and a rich landscape experience. On the west side facing the fields, a group of guestrooms with a view of the surrounding landscape are set up, with the courtyard walls hoisting up the living space, vertically dividing the living functions inside. On the first floor, walls enclose the private courtyards and other dynamic spaces, such as the living rooms, dining rooms and spas, while the volume on the second floor hosts a more private bedroom space that is visually oriented toward the fields. The courtyard of the public resting area, which faces a canal to the east, creates a tension between the longitudinal walls and the horizontal space covered by a grid beam structure. Plants pierce through the stacked and extended walls and the building eaves, adding vibrant green life to the scene. Combined with the water feature, they create a tranquil atmosphere that blends in with the surrounding environment.

Rendering of public lounge

View of guestroom construction site

Rendering of public courtyard

1
2 | 3

1. Rendering of public lounge
2. Rendering of spa in guestroom
3. Interior rendering of guestroom

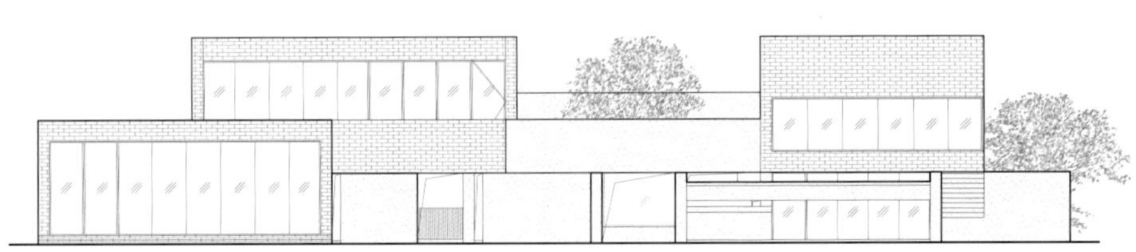

West elevation of field-view guestroom

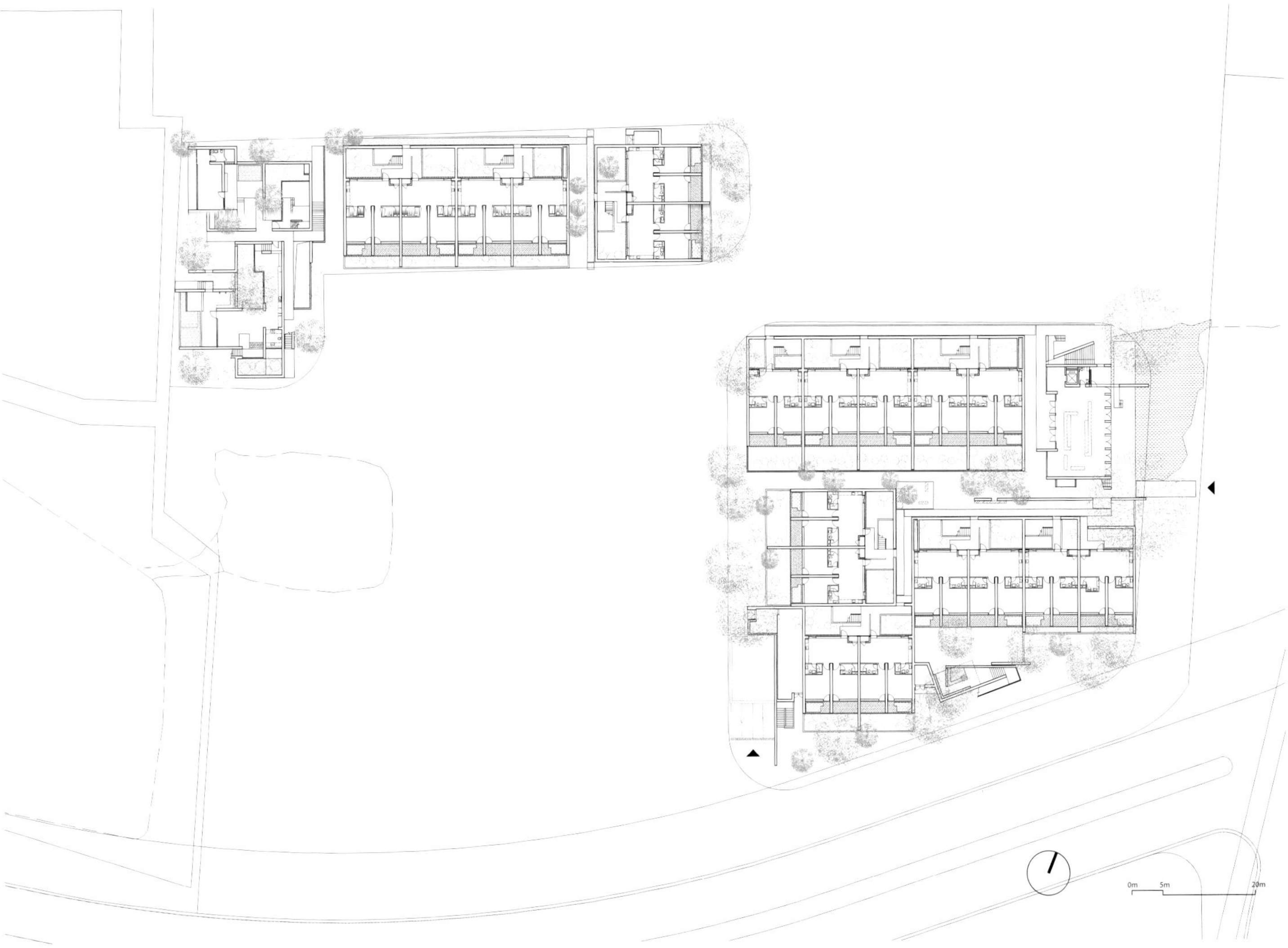

First-floor plan

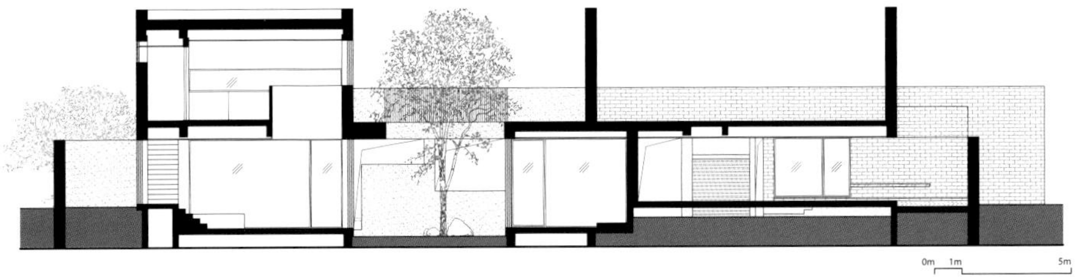

Section of field-view guestroom

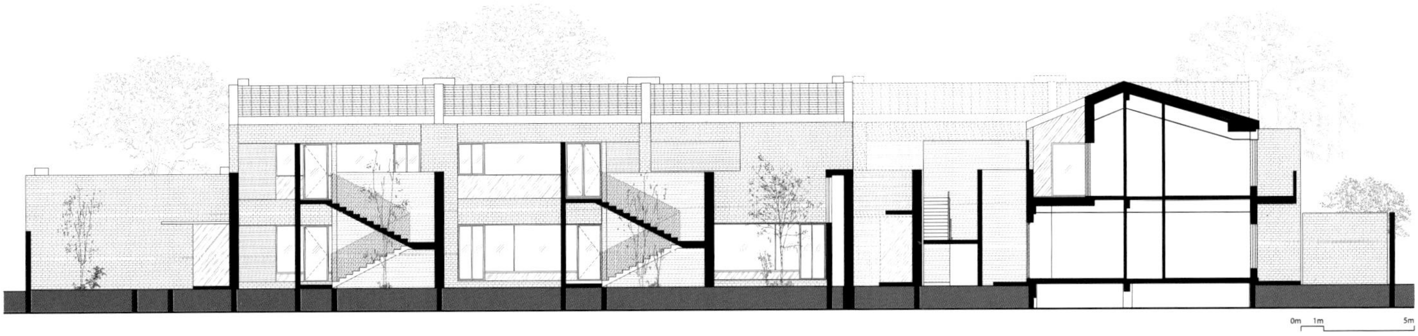

Section of courtyard-view guestroom

Ge Ming Studio

Architect: Ge Ming Studio
Principal architect: Ge Ming
Design team: Chen Jieping, Jiang Menglin, Zhang Yinan, Han Siyuan, Liu Xiaodan
Area: 24,623 square meters
Floor area: 7,652 square meters
Completion: In progress
Photography: Tian Fangfang

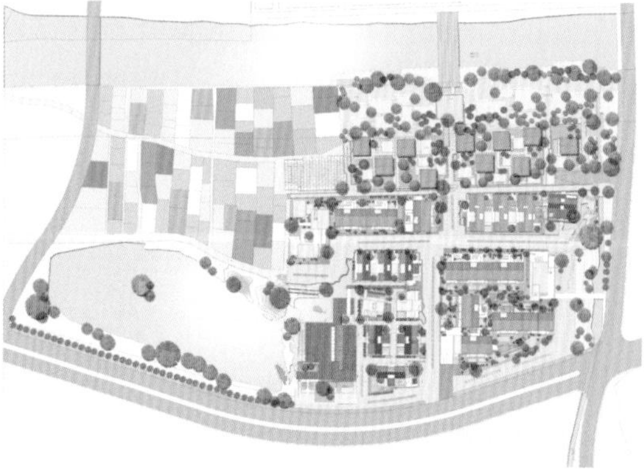

Site plan

Exterior rendering of Hu Shan pavilion

Interior rendering of Hu Shan pavilion

The team led by Professor Ge Ming was mainly responsible for the design of the northeast and southwest areas of the Expo Village, which highlight the concepts of fields, gardens, clusters, and huts to recreate a traditional landscape painting with lakes and mountains. The single building complex also emphasizes a modular construction concept with a structural organization that can be separated or combined to add spatial levels and improve usage flexibility. In the village, this concept stresses the atmospheric integration of alleys, courtyards, and houses, forming a three-dimensional pattern of paths and yards through the integration of aboveground and underground spaces.

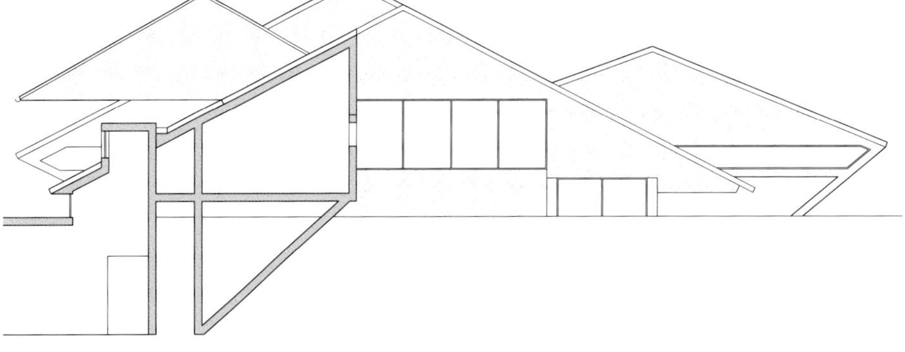

Section of Hu Shan pavilion

Interior rendering of Da San Zhai (three big guestrooms)

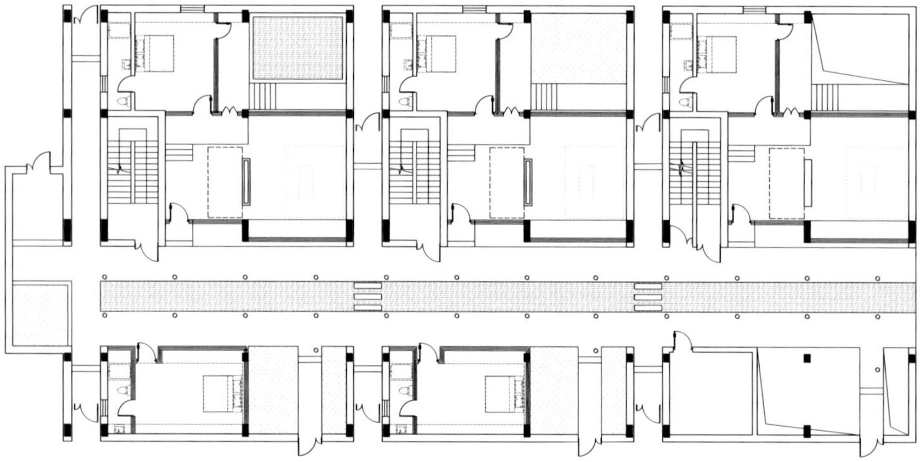

First-floor plan of Da San Zhai (three big guestrooms)

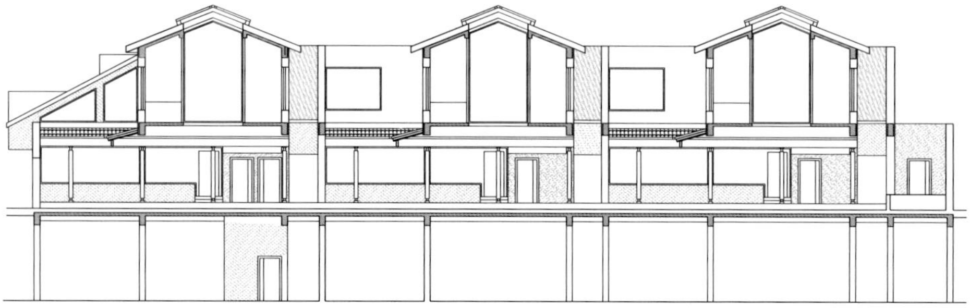

Elevation of Da San Zhai (three big guestrooms)

Rendering of Xiang Yuan (alley garden)

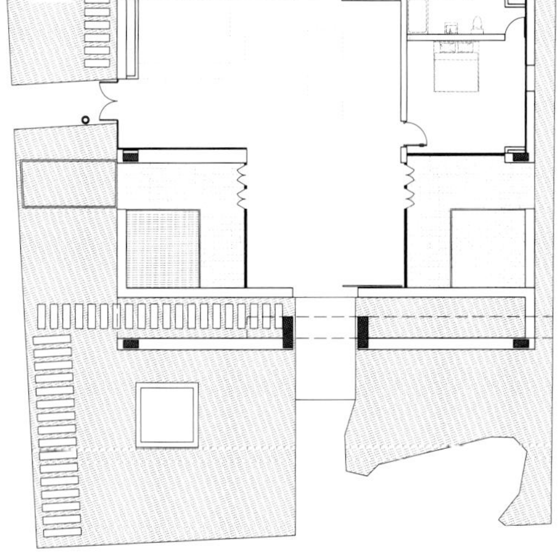

First-floor plan of San Fang

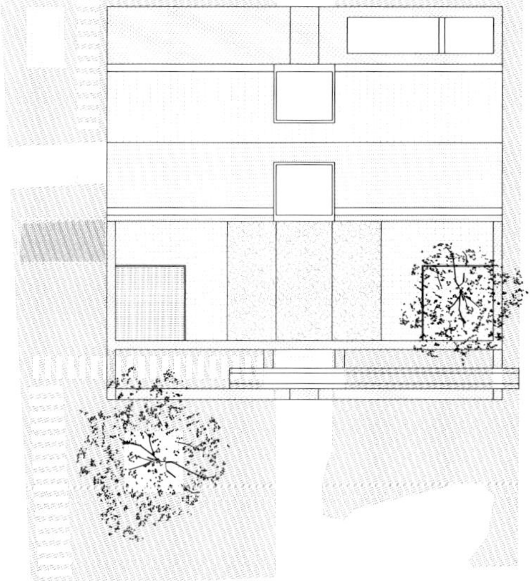

Second-floor plan of San Fang

Scenic Architecture Office

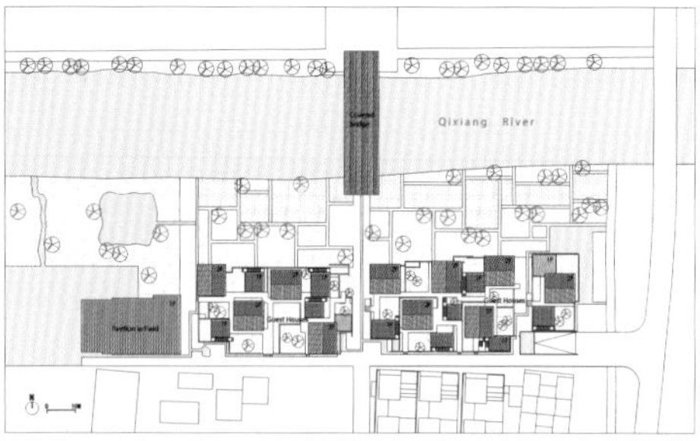
Site plan

Architect: Scenic Architecture Office
Design team: Zhu Xiaofeng, Li Qitong, Zhou Yan, Zhang Xuan
Completion: In progress
Photography: Tian Fangfang

The Expo Village lies in the shadow of Mount Xian, with the terrain rising from north to south. The northern area of the Expo Village faces the Qixiang River to the north, with a parking lot for the Horticultural Exposition on the other side. As an organic section of the Expo Village, the building settlement of the northern area needs to be in harmony with the entire village, while resonating with the site's hydrological terrain, the parking lot north of the village, the green riverside, and the fields west of the village. To that extent, a covered pedestrian bridge is built across the Qixiang River to connect the site with the parking lot. The buildings themselves are split into four groups, extended along a small street. Three eastern groups host ten guesthouses with courtyards, while a western group hosts a small pavilion among fields where families with children can pick vegetables and rest. The covered bridge and the four building groups form a total of three lanes that serve to guide rainwater from the mountain to the river, as they also lead people southward from the parking lot into the village and connect the interior of the village with the river.

Courtyard House with Shadow Walls

Hollowed-out brick walls surround the courtyard guesthouses and show-off eye-level openings that are filled with glass bricks, creating and attractive design that also respects privacy. Each guesthouse complex consists of a two-story house with a pitched roof, a one-story house with a flat roof, and a walled-off courtyard. Their design language emphasizes the difference between a structure and its contents, giving the buildings a formational lightness both inside and out. This lightness is further enhanced by the separation of the first-floor courtyard wall from the second floor, giving the effect that the pitched roof house is floating above the courtyard.

Entering the guesthouse from the alley, a winding corridor leads to the first floor of the pitched roof house, which locates a shared living room, dining room, and an open kitchen designated for the rooms on the second floor and the flat roof house. While the pitched roof house (with its balcony and main courtyard), the flat roof house (with its terrace and side courtyard), and a hot spring pool are all carefully designed to provide privacy, they also create an intimate connection and spatial flow through the duality of their interiors and exteriors. Although all ten guesthouses share a homogenized living experience, each has its own unique interior courtyard and exterior landscape, based on the different orientations of the buildings and courtyards. Depending on operational needs, the ten guesthouses can also be divided into twenty guestrooms by using the pitched and flat roof houses separately. Furthermore, the guesthouses can also be turned into combined courtyards (about three to five) through openings in the walls, providing even more possibilities for individual guests and group tours.

Pavilion in the Fields

The Pavilion in the Fields in the northwest corner of the Expo Village is a steel-framed, single-story stilt house with rice paddies to the north and west. Pointed arches derived

Aerial rendering

from the shape of haystacks are scattered across the field as structural units to support the roof. The sloping roof structure is made of 1-centimeter-thick, 350-millimeter-tall steel folded plates, on top of which lie translucent polycarbonate panels for drainage. The upper grid of the folded plate provides natural light to the space under the canopy, while the lower grid is used for equipment ducts and planters that allow climbing vines to trail and create soft lighting within the structure. Under the roof cover, indoor and semi-outdoor spaces can be flexibly transformed through sliding doors. Natural ventilation equipment for greenhouses and air conditioning integrated into the low walls provide a combination of passive and active temperature control for the indoor spaces. The cohesion and intimacy of the small huts under the canopy are ideal for gardening classes and group discussions, while the open space in between the huts that faces the rice fields is more suitable for craft workshops and casual gatherings. In this design, the contemporary pavilion forms a symbiotic relationship with the site and its climate, organically blending the structural space with rural nature, triggering its users to perceive and resonate with the surrounding rice paddies and mountains beyond a purely visual sense.

A Hanging Rainbow

The covered bridge over the Qixiang River spans 36 meters and functions as a pedestrian entrance to the northern part of the village. The bridge not only provides convenient access, but also serves as a place for visitors to gather, rest, and socialize; the space under the bridge also needs to be of a certain height in order for boats to pass through. Considering the height difference between the revetment and the water level, the bridge needed to be raised or arched in the middle. Combining these two design requirements, the 8-meter-wide bridge deck is divided into nine 4-by-8-meter platforms—like nine connected pavilions that gradually rise and fall. The most appropriate structural form for this design idea was to use the sloping roof of the bridge as the main arch to suspend the nine separate platforms. Through the joint efforts of the architects and structural engineers, steel trusses arranged along the double gable roof form a folded plate arch, which transforms the vertical load of the suspended platforms into internal force that is transferred to the sides of the arch structure.

Finally, the gravity and lateral thrust are passed on to the foundation on the revetment through the U-shaped concrete bridgehead. The nine suspended platforms are light and permeable, connected by ramps and steps along a central passage. They also provide areas for rest and market stands on either side. The bridgeheads on both sides are simple and solid; the design continues the double gable roof to cover the bridge's shear walls, turning the bridgehead into two semi-outdoor cabins, presenting the pedestrian bridge with the imagery of a village and the warmth of home.

Axonometric diagram of guestroom

First-floor plan

1. Covered bridge
2. Pavilion in field
3. Lobby
4. Guestroom
5. Courtyard
6. Canteen
7. Tearoom
8. Recreation room

View of guestroom construction site

Second-floor plan

1. Guestroom
2. Terrace
3. Roof garden

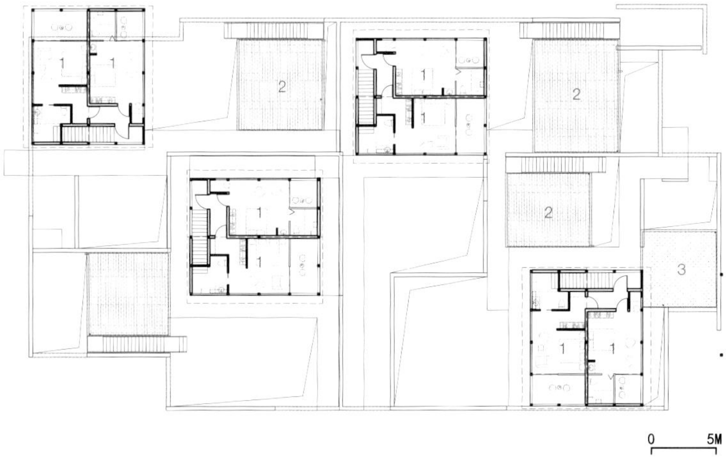

Longitudinal section of village

Rendering of guestroom

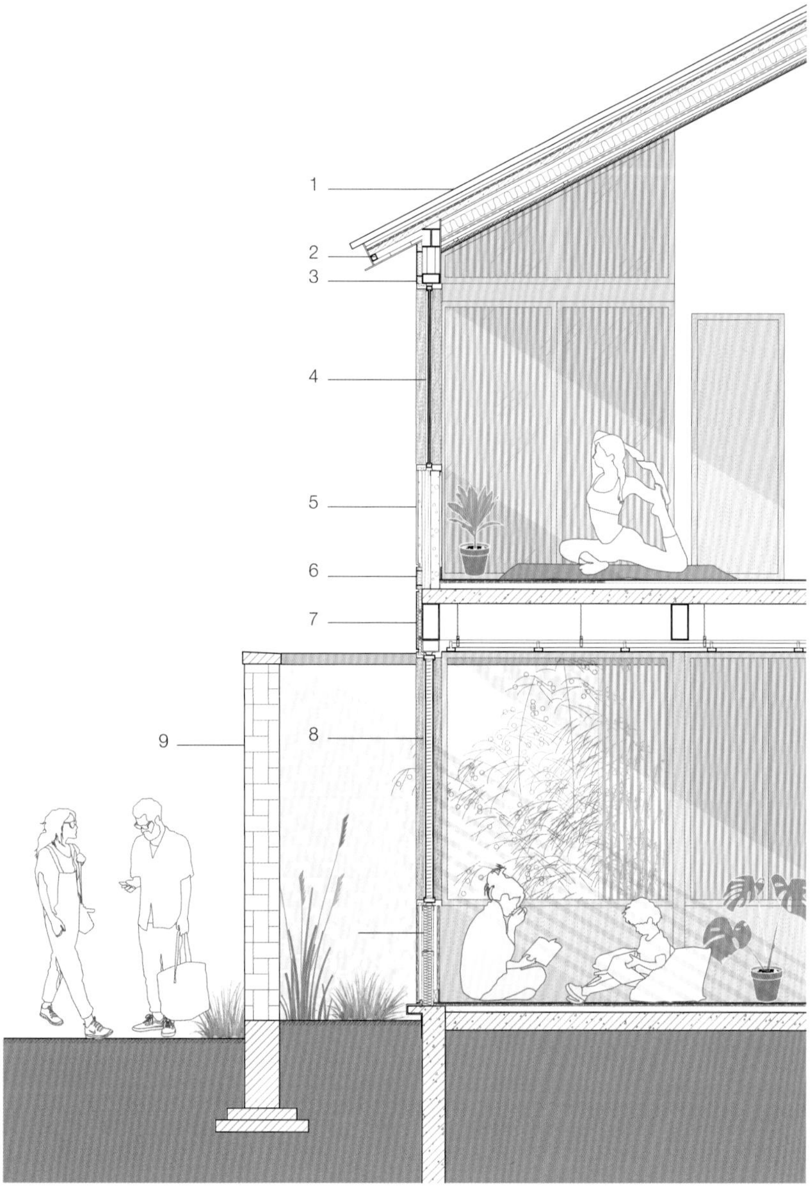

Construction detail

1. Traditional-style small blue-black tile
2. Dark-gray aluminum board
3. Steel sheet in wood-texture PVDF coating
4. Insulated low-iron tempered and laminated low-e glazing, with wood grill
5. Advanced white inorganic texture paint
6. Light-gray aluminum board
7. Ceramic fritted low-iron insulated low-e glass, with built-in aluminum louver
8. Light steel keel, high grade solid wood wall
9. Blue-black bricks with glass bricks in between

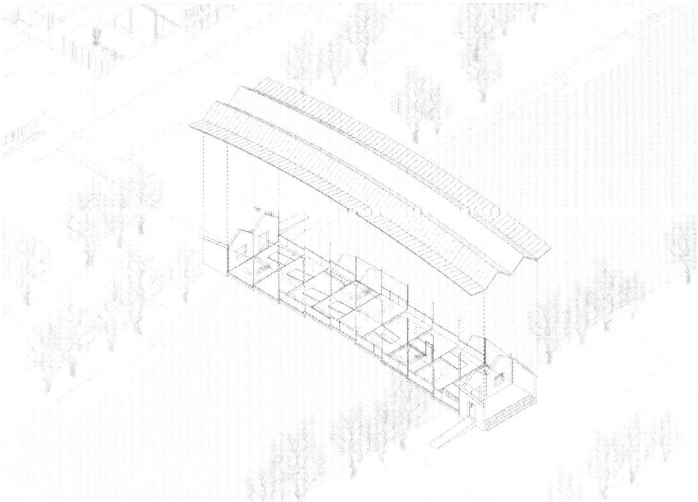

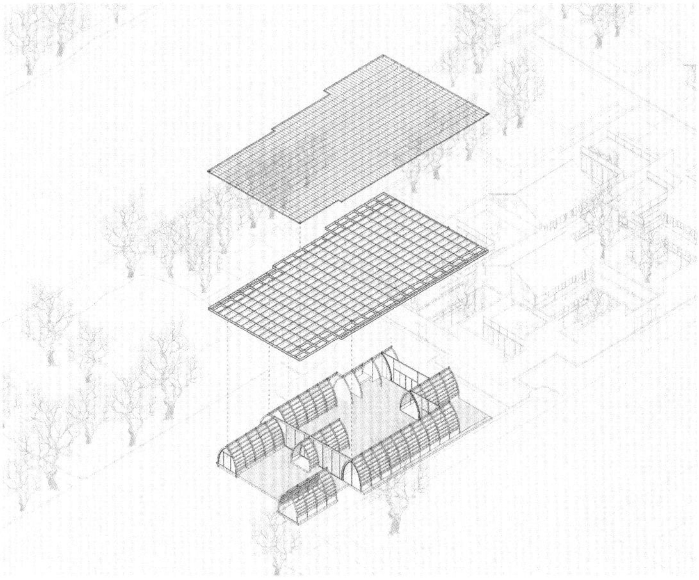

1. Exploded diagram of Qi Xiang bridge
2. Exploded diagram of pavilion
3. Rendering of Qi Xiang bridge
4. Rendering of pavilion

The Second Entrance Building

Totao Design

Architect: Totao Design
Principal architect: Luo Jianli
Design team: Li Song, Dai Jing, Gan Hao, Ding Mengxiong, Sun Qian, Feng Xiao, Wang Xun, Wu Yaming
Interior design: Fan Architectural Firm (FANAF)
Landscape design: DG Landscape Design Studio
Construction drawings: Nanjing Yangtze River Urban Architectural Design Co. Ltd
Completion: In progress
Photography: Tian Fangfang

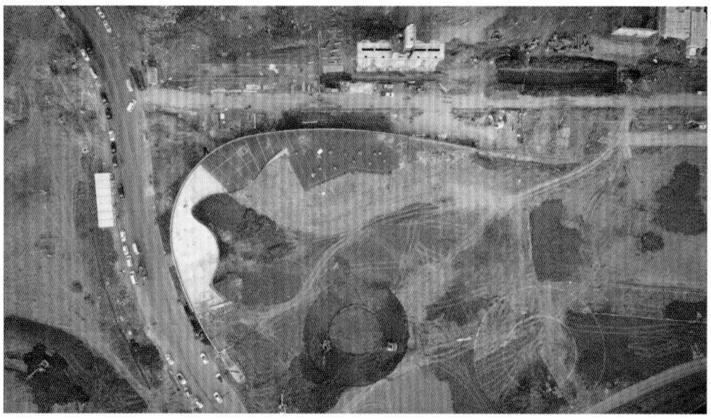

Site plan

The second entrance building is surrounded by hills on the south, east, and west sides, naturally forming a north-facing entrance to the park. The site is surrounded by diverse geological features, rural settlements, industrial remains, and several linear traces of the transformation to nature caused by humans, such as the West-East Gas Pipeline, the Beijing-Shanghai high-speed railway, a farmland boundary, the Qixiang River, and a mining railway.

The building design is conceptualized as a "smile of the earth," gracefully drawing a curved "smile" along the existing boundary of the farmland to welcome visitors into the park. The ground is slightly raised along this curve to create a multifunctional service area underneath, while the rooftop hosts a sky garden from where visitors can admire the breathtaking surrounding of majestic mountains.

To coexist with nature, the building for entrance No. 2 employs a more relaxed design approach that minimizes human intervention on the environment; it exhibits more harmonious and optimistic traces of human activity befitting of current environment-conscious times to lead a Horticultural Exhibition of a new era.

View of second entrance building construction site

Aerial rendering of second entrance building

Ground-floor plan of second entrance building

1. Ticket office
2. Art space
3. Service center
4. Women's restroom
5. Nursing and baby care room
6. Men's restroom
7. Equipment room

View of digital design construction site

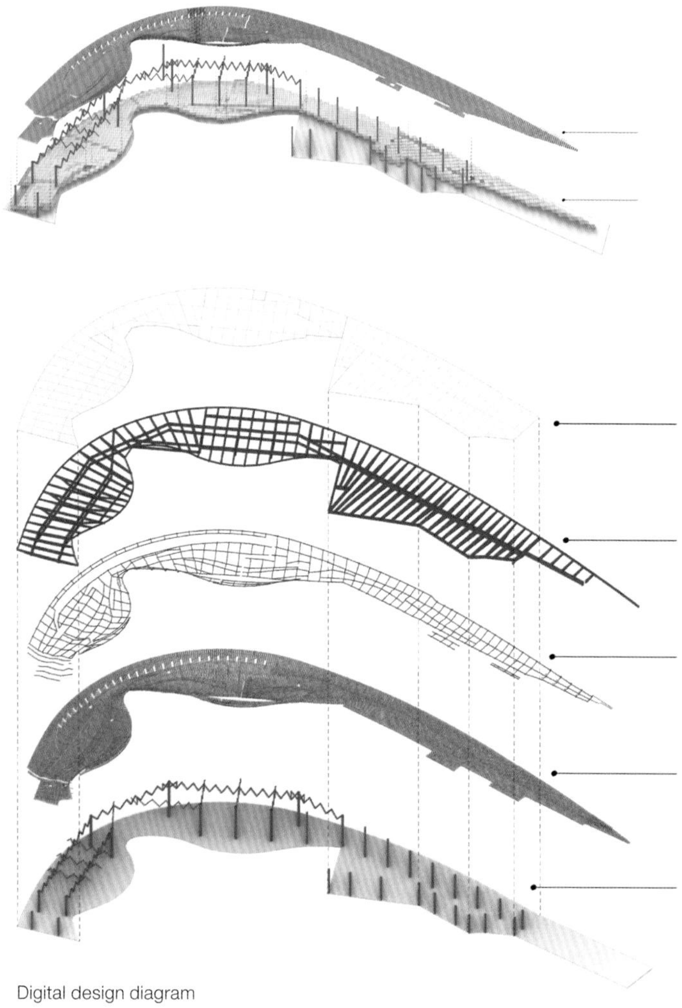

Digital design diagram

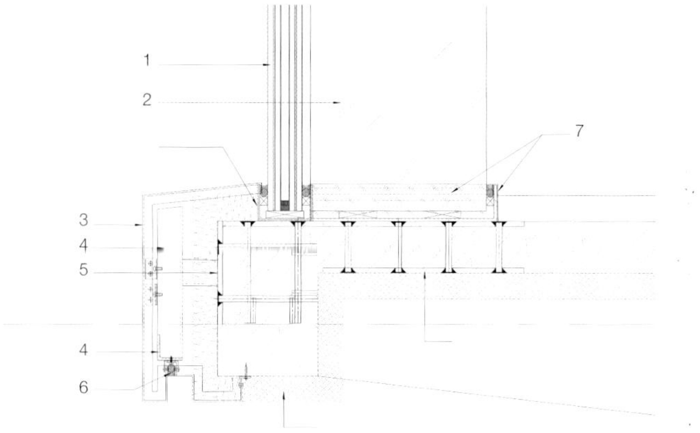

Details of construction

1. Tempered laminated glass (heat bent glass)
2. Tempered laminated glass (glass ribs)
3. 3 mm fluorocarbon-coated aluminum steel
4. 50x50x4 hot-dipped galvanized rectangular angle
5. Pre-embedded hot-dipped galvanized parts
6. Foam stick and weather-proofing sealant
7. Covered with 1.2 mm stainless-steel plate

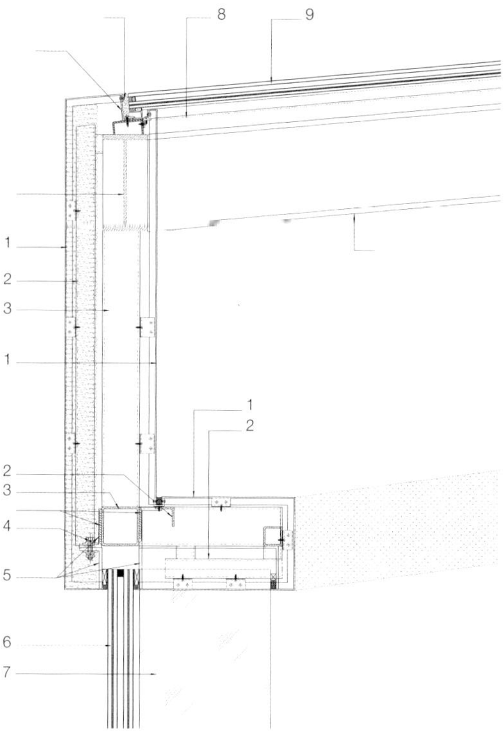

Details of construction

1. 3 mm fluorocarbon-coated aluminum steel
2. 50x50x4 hot-dipped galvanized rectangular angle
3. 100x100x5 hot-dipped galvanized rectangular steel pipe
4. M12 stainless-steel bolts
5. 10 mm galvanized bending steel sheet
6. Tempered laminated glass (heat bent glass)
7. Tempered laminated glass (glass ribs)
8. 40x60x40x4 hot-dipped galvanized bending channel
9. Hollow laminated tempered glass

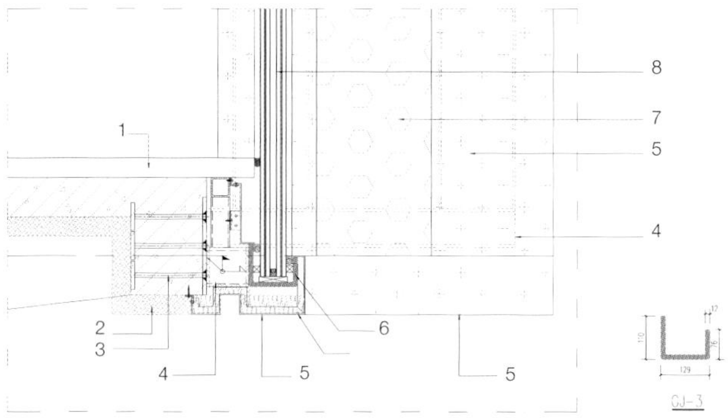

Details of construction

1. Indoor floor
2. Waterproof mortar
3. 400x250x12 hot-dipped galvanized pre-embedded parts
4. 100x100x8 hot-dipped galvanized rectangular steel pipe
5. 3 mm fluorocarbon-coated aluminum steel
6. Hot-dipped galvanized bending channel
7. 3 mm fluorocarbon-coated aluminum steel (perforated plate)
8. Tempered laminated glass (heat bent glass)

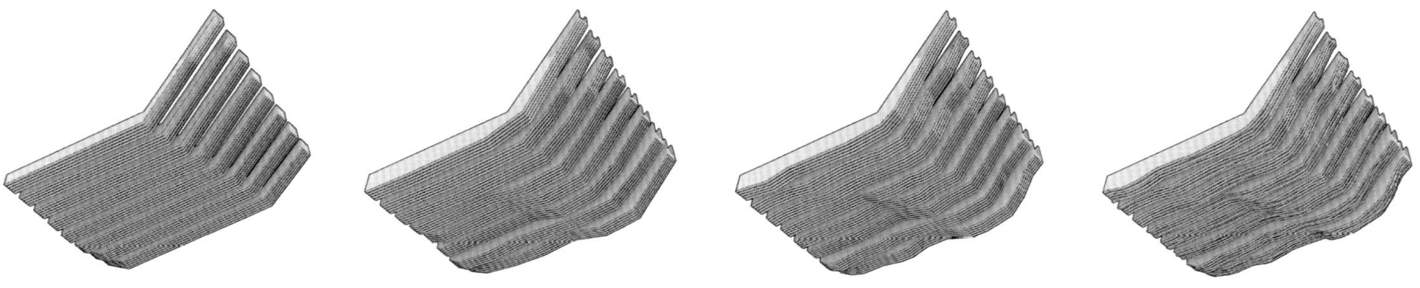

Initial geometry

Level one:
Volumetric formations

Level two:
Adding complexity to
individual beams

Level three:
Adding complexity to
individual boards

Form generation diagram

The Third Entrance Building

Totao Design

Architect: Totao Design
Principal architect: Luo Jianli
Design team: Li Song, Gan Hao, Ding Mengxiong, Sun Qian, Wu Yaming
Interior design: Fan Architectural Firm (FANAF)
Landscape design: DG Landscape Design Studio
Construction drawings: Nanjing Yangtze River Urban Architectural Design Co. Ltd
Completion: In progress
Photography: Tian Fangfang

Site plan

The third entrance building is located in the east of the expo park, hidden among quiet, serene rolling hills. The design concept is characterized by a "landscaped wall," which is a long stone wall placed along an existing road, that retains all of the large trees within the site. The long horizontal line of the design echoes the subtle ups and downs of the terrain and defines the internal and external boundaries of the park. The wall also functions as a footbridge, connecting the park's ticket office with the tour-train station (where visitors can embark on a sightseeing train ride), while also leading visitors directly to a natural forest. The wall is made of colored natural stones, created through modern processing methods; they are arranged in an attractive pattern to form a giant landscape mural.

This simple and modern architecture stands in harmony with the natural hilly landscape, serving not only as a contemporary expression of the traditional Chinese view of nature, but also implying a representative image of Nanjing as a city harmoniously bound by mountains, rivers, and forests.

Sketch of design concept

Night rendering of third entrance building

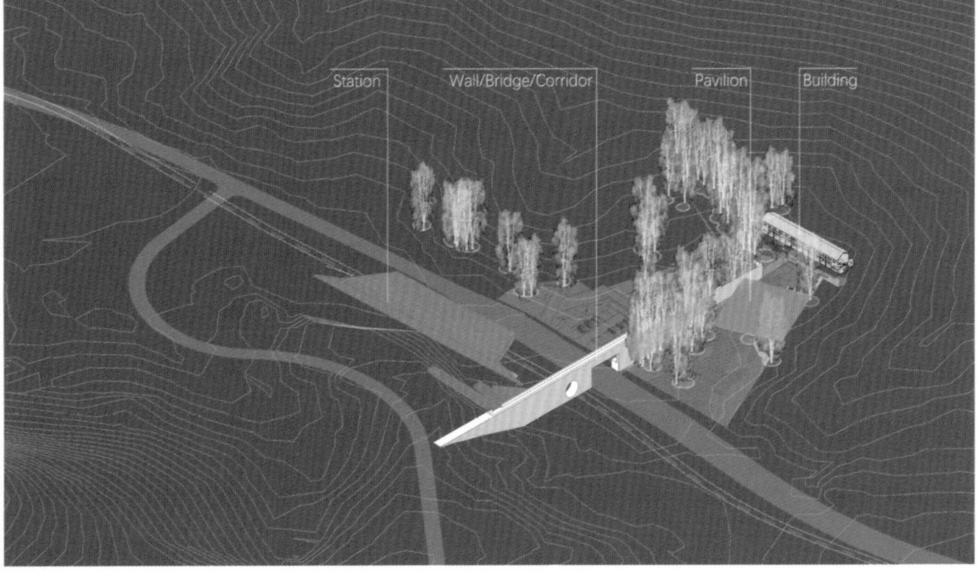

Constitution analysis diagram

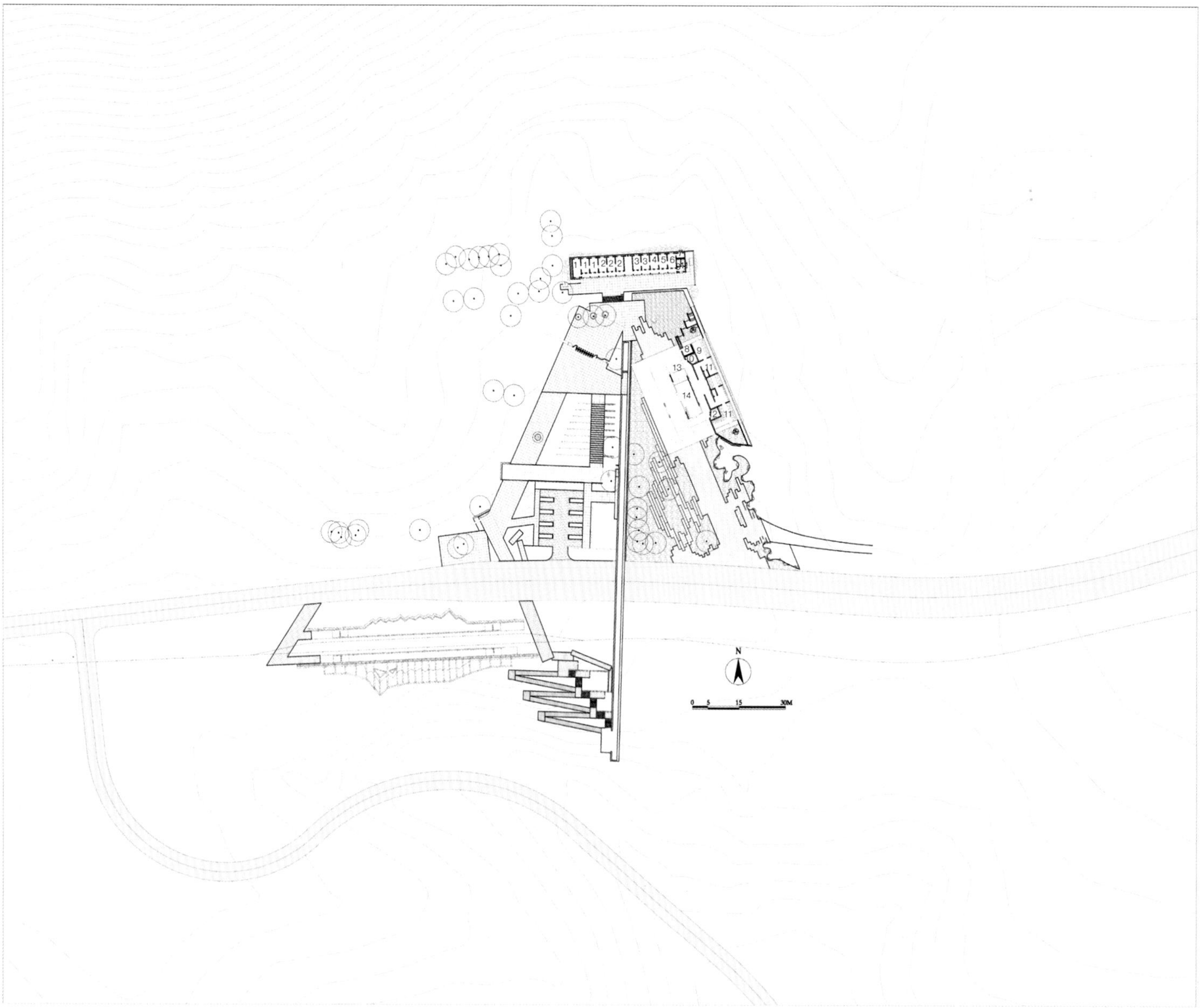

Ground-floor plan

1. Supermarket
2. Creative space
3. Information desk
4. Lease/deposit
5. Communication service
6. Team reception
7. Equipment room
8. Management room
9. Men's restroom
10. Additional/accessibility restroom
11. Women's restroom
12. Nursing and baby care room
13. Manual ticketing
14. Ticket center

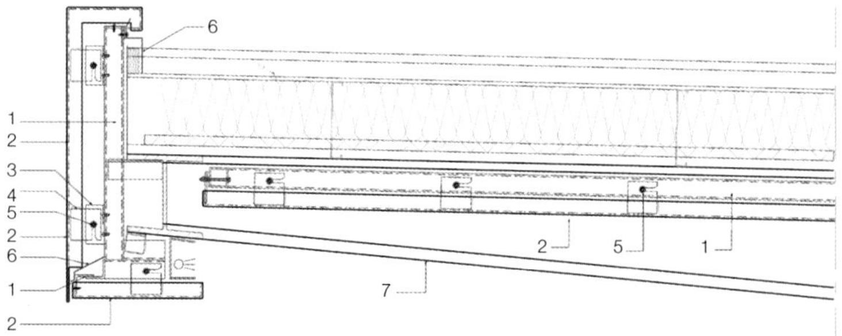

Detail of roof

1. 50x50x4 galvanized steel square tube
2. 5 mm trimmed steel plates
3. 4 mm U-shaped steel parts
4. 4 mm galvanized steel pendant
5. M8x65 stainless-steel bolts
6. 1.5 mm galvanized steel plate
7. Main steel structure (anti-corrosion fluorocarbon coating)

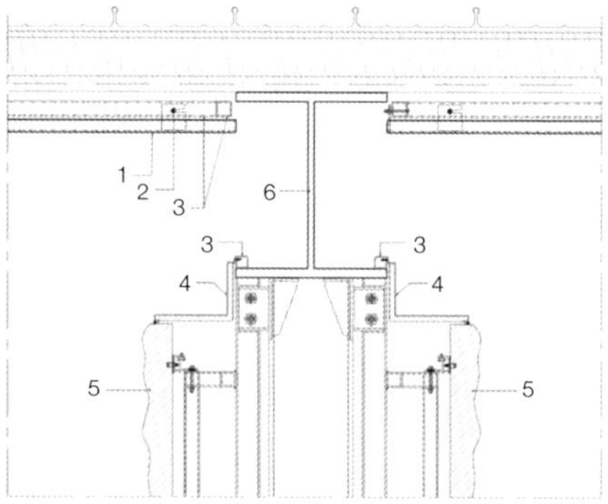

Detail of roof

1. 5 mm trimmed steel plates
2. M8x70 stainless-steel bolts
3. 50x50x4 galvanized steel square tube
4. 3 mm trimmed steel plates
5. Stone curtain wall
6. Main steel structure (anti-corrosion fluorocarbon coating)

Exterior rendering of third entrance building

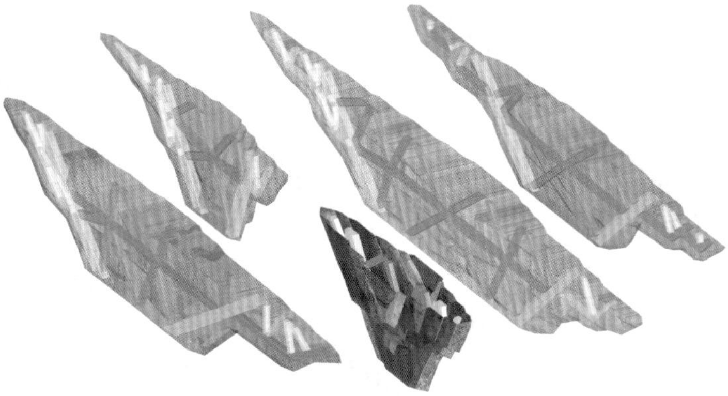

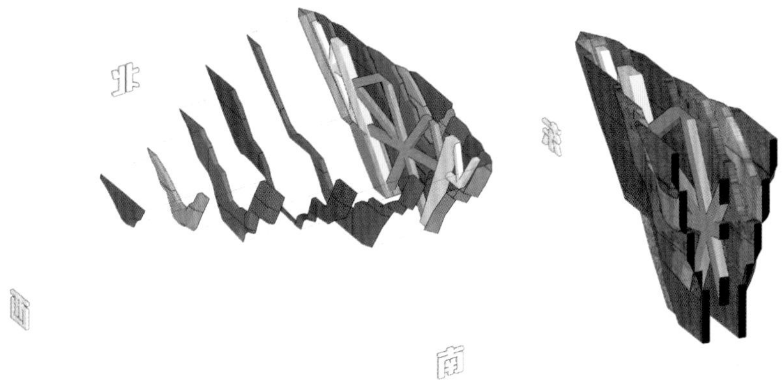

Axonometric diagram of structure

ARCHITECTURE
CHINA

Toilet Revolution

Responsive Practices of the Toilet Revolution in Contemporary Chinese Cities

Introduction: Toilet Revolution in Urban Contexts

The history of toilets stretches as far back as the history of human civilization. By the time the Skara Brae settlement (3100 BC to 2500 BC) sprang up in Scotland, people had already moved their personal business indoors, after which toilets became a unique space for communities and residential buildings. Insofar as they provided relief for basic needs, toilets were also overlooked in traditional urban history and architectural history because of its relation to negative associations: "filthy," "murky," "damp," and such. As Rem Koolhaas said, "No architectural treatise declares the toilet as the primordial element of architecture, but it might be the ultimate one." [1]

In real historical practice, efforts at improving toilets and its usage have never ceased. A London watchmaker, Alexander Cummings, designed the first flush toilet in 1775 and subsequent technological advancements led to the prototype of the contemporary flush toilet. However, most developing countries, including China, primarily used the more traditional pit toilets up until the 1970s. As China experienced breakneck growth following its period of economic reforms, toilets became an increasingly glaring obstacle to elevating the standard of life for both urban and rural residents. It was against this backdrop that the "toilet revolution," now an element of modern-day Chinese architectural practices, slowly gained steam.

UNICEF first proposed the concept of the toilet revolution in 1997, calling upon the global community to focus on the toilet safety and hygiene issues facing impoverished populations. Despite that, in 2015, there were still 2.4 billion people across the world who relieved themselves in deplorable conditions—and of those, 950 million for whom open defecation was the only choice. Many philanthropists like Bill Gates have extended their generosity toward bettering society and helping others, even so, the problem of toilets has remained fundamentally unresolved in the last century. As designers and planners, architects need to approach this global issue through new methods, while reducing this any hazards as much as possible through technological and economic innovations.

China turned its attention to the toilet problem during the Patriotic Health Campaign in the 1960s. The China National Tourism Administration proposed the idea of a toilet revolution in 2015 before implementing a wave of toilet updates and renovations at major tourist attractions around the country. Policy from the federal level down then expanded the toilet revolution into urban and rural communities, which provided a common point for campaigns aimed at revitalizing rural villages and renovating cities.

Today, four related, yet distinct initiatives drive the actual practices of China's toilet revolution: the first is making indoor flush toilets universal during urban renovations; second, developing infrastructure in rural areas, primarily through hazard-free biogas toilets and the improvement of pit latrines; third, upgrading the quality of public toilet services at tourist spots and areas; and fourth, allowing public access to restrooms at government agencies, institutions, and public service facilities.

On the whole, the toilet revolution remains concentrated in private and communal restrooms in rural areas and old shantytowns. Public restrooms in urban open spaces command less attention, even though existing restrooms can have an impact on a city's overall improvements because of cleanliness and image issues. Architects face three main difficulties in bringing the toilet revolution to the cities. First, there needs to be a comprehensive way of thinking in order to defuse and integrate the conflict between restroom spaces and urban interfaces. Second, the functional designs of public toilets should start with considering the users' bodily posture, positioning, and motion paths. Finally, the key to popularizing the design lies in extending the revolution over a greater area and the design scope, which is shaped by the choice of materials, structure, and construction mode during the building process.

The public toilet design practices that were introduced began with the urban renewal campaign spearheaded by the local governments in Kunshan and Quzhou, located in Jiangsu Province and Zhejiang Province, respectively. Both are economically developing areas situated on the coast of Eastern China with relatively good infrastructure. Their municipalities have devoted more efforts toward improving public toilets in their respective cities as a way of adapting to the area's accelerating urbanization. Thirty-over design projects provided by twenty-two architects and firms offer a glimpse of the intersection between design and the toilet revolution, and the way architects used their own strategies to respond to different urban dilemmas and social demands.

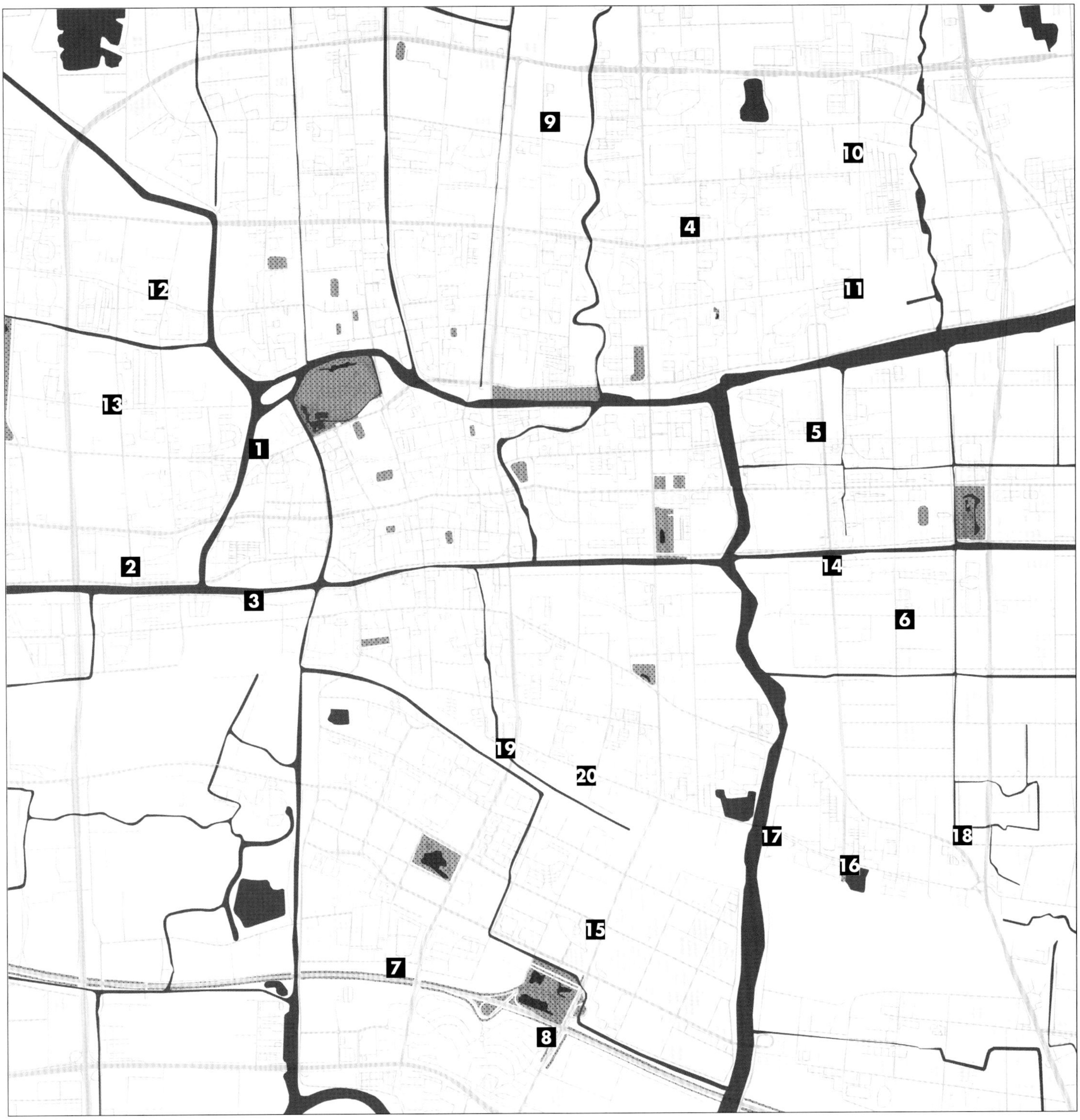

Master plan of Kunshan project

No. 1, 20

Shui Yanfei/
NATURALBUILD

No. 2, 6

Huang Yujia/
YJ Atelier

No. 3, 17

Fan Jiujiang/
Continuation Studio

No. 4, 14

Huang Mingjian/
Design Hub

No. 5, 10

Ruan Hao/
LYCS Architecture

No. 7, 15

Wang Hao/
Rùn Atelier

No. 8, 11

Fan Beilei/
genarchitects

No. 9, 12

Liu Kenan, Zhang Xu/
Atelier XÜK

No. 13, 18

Qi Shanshan/
STUDIO QI

No. 16, 19

Li Danfeng, Zhou Jianjia/
YEAS

Master plan of Quzhou project

No. 1

Chen Haoru/
Atelier Chen Haoru

No. 2

Yuan Feng/
Archi-Union

No. 3

Chen Lichao/
Atelier Chen Lichao

No. 4

Li Xinggang/
Atelier Li Xinggang

No. 5

Zhang Ke/
standardarchitecture

No. 6

Zhuang Shen/
Archmixing

No. 7

Zhang Bin/
Atelier Z+

No. 8

Liu Yichun/
Atelier Deshaus

No. 9

Chang Yung Ho/
Atelier FCJZ

No. 10

Ge Ming/
Ge Ming Studio

No.11

Zhang Lei/
AZL Architects

No. 12

Wang Shu/
Amateur Architecture

Land, Landscape and Topography

Unlike their implementation in rural areas, public toilet designs in the city must first adhere to the rich and complex spatial qualities of contemporary cities. The complexities of these spaces are manifested in large urban populations and jam-packed residential structures, as well as the unique local building scales, social functions, and environmental efficacy of the different urban areas. With buildings and sites so tightly surrounded by such spaces, the focus on locality and temporality forces urban constructions to become active "responsive constructions;" buildings also become the synthesis of what architect David Leatherbarrow calls "a network of topographical relationship."[2] Beyond the building itself, this responsive character is also reflected in the public toilet design practices within modern Chinese cities in which architects face two kinds of environmental conditions.

The first category is a city's built environment, including interwoven networks and existing architectural textures. For example, architect Wang Shu designed public restrooms situated in a roadside green space just north of a residential community at a major intersection in Quzhou. This type of linear space is not uncommon in the architectural environment of modern-day China. Chinese neighborhoods are generally closed off with a few designated entrances, using either surrounding greenery or walls as partitions from the city streets. As a result, the streets encircling these communities become walkways with no sign of life, and pedestrians lack access to immediate services, including convenient public restrooms.

Wang Shu's strategy breaks down the toilet building into independent, albeit inter-connected, rooms and then reassembles them based on the linear arrangements of the nearby apartment buildings. That, together with the slightly raised green belt, marks the transitional boundary from the residential area into the city streets. Each room sits at a forty-five-degree angle from the street to better protect the restrooms and prevent passersby from catching sight of the interior. The entire structure is eye-catching and made to look like the bus stations commonly found throughout the city. Even though the shape of the restrooms emerged in response to the monotonous urban space, this structure also shatters the dullness of the existing street through its arrangement of materials and walls, as well as its Chuan-Dou style timber structure, and its continuous, semi-translucent roof.

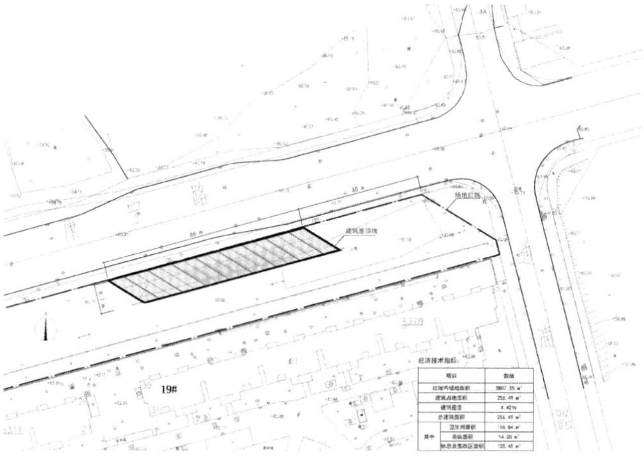

Master plan of No. 12 toilet (Quzhou) © Amateur Architecture

Rendering of No. 12 toilet (Quzhou) ©Amateur Architecture

Section of No. 12 toilet (Quzhou) ©Amateur Architecture

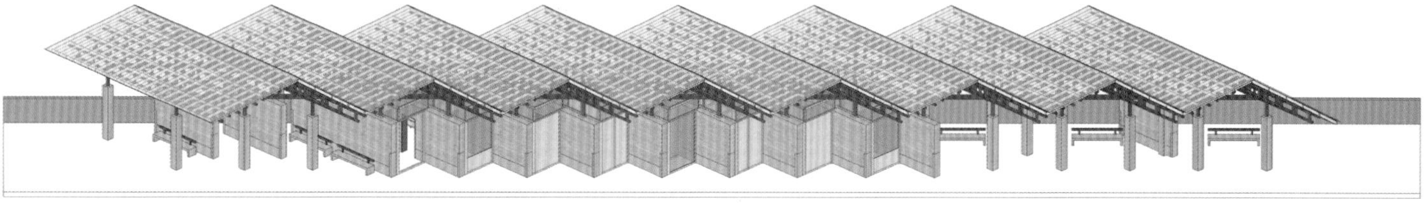

Axonometric diagram of No. 12 toilet (Quzhou) ©Amateur Architecture

Rendering A of No. 10 toilet (Quzhou) © Ge Ming Studio

Rendering B of No. 10 toilet (Quzhou) © Ge Ming Studio

Sketch by Ge Ming © Ge Ming Studio

Ge Ming's project presents another example of using urban "scrap" spaces, though it is far smaller than Wang Shu's. Buildings obstruct three sides of the site and the surrounding streets, which are more private and compact, thus forcing Ge Ming to move away from Wang Shu's open, conspicuous design, toward creating a deep, serene site with a more relaxing atmosphere for visitors. To this end, he used the trees and the nearby buildings; the modest dimensions also supplemented the gaps between the woods.

The largest tree there bisects the building's core space, affecting the raised roof and composition of the path. Inspired by classical Chinese paintings, the architect establishes a minimalistic, understated relationship between the greenery and the architecture, thereby transforming them into a forest in the midst of a bustling city.

Model of No. 10 toilet (Quzhou) © Ge Ming Studio

Master plan of No. 10 toilet (Quzhou) © Ge Ming Studio

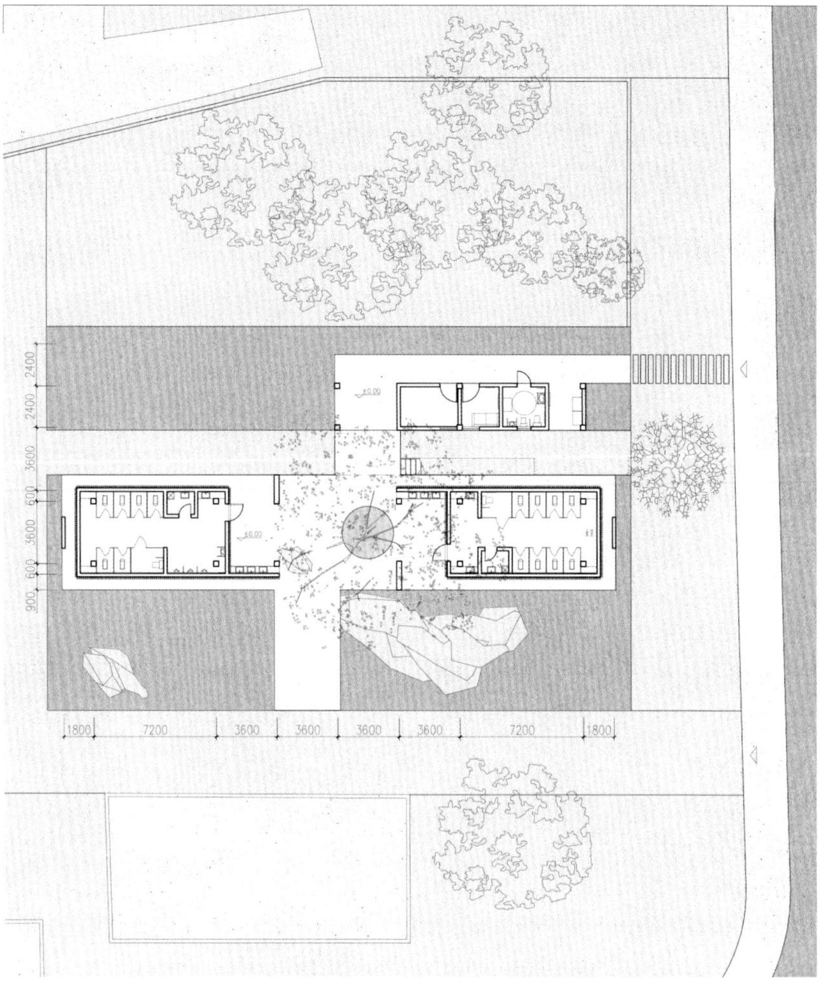

Floor plan of No. 10 toilet (Quzhou) © Ge Ming Studio

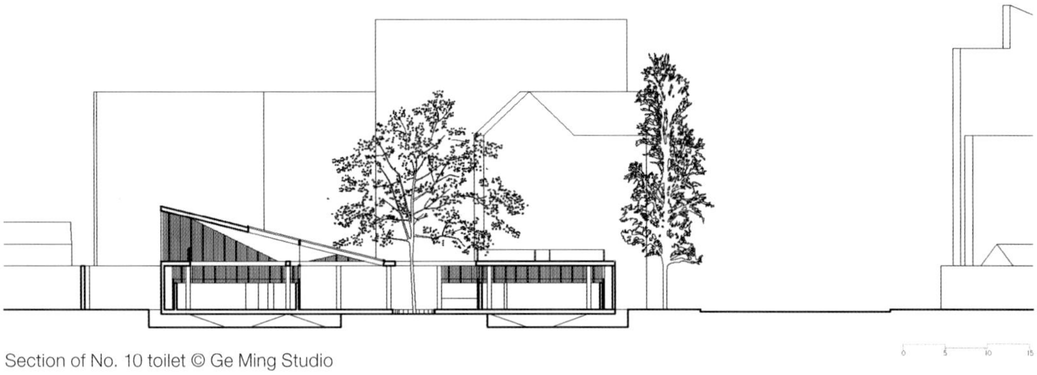

Section of No. 10 toilet © Ge Ming Studio

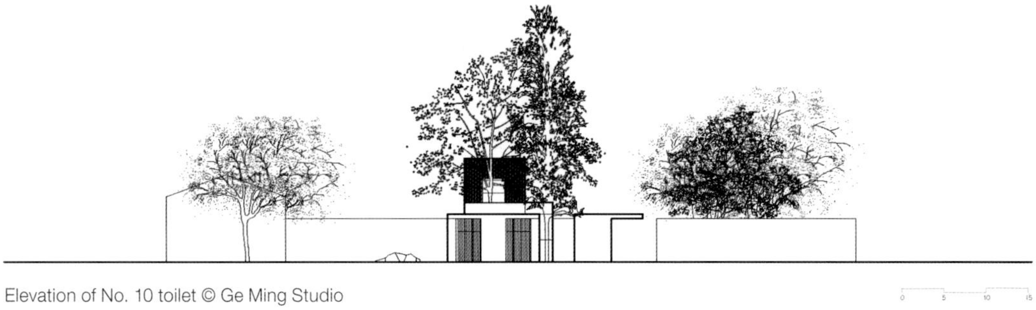

Elevation of No. 10 toilet © Ge Ming Studio

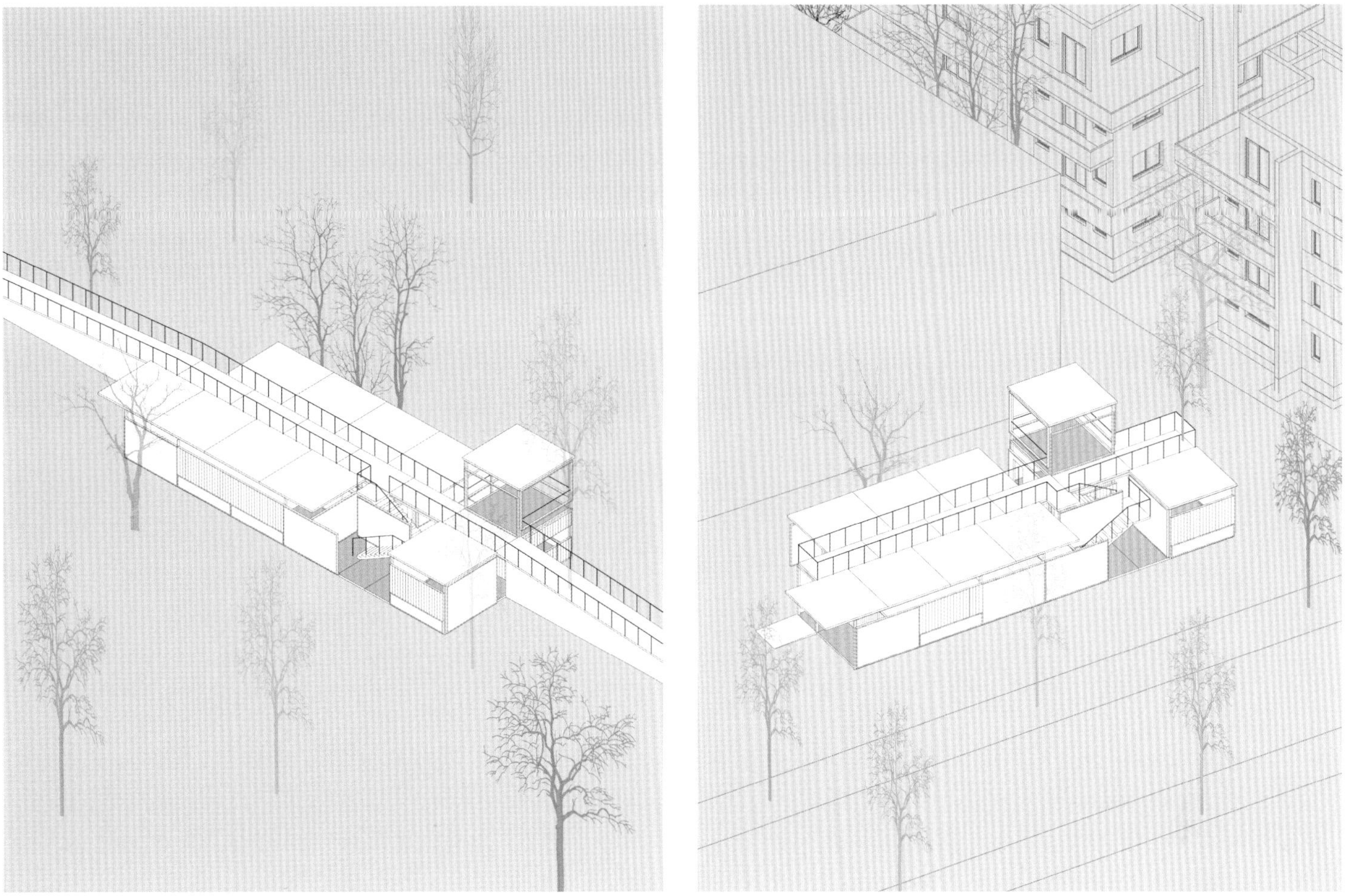

Axonometric diagrams of No. 4 toilet (Quzhou) © Atelier Li Xinggang

The second type of environmental condition is a city's natural settings. The growing ecological consciousness has turned parks and waterfront areas into leisure destinations for city residents and a main setting for public restrooms. The way architecture adapts to the environment is also a consideration of the way such natural spaces respond to urban landscapes. In Li Xinggang's project, the waterfront park restrooms have been conceived as a creeping walkway and an observation platform with panoramic views, extending the structure as a landscape in the city.

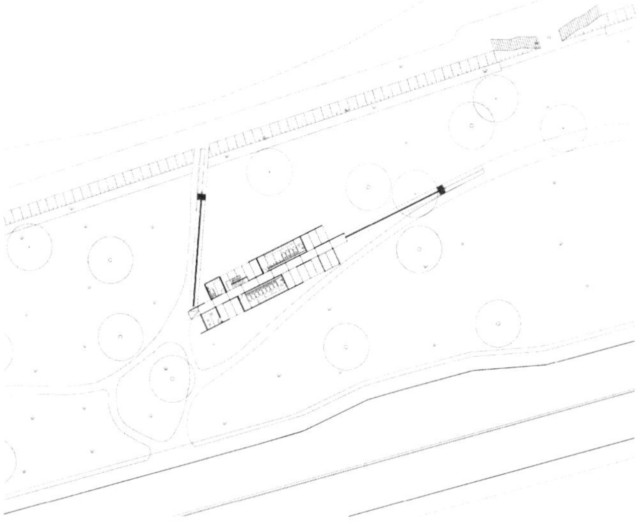

Master plan of No. 4 toilet (Quzhou) © Atelier Li Xinggang

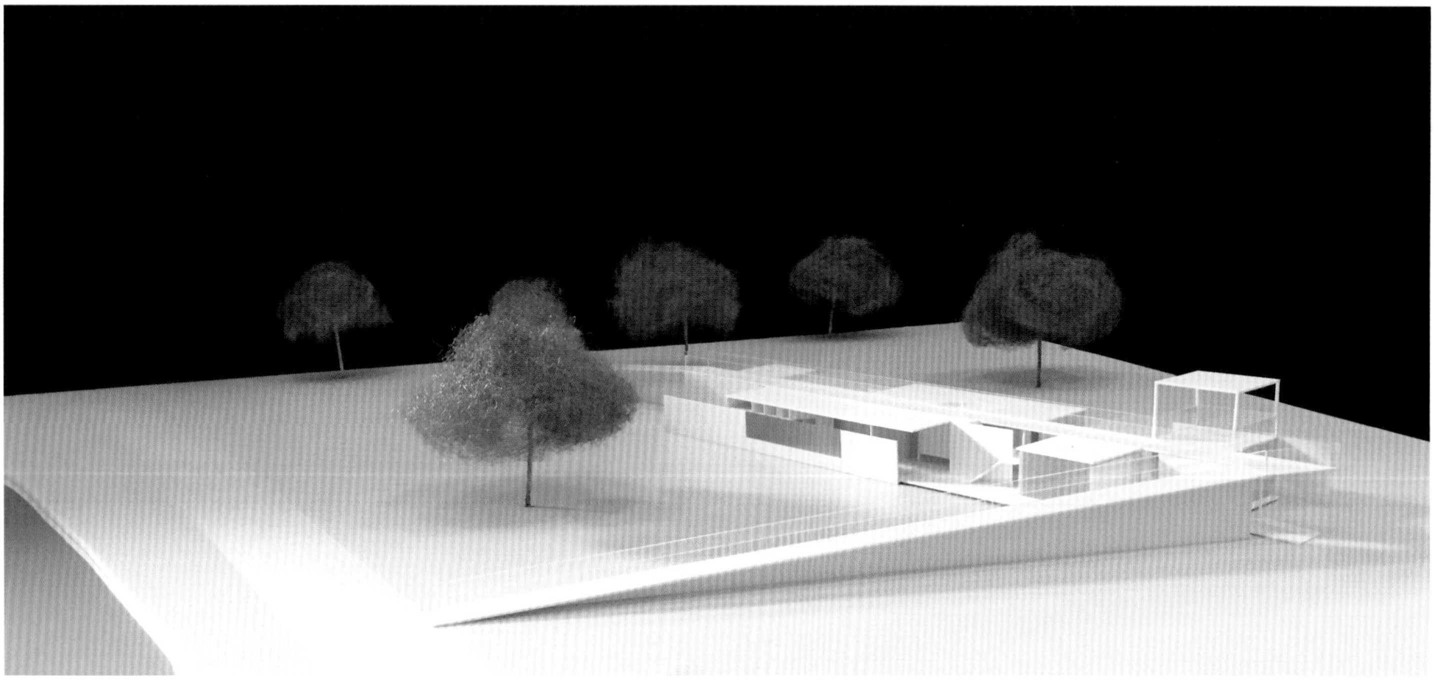

Model of No. 4 toilet (Quzhou) © Atelier Li Xinggang

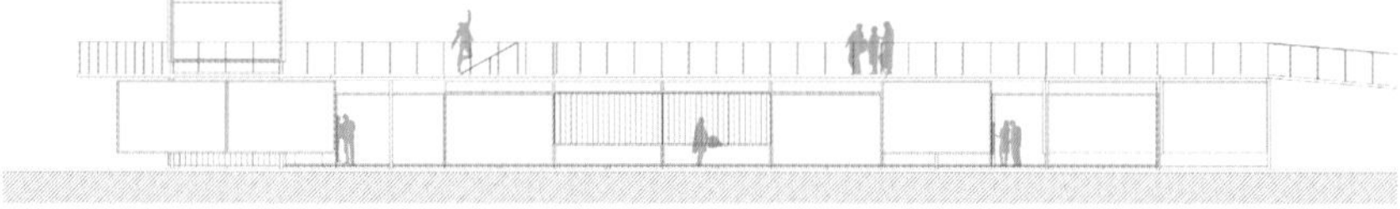

Section of No. 4 toilet (Quzhou) © Atelier Li Xinggang

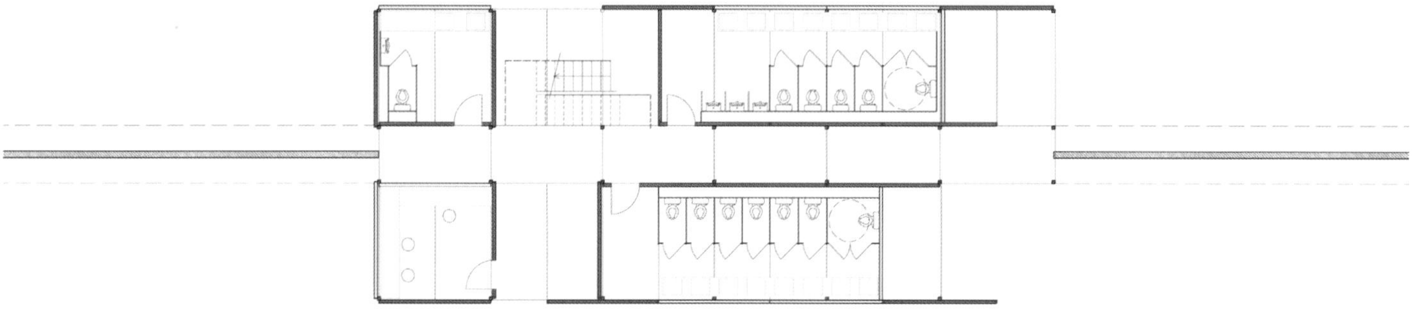

Floor plan of No. 4 toilet (Quzhou) © Atelier Li Xinggang

Rendering A of No. 8 toilet (Quzhou) © Atelier Deshaus

Rendering B of No. 8 toilet (Quzhou) © Atelier Deshaus

The project by Atelier Deshaus is another impressive example. Unlike the strategies of other architects, this design planted the structure directly into the hillock, rather than sidestepping the raised terrain. The architects cited Japanese aesthete Jun'ichirō Tanizaki's take on restrooms; he said that "toilets are best placed close to the earth in a spot inextricably linked to nature, as there is no parallel to taking care of business outside under the sky." The building is connected to the earth, its original form reconstructed through the raised roof. The roof supports and stylobates carve out a house within the forest. By digging into the hillock to produce four dispersed stylobates, the architects cleverly balanced the force of the land with the lateral force facing the buildings. This allows the slender pillars and the four interior structural walls to better support the expansive roofs, between which sunlight, rain, and upstretched branches pass. This successfully casts the building as more natural and more local, both visually and structurally.

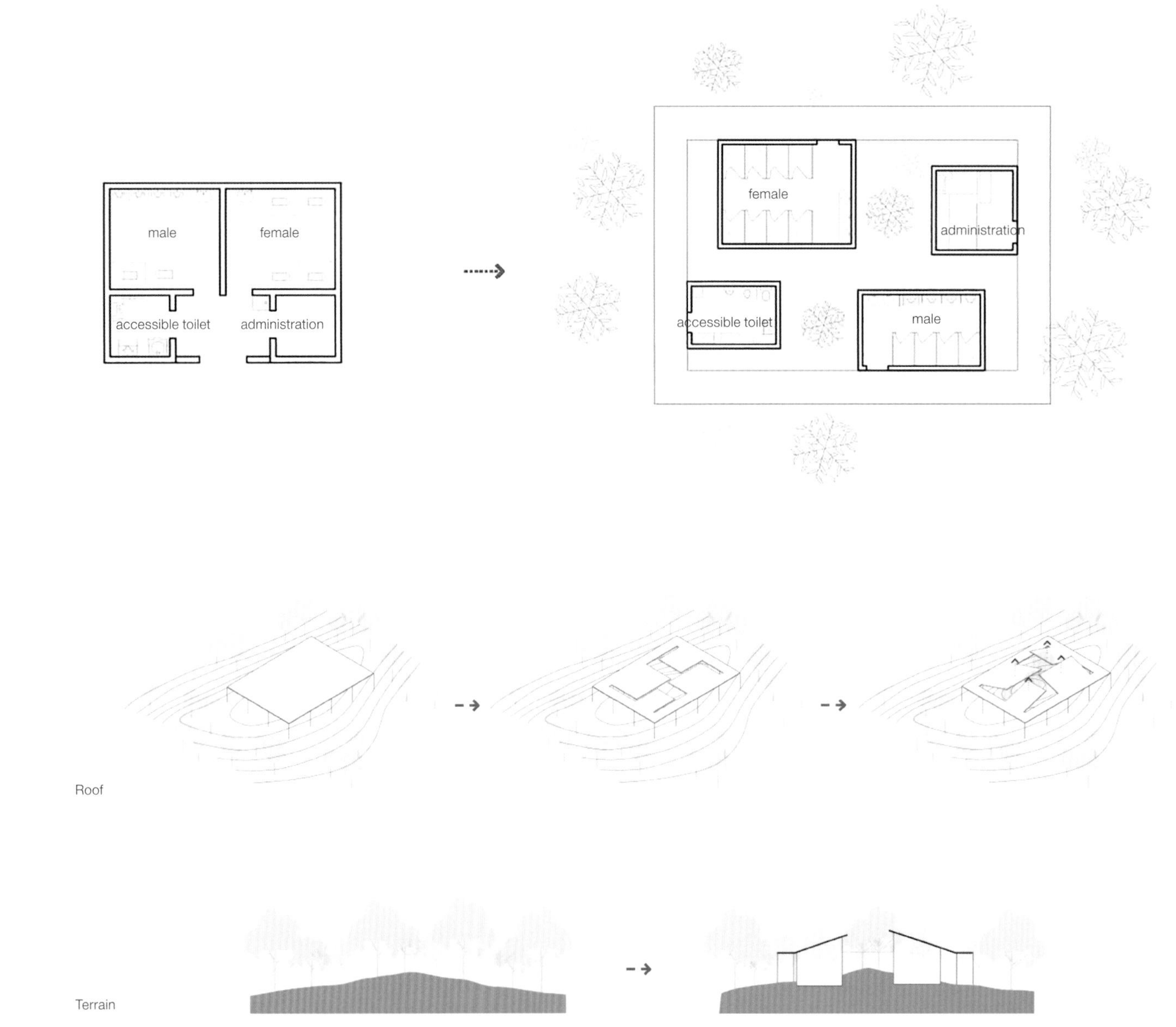

Conceptual diagram of No. 8 toilet (Quzhou) © Atelier Deshaus

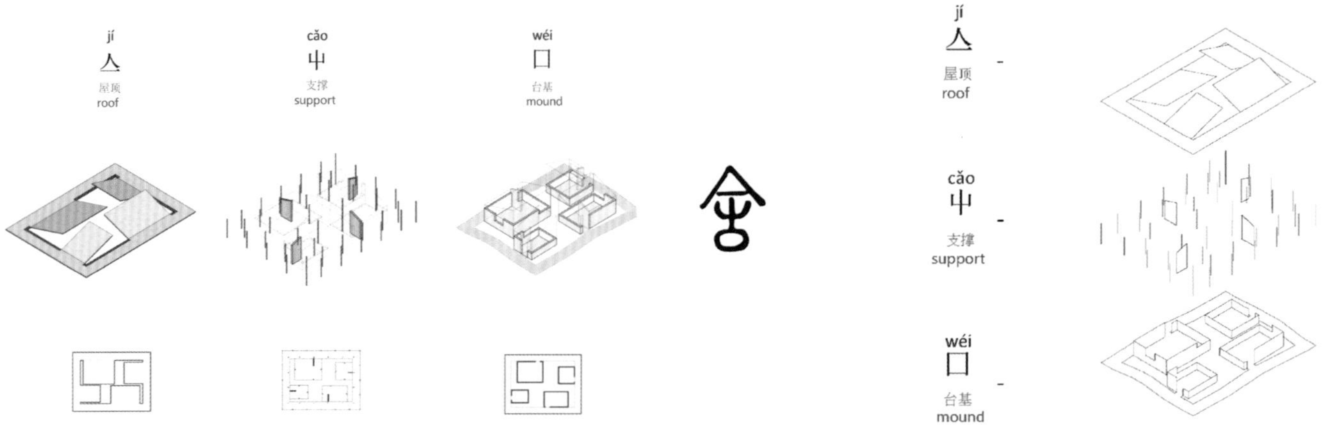

"She (house)," the design concept of No. 8 toilet (Quzhou) © Atelier Deshaus

Rendering C of No. 8 toilet (Quzhou) © Atelier Deshaus

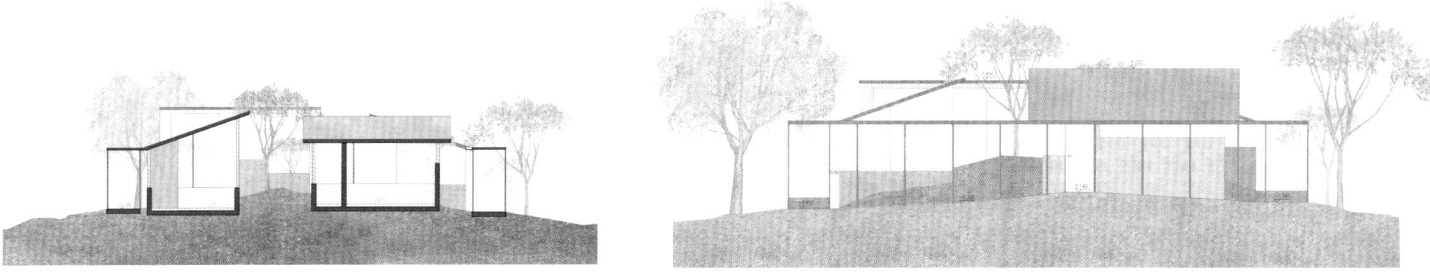

Sections of No. 8 toilet (Quzhou) © Atelier Deshaus

Interior views of No. 8 toilet (Quzhou) © Atelier Deshaus

Rendering of No. 3 toilet (Quzhou) © Atelier Deshaus

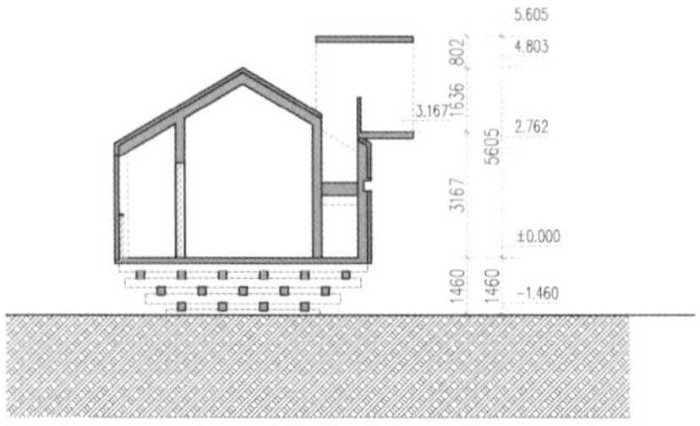

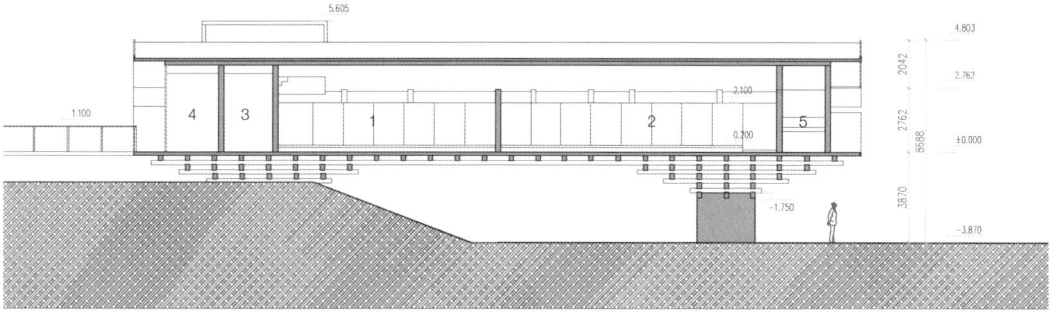

Sections of No. 3 toilet (Quzhou) © Atelier Deshaus

1. Men's toilet
2. Women's toilet
3. Accessible toilet
4. Baby care room
5. Administration

Chen Lichao's riverside restrooms, perched on a riverside with a height discrepancy of nearly two meters, also faced site conditions similar to the projects of Li Xinggang and Atelier Deshaus. However, in a departure from the latter's approach, the architects in this project drew from the topographical strategy of traditional covered bridges. They assembled a cantilevered bridge from prefabricated concrete components and converted the restrooms into a public viewing corridor suspended above the river. A framed view of the city awaits at the end of the corridor, while on the other side, residents can climb to the loft for a view of Qu River.

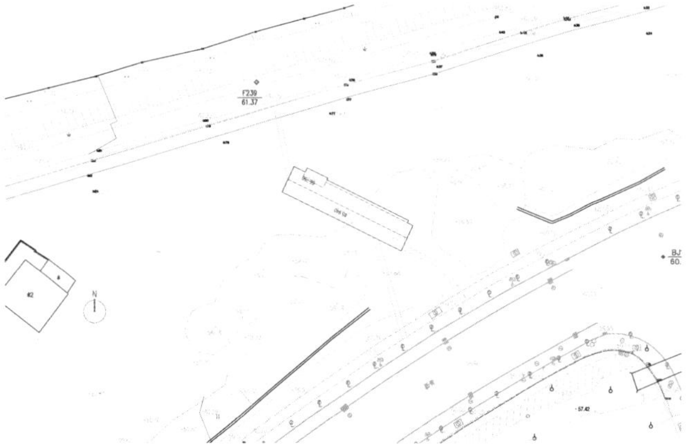

Master plan of No. 3 toilet (Quzhou) © Atelier Deshaus

Annexation, Internalization and Consolidation

Turning public restrooms into a part of the city landscape is an effective design tactic, but it may not always overturn the pre-existing negative connotations that restrooms bring with them. Acknowledging that users naturally repudiate such service facilities, architect Zhuang Shen used years of urban fieldwork and theory to propose intervening the spatial practices of ordinary cities by way of a "breakdown" method: breaking restrooms down into city-facing parts and functional interiors. He advocated that such an approach would broaden the possibility of including restrooms in urban spaces while skirting the negative perceptions that restrooms cast upon their surroundings.

This site is similar to Wang Shu's, however, its northern end neighbors a government office building. Many people, mainly residents running errands, pass by here every day. As a result, the design had to start with considering the convenience and hybridity of the restroom itself, which is situated at a street corner. Zhuang Shen referred to this building as one "with only the interior and no backside." As a smart city station, a lateral hallway on the restroom exterior offers essential services to residents, including a waiting area for transportation, a phone charging station, information services, and vending machines. For the restroom behind the hallway, the architects focused on integrating the skylight, exhaust ducts, and cooling system, to provide users with comfort and cleanliness.

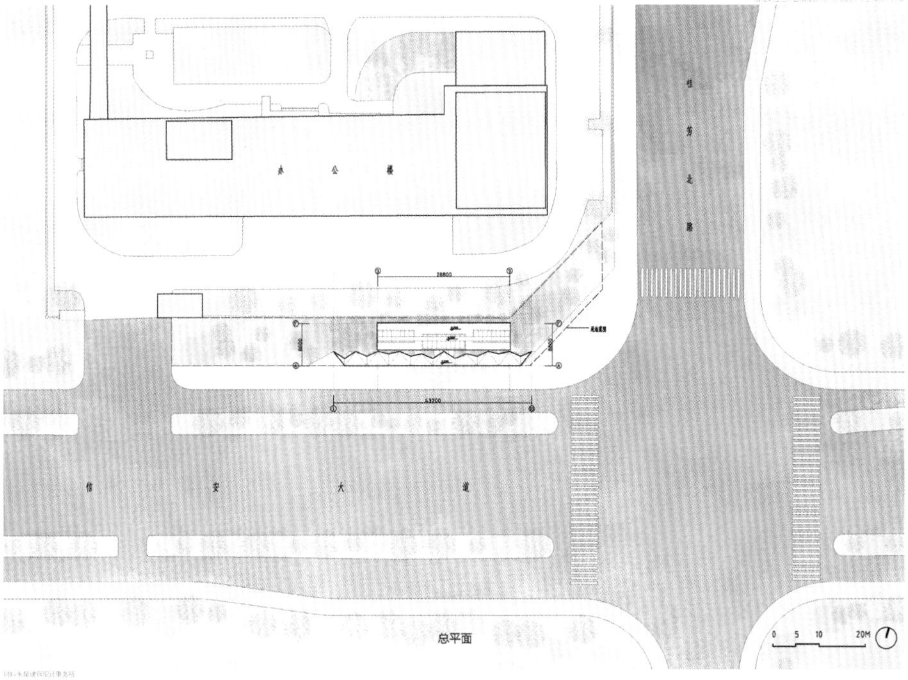

Master plan of No. 6 toilet (Quzhou) © Archmixing

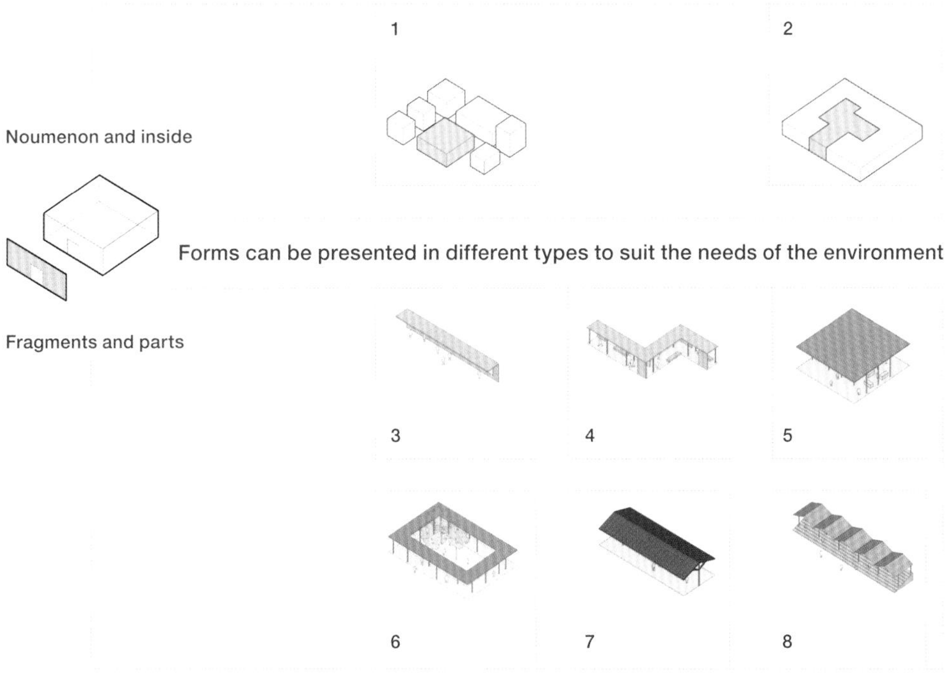

1. Independent form functioning as a volume within its own environment
2. Partial form filling up the gaps of building or city
3. Station placed on the roadside for pedestrians to rest
4. Gallery layout in the landscape for people to walk around
5. Market or city parlor covering a wide area for crowds to gather
6. Courtyard in garden-enclosing landscape for people to enjoy the scenery
7. Traditional construction where traditional material structure matches the surrounding environment
8. Special types that adapt to specific terrain or behavioral needs

Conceptual diagram of No. 6 toilet (Quzhou) © Archmixing

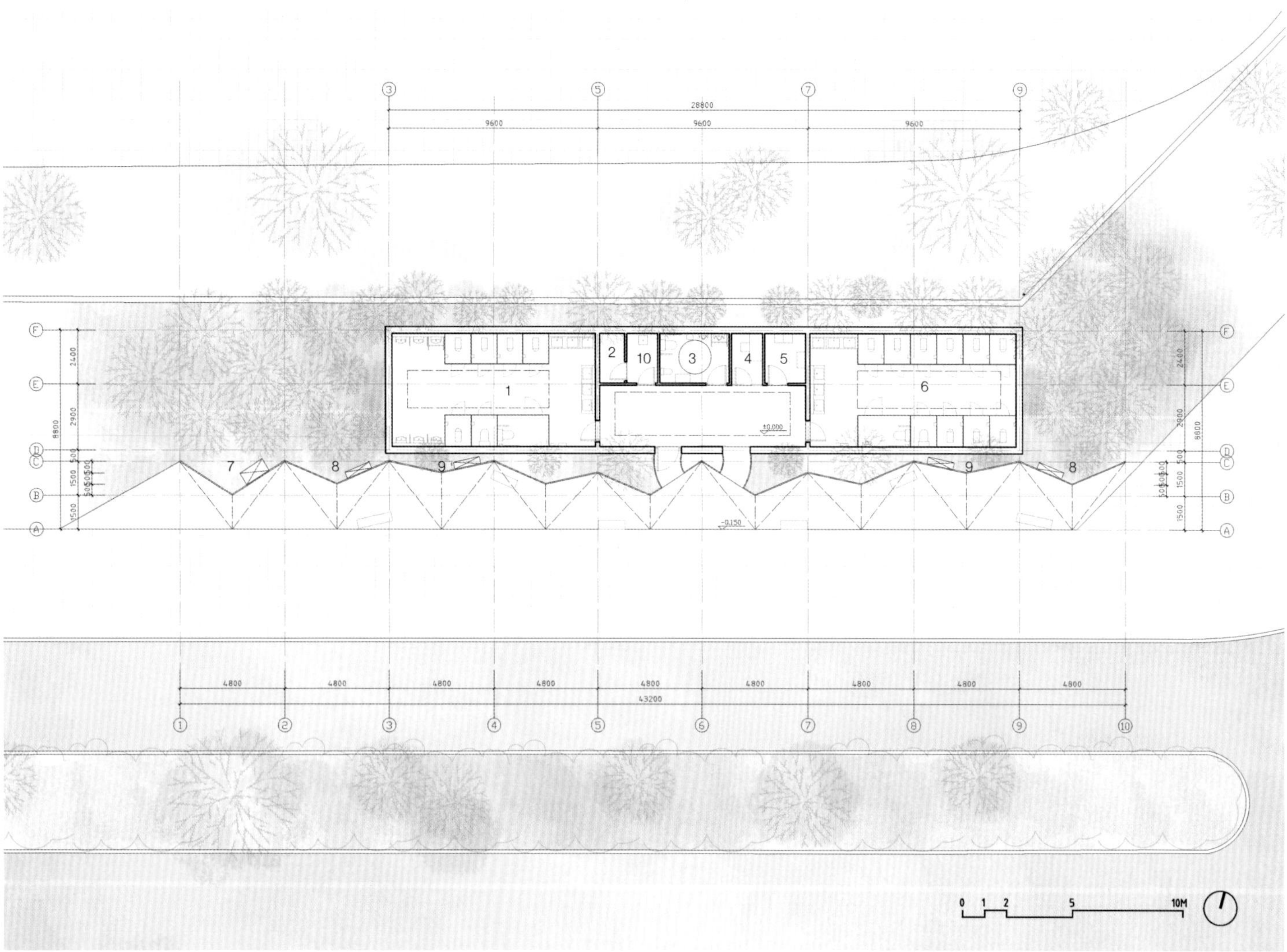

Floor plan of No. 6 toilet (Quzhou) © Archmixing

1. Men's toilet
2. Equipment room
3. Accessible toilet
4. Administration
5. Baby care room
6. Women's toilet
7. Vending
8. Interactive screen
9. Charging/WIFI area
10. Cleaning equipment room

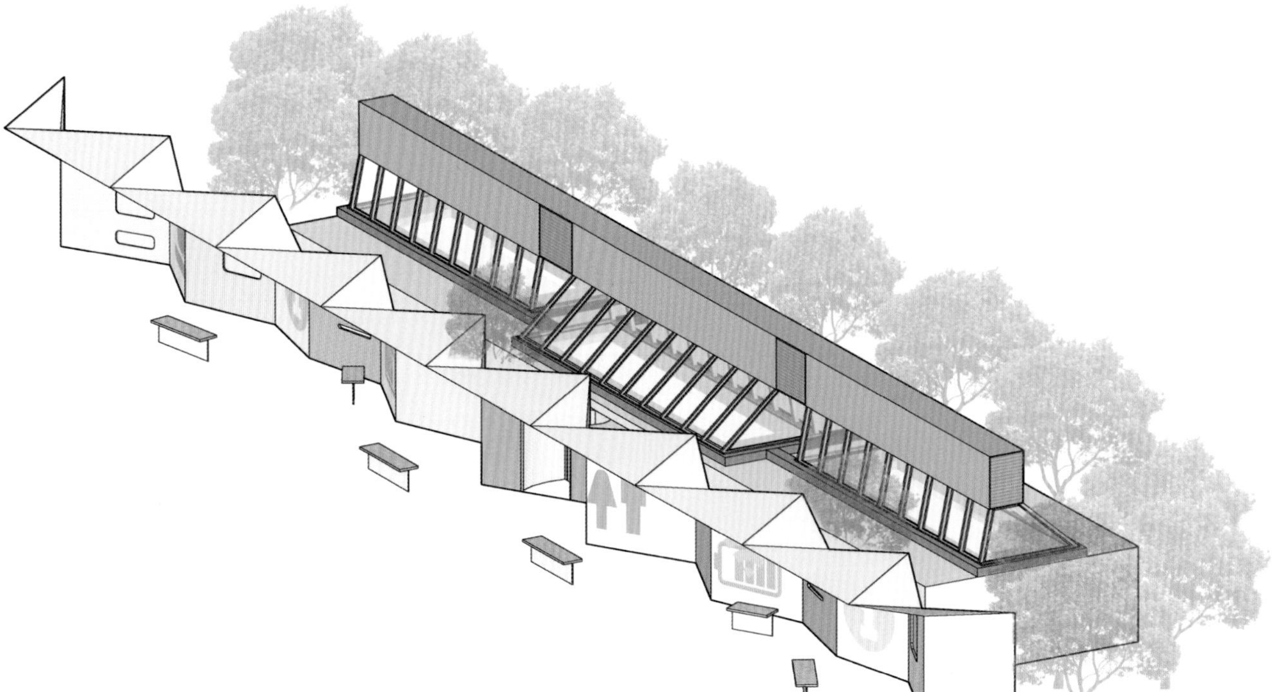

Axonometric view of No. 6 toilet (Quzhou) © Archmixing

Renderings of No. 6 toilet (Quzhou) © Archmixing

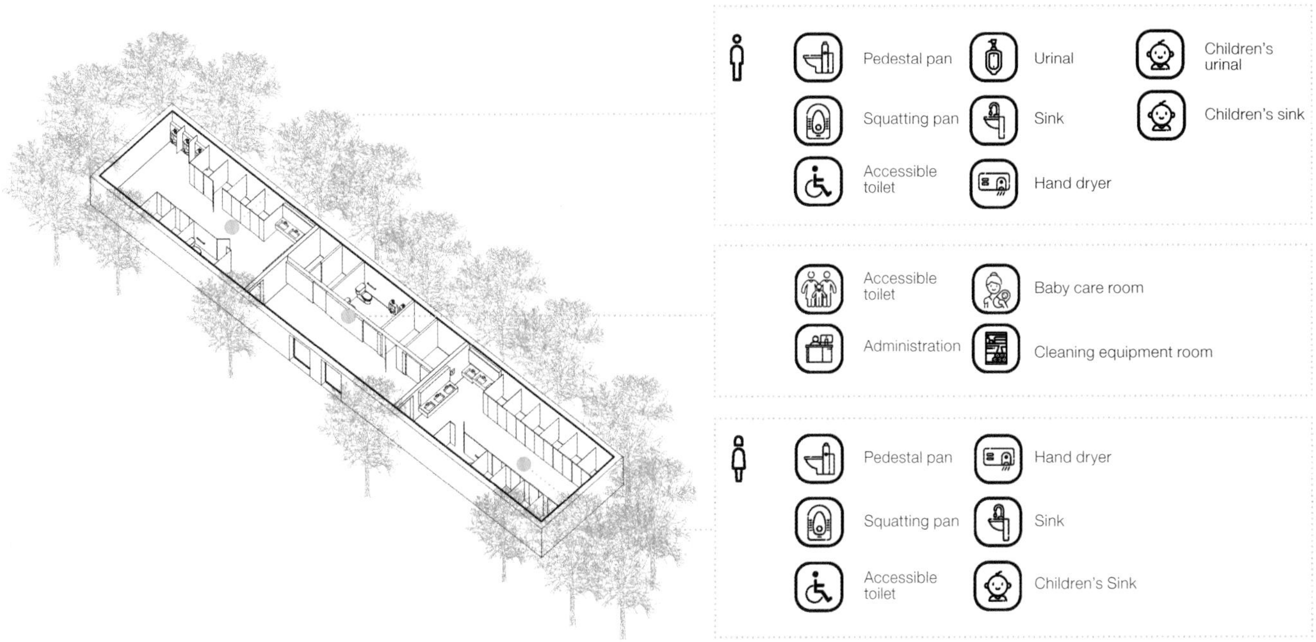

Annexed functions of No. 6 toilet (Quzhou) © Archmixing

Rendering of No. 7 toilet (Quzhou) © Atelier Z+

Interior of No. 7 toilet (Quzhou) © Atelier Z+

Section of No. 7 toilet (Quzhou) © Atelier Z+

That route of thought led to different modes of expressions in different environments. Apart from adapting to the terrain, Zhang Bin's design juxtaposed multiple functions to discreetly tuck away the restrooms. The toilet facilities are concealed by a rounded, looming "theater" that faces the lake and its seasonally changing scenery. The organization of the walking paths also reveals the separation between the outer areas and the interior. As visitors stroll by the lake, they will arrive at a half-spherical structure. Some may use the restrooms, but those that pause to rest won't feel discomfited by the nearby restrooms, thanks to the clean separation created by the curved walls.

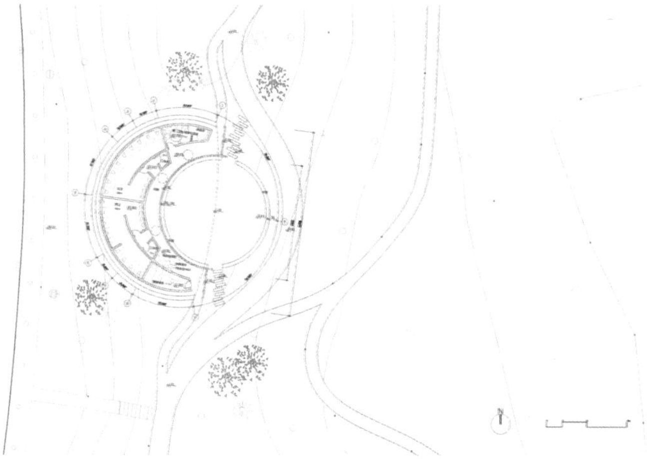

Master plan of No. 7 toilet (Quzhou) © Atelier Z+

Rendering of No. 11 toilet (Quzhou) © AZL Architects

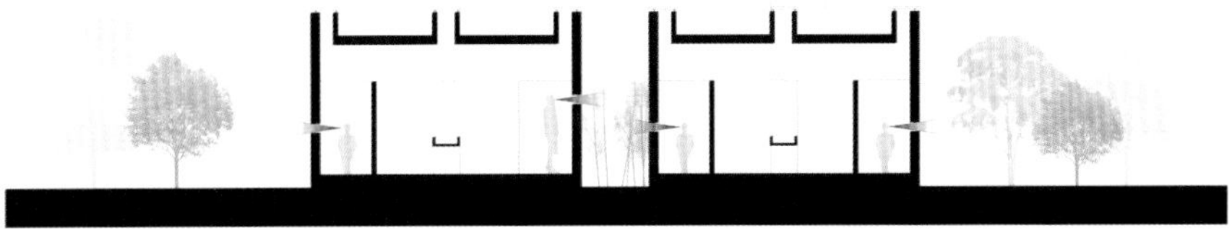

Section of No. 11 toilet (Quzhou) © AZL Architects

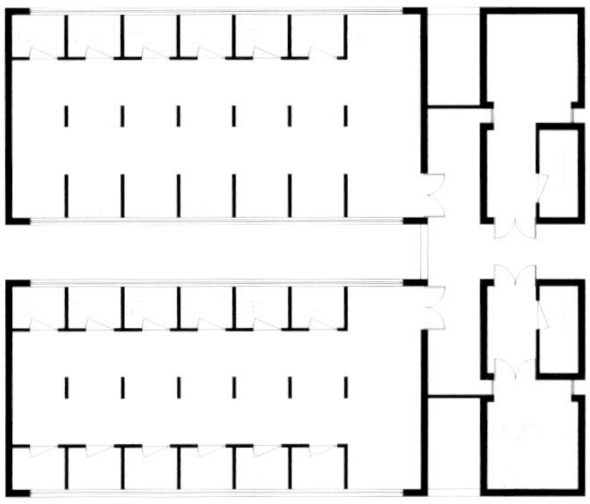

Floor plan of No. 11 toilet (Quzhou) © AZL Architects

Zhuang Shen and Zhang Bin concealed the restrooms within the overlap of daily urban functions, but Zhang Lei and Yung Ho Chang dissolved the unfavorable connotations of toilets through integrating morphological abstractions instead. The site of Zhang Lei's project differed from that of other architects. It was a farmland located in a still undeveloped part of the city, sparsely surrounded by buildings and dotted with residential neighborhoods, near a village that was awaiting demolition. The previous restrooms presented a rather typical structure—one-story and brick—and were unhygienic inside. Without surrounding trees or buildings to obscure it, the architects integrated the new restroom space into an abstract, autonomous whole, and used the exterior to reduce the negative associations toward restrooms. Four closed, sculptural blocks form the new bathroom, which has transverse windows installed at waist-height to protect users' privacy.

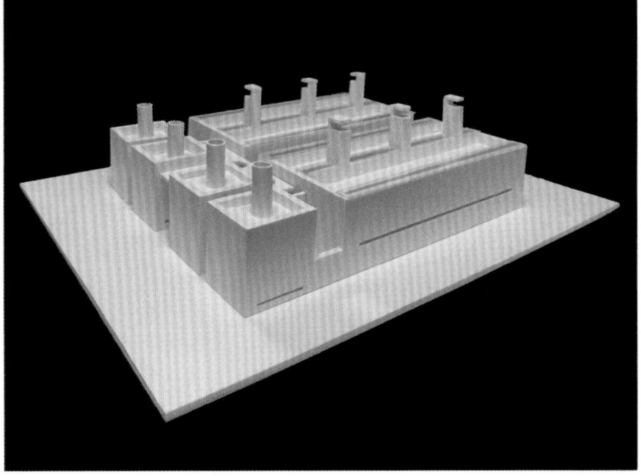

Model of No. 11 toilet (Quzhou) © AZL Architects

Another similar design project is the one by Atelier FCJZ. Pedestrians perceive only a tall, abstract brick box, its structural methodology seemingly making the eastern- and western-facing walls levitate. In the dense interior of the box, the central skylight evokes memories of historical Siheyuan courtyard residences.

Body, Place and Public Space

Aside from adapting to different urban environments, the basic function of public restrooms directly links to the lives of urban residents. The juxtaposition of functions acts as a buffer to reduce the negative perception of a restroom while creating a venue for other activities. Li Xinggang, Zhuang Shen, and Zhang Bin's projects provided users with services beyond the restroom itself. In No. 14, Design Hub's project, the architectural form is defined based on the relationship between interaction and space, as well as the private and the shared. The architects used studies of people's bathroom habits to gain a series of visual clues in pictorial form, including the different gender-based needs that people have of restroom spaces, the mundanity of waiting in line, and the historic significance that restrooms have in communities. After reconstructing this visual language, the architects reduced these fundamental functions into the smallest possible units and dispersed them. That arrangement enclosed the corridor, courtyard, and other spaces, while encouraging users to interact as they waited. Each unit has its own entrance, ventilation, and skylight. Its morphological combination diluted the public restroom as a whole, forming a micro-village on the site. YEAS' Project No. 16 represents a similar example.

Floor plan of No. 14 toilet (Kunshan) © Design Hub

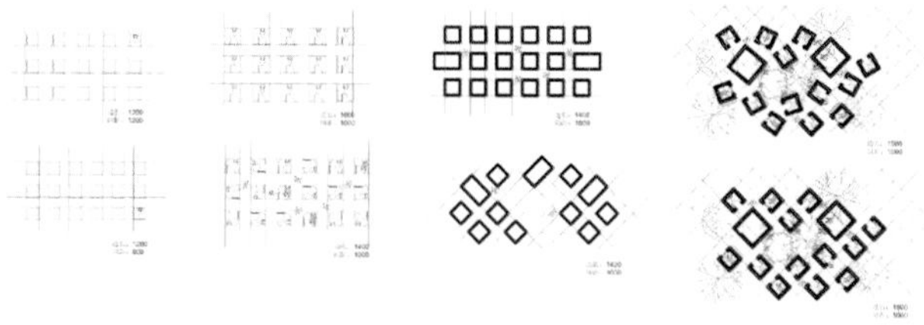

Conceptual diagram of No. 14 toilet (Kunshan) © Design Hub

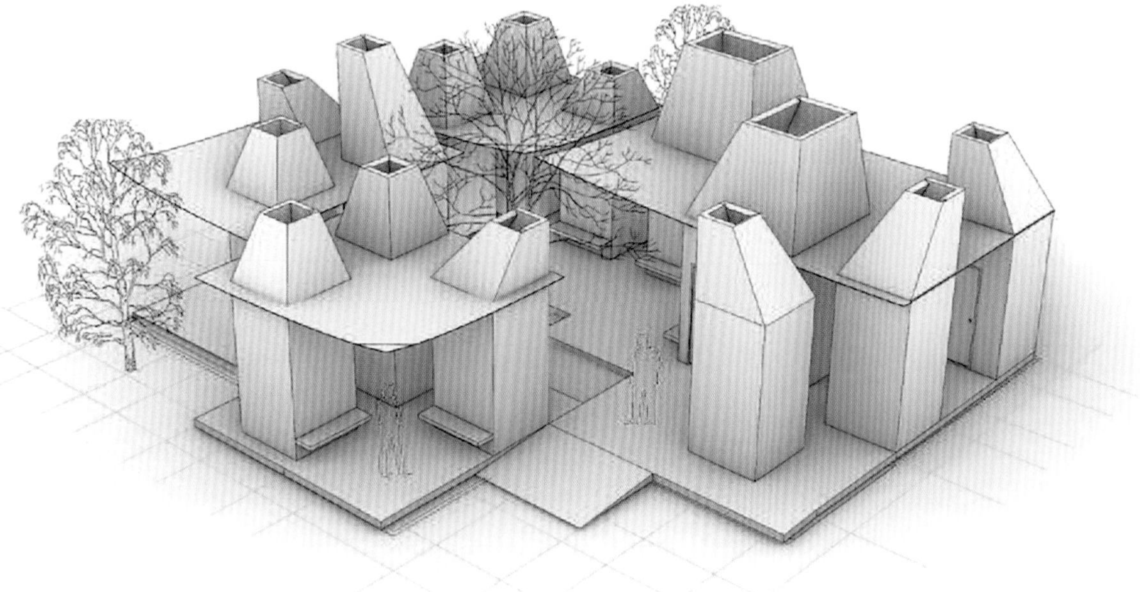

Rendering of No. 14 toilet (Kunshan) © Design Hub

Interior A and B of No. 14 toilet (Kunshan) © Design Hub

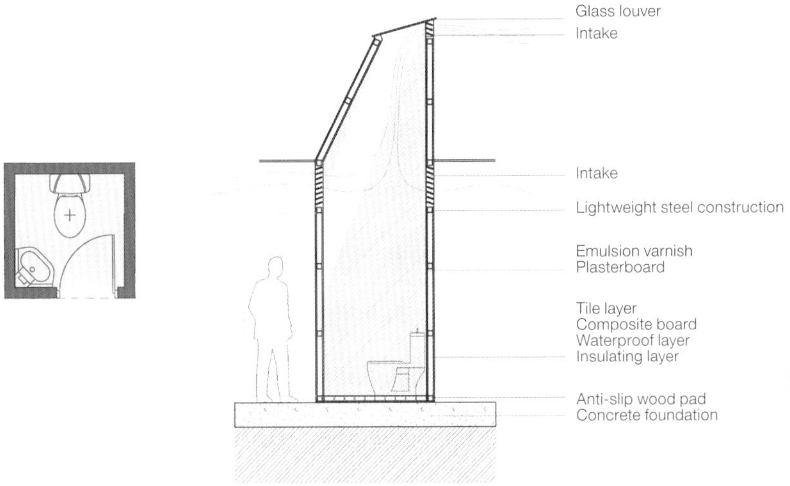

Details of No. 14 toilet (Kunshan) © Design Hub

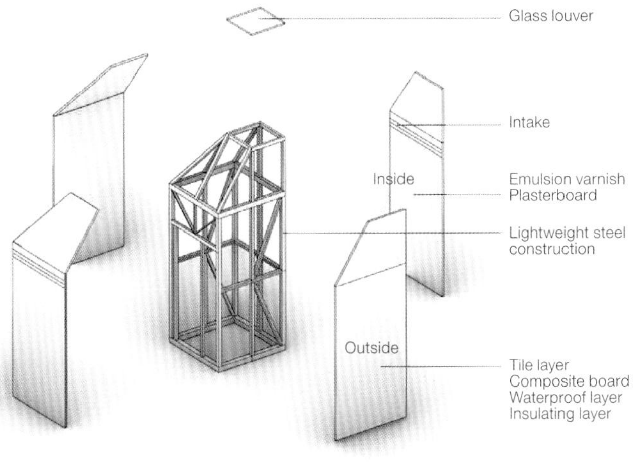

Structure of No. 14 toilet (Kunshan) © Design Hub

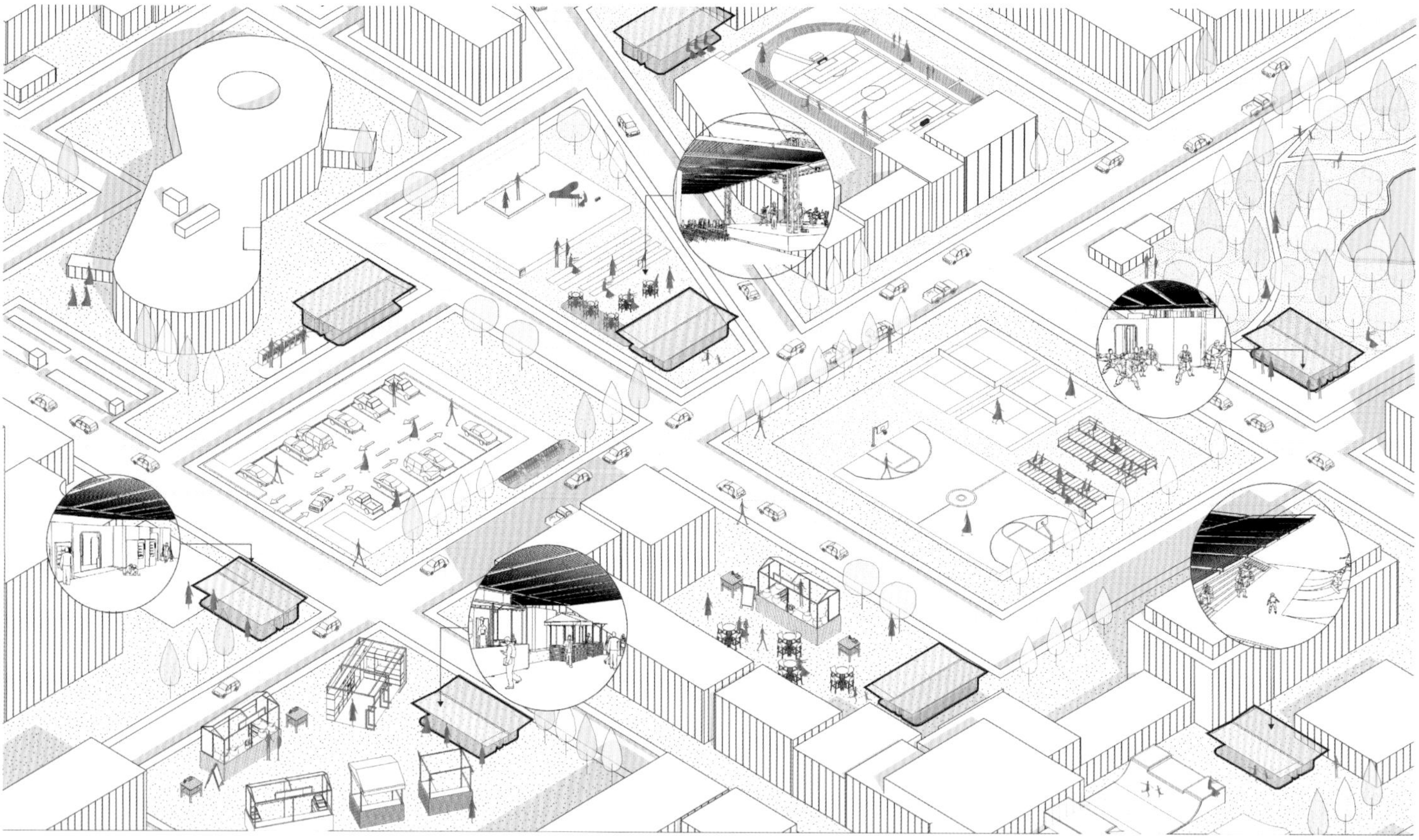

Scenic application of No. 3 and 17 toilets (Kunshan) © Continuation Studio

Two different urban environments of No. 3 and 17 toilets (Kunshan) © Continuation Studio

Continuation Studio's "seesaw pavilion" diverges sharply from Design Hub's solutions in form and structure, but their core designs are similar in offering city residents an "ordinary experience among extraordinary spaces." The structural body of that project comprises a magnified seesaw, paralleled and duplicated across the structure, which contains the restroom and a free space. The latter is the studio's effort at creating a multifunctional space, using a flexible architectural system and affordable materials to ensure that it can accommodate all varieties of events. It can adapt to ticketing, gaming, fairs, hawking or vending, as well as other functions at parks, schools, markets, and other sites.

Rendering A of No. 3 and 17 toilets (Kunshan) © Continuation Studio

Rendering B of No. 3 and 17 toilets (Kunshan) © Continuation Studio

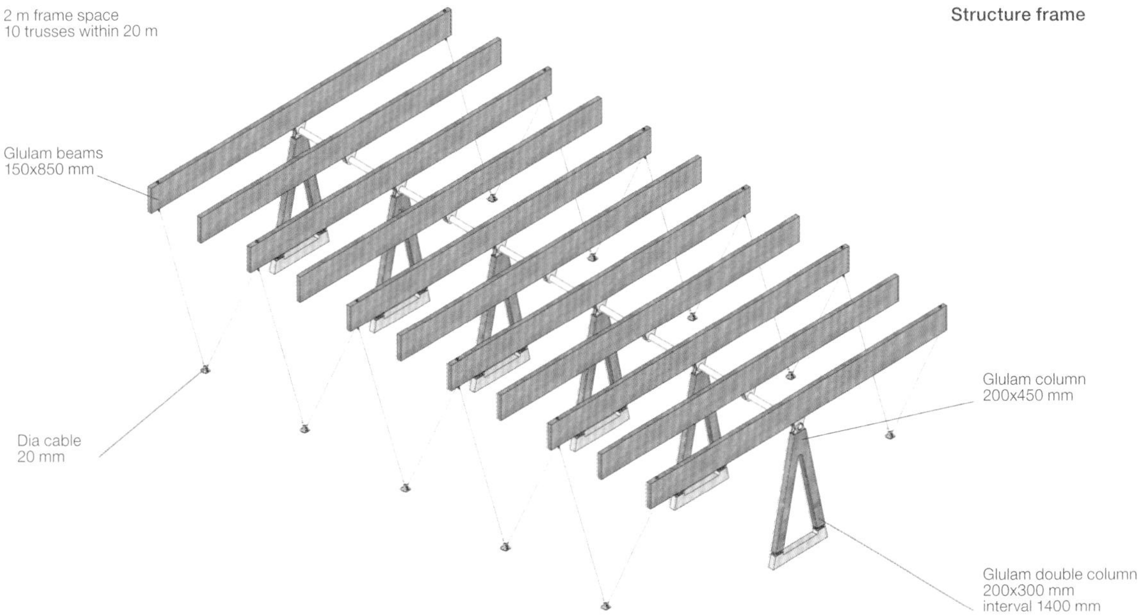

Structure of No. 3 and 17 toilets (Kunshan) © Continuation Studio

Section of No. 7 and 15 toilets (Kunshan) © Rùn Atelier

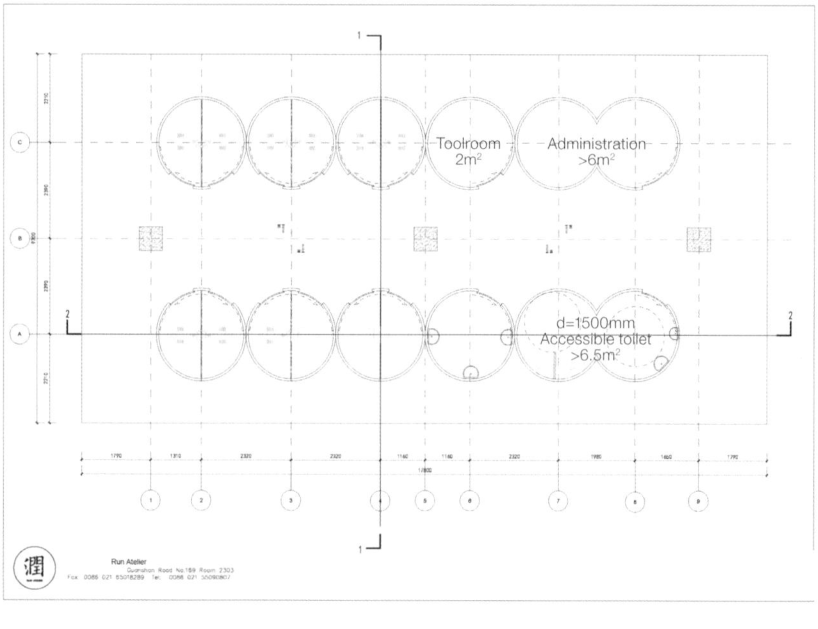

Floor plan of No. 7 and 15 toilets (Kunshan) © Rùn Atelier

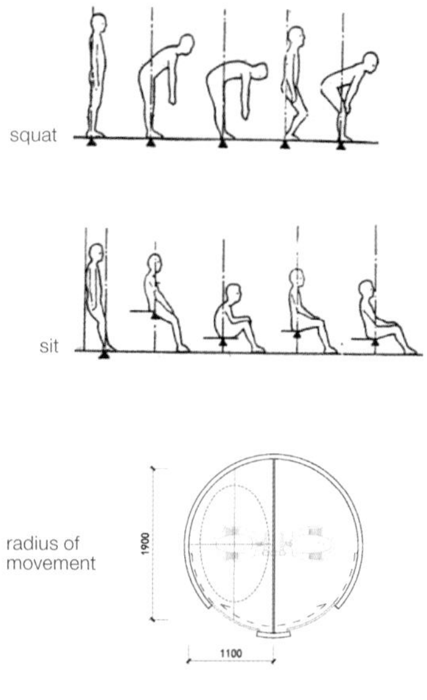

Relationship between body movement and capsule toilet © Rùn Atelier

The architects of Continuation Studio poured just as much thought into the everyday functionality of the restrooms, thinking about the actual dimensions, atmosphere, and usage of the toilets and relating them closely to the bodies, behaviors, and feelings of the users, which signals the architects' anthropological concern for public urban spaces.

Among all the bathroom designs, Rùn Atelier's circular toilets stand out. Measuring nearly 2 meters in diameter, the circular space is partitioned into two restrooms. The dimensions are determined by the average person's radius of motion, thereby allowing most users to stand, sit, or squat without compromising comfort or resulting in a sense of envelopment in the relatively narrower space. Accounting for the motion and flow of users with disabilities, the enhanced toilet is also specially fitted to the curved walls.

Design Hub's Project No. 4 also reflected on the emotional impact that a sharp-edged interior would have on its users. In its layout, the inward-facing walls enclose three primary functional spaces and a central atrium that improves ventilation.

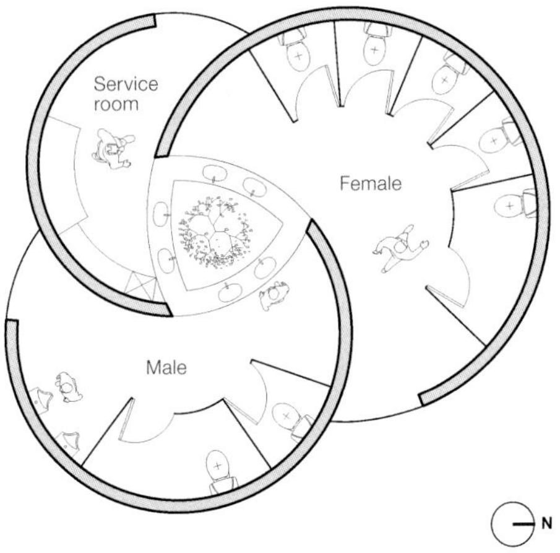

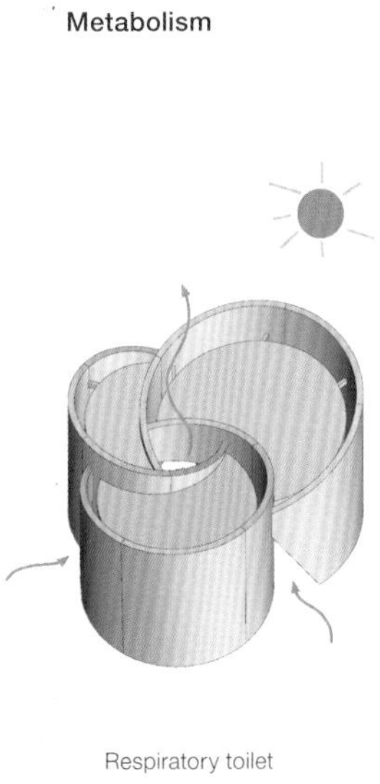

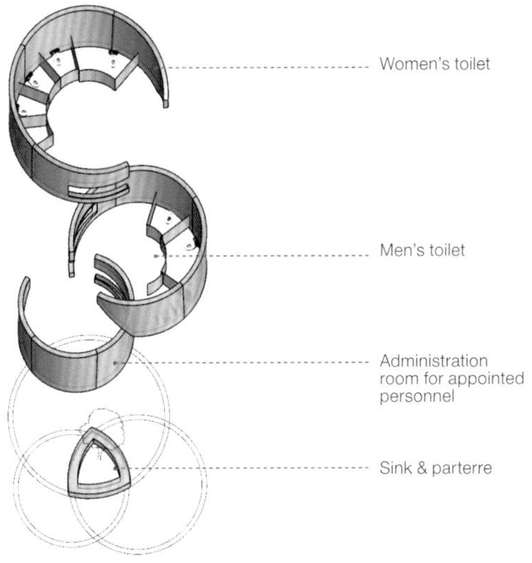

Floor plan of No. 4 toilet (Kunshan) © Design Hub

Structure of No. 4 toilet (Kunshan) © Design Hub

Conceptual diagram of No. 4 toilet (Kunshan) © Design Hub

Materials, Structure and Building System

Lastly, architects have to face the challenge of quickly, safely, and economically building the urban infrastructure of restrooms. At the same time, smaller building dimensions give them a rare opportunity to experiment with new materials, structures, and architectural systems. In designing restrooms, most architects primarily use industrialized materials such as corrugated sheet metal, PC light panels, and precast concrete that present low costs, yet offer stable performance and ease of construction. Genarchitects even compared how users experience the textural differences of the outer wall materials, such as weather-resistant cotton canvas, dry stone, and wooden shingles. Naturalbuild incorporated glass fibers into the double-layered, semi-translucent corrugated panels, while creating a clean, bright atmosphere with evening lights; Qi Shanshan's project featured a semi-translucent building skin, except that she combined perforated aluminum sheets with glass bricks, or used transparent glass fiber-reinforced concrete; YEAS used mirrored walls to disperse the abstracted building blocks into a pleasant, natural setting, while LYCS Architecture and Chen Haoru used ecological materials like bamboo, rammed earth, and cobblestones.

Building structures take on greater flexibility in these types of practices. Projects by Deshaus, Continuation Studio, and Rùn Atelier all reflect the architects' creativity in this area. In Continuation Studio's Project No. 17, the swings hanging from the eaves of the building create an ambiguous relationship with the roof fasteners and reinforce the feeling of being suspended. Rùn Atelier's circular restrooms are preassembled structures, similar to YJ Atelier's cylinders. The illusory appearance of the building suggests that all the individual units were made from ordinary, precut concrete tubes. In reality, they more closely resemble a collection of three-pronged rings, with the entrance and walls added based on specific needs. In another of their designs that reflects the architects' sensitivity towards structure, the interaction between the setting and the flow of people results in a design where the T-shaped walls—comprising seven groupings of different sizes and orientations—stagger and shift, the concrete roof undulating with them.

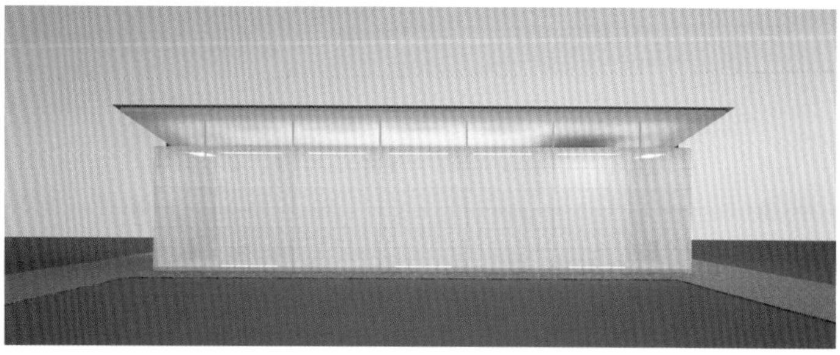

1. Model of No. 8 toilet (Kunshan) © genarchitects
2. Rendering of No. 1 toilet (Kunshan) © NATURALBUILD
3. Floor plan of No. 13 toilet (Kunshan) © Stud
4. Rendering of No. 4 toilet (Kunshan) © YEAS

Structure concept

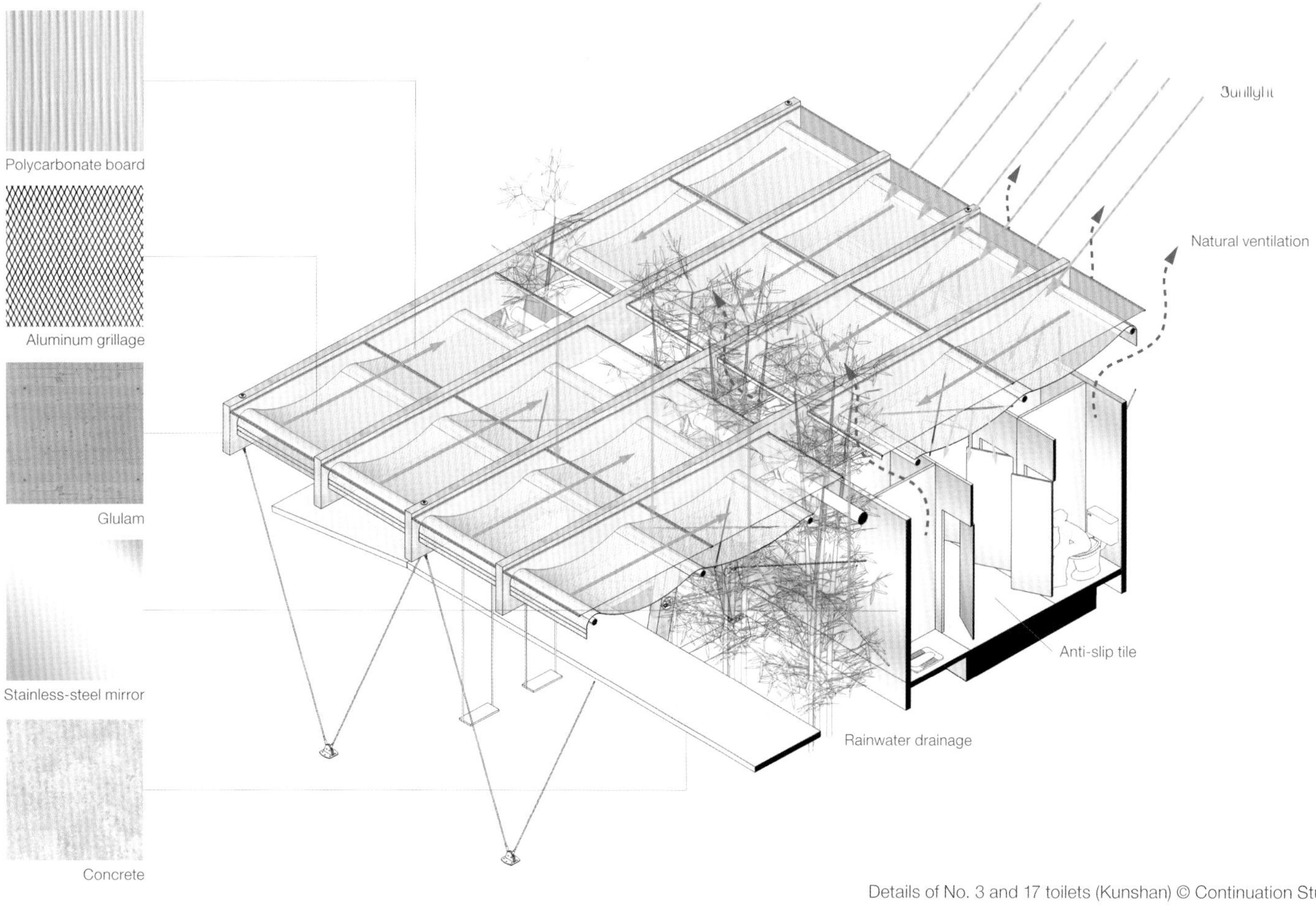

Details of No. 3 and 17 toilets (Kunshan) © Continuation Studio

Rendering of No. 3 and 17 toilets (Kunshan) © Continuation Studio

Interior of No. 2 toilet (Kunshan) © YJ Atelier

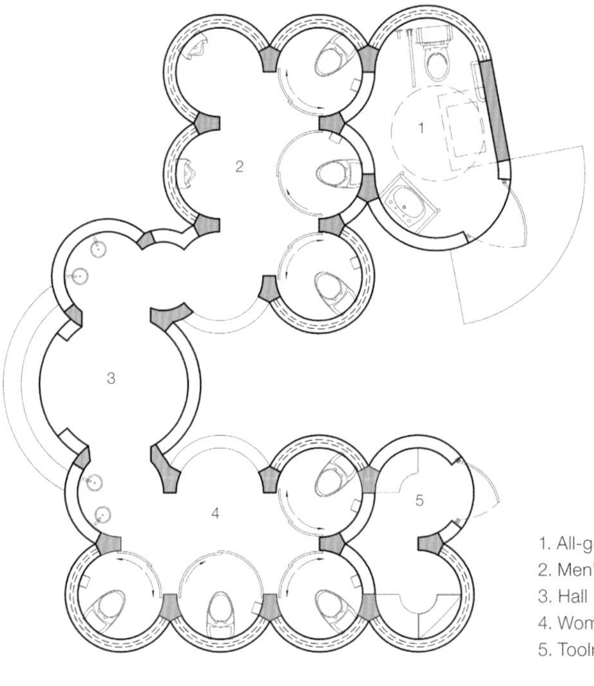

1. All-gender toilet
2. Men's toilet
3. Hall
4. Women's toilet
5. Toolroom

Floor plan of No. 2 toilet (Kunshan) © YJ Atelier

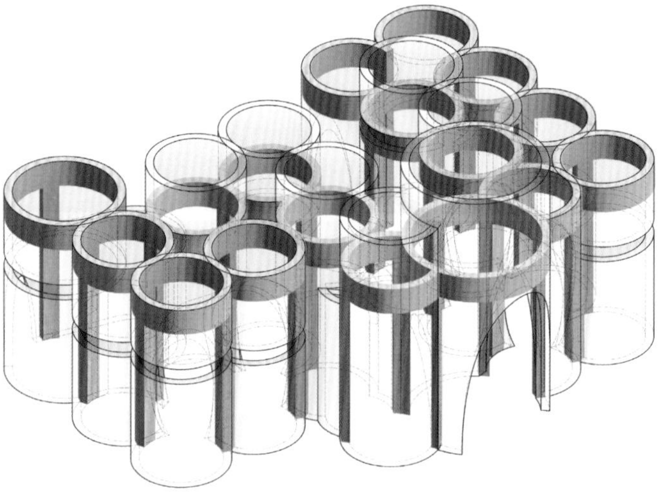

Structure of No. 2 toilet (Kunshan) © YJ Atelier

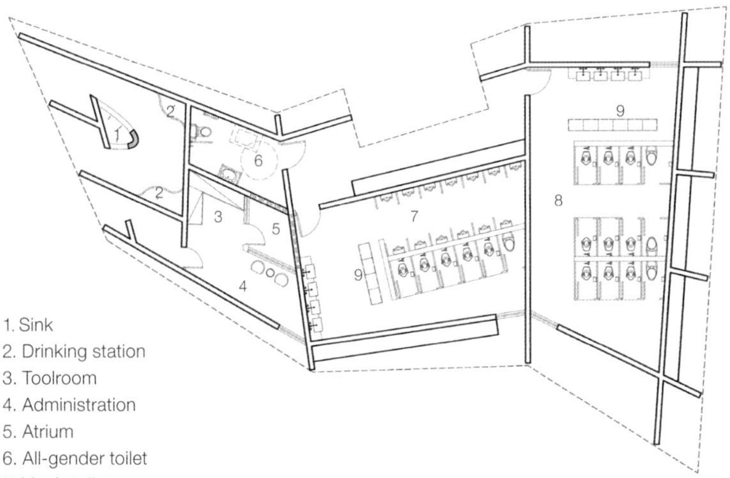

1. Sink
2. Drinking station
3. Toolroom
4. Administration
5. Atrium
6. All-gender toilet
7. Men's toilet
8. Women's toilet
9. Seats/waiting area

Floor plan of No. 6 toilet (Kunshan) © YJ Atelier

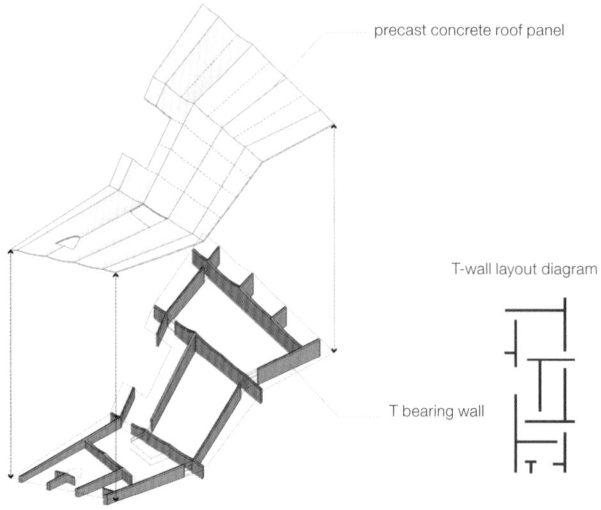

Structure of No. 6 toilet (Kunshan) © YJ Atelier

Building system of No. 9 and 12 toilets (Kunshan) © Atelier XÜK

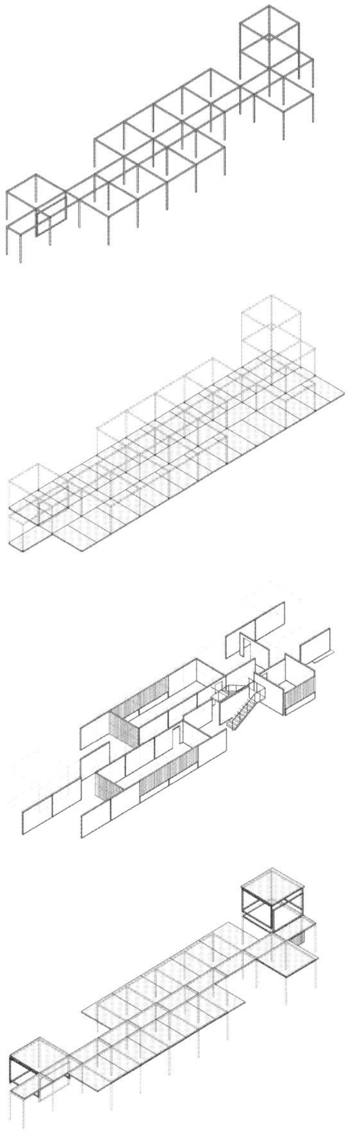

Building system of No. 4 toilet (Quzhou)
© Atelier Li Xinggang

Rendering of No. 9 and 12 toilets (Kunshan) © Atelier XÜK

Interior of No. 9 and 12 toilets (Kunshan) © Atelier XÜK

Interior of No. 2 toilet (Quzhou) © Archi-Union

Conceptual diagram of No. 2 toilet (Quzhou) © Archi-Union

Rendering of No. 2 toilet (Quzhou) © Archi-Union

Of course, well-designed public restrooms could become more widespread amid increasing urbanization if we could combine affordable materials and flexible structures within a mature architectural system. The projects by Atelier XÜK and Li Xinggang explored the use of standardized modules and swifter construction processes to adapt to a protean urban environment. Atelier XÜK's construction plan can be split into six steps: placing the concrete floor beams, setting concrete slabs, installing soundproof walls, placing wooden compartments, erecting thin steel columns, and covering the columns with steel roofing. Most of the modular parts were preassembled, minimizing the wet construction needed on-site. Because of the standardized modules, it is relatively easier to add, demolish, or relocate the structure.

Wang Hao's building proposal improved upon traditional timber architecture. Glulam and metal connectors prevent cracks in the timber, strengthening its load-bearing capacity while making it easier for local factories to standardize production and accelerate construction. Philip F. Yuan's design utilized an abstract strategy for its form, similar to Zhang Lei's. Creating the building's intersecting arches might seem insurmountable through the lens of traditional architectural logic, but 3D printing enabled the quick installation of prefabricated modules, which made it easier to create these irregular spaces.

Afterword

When design intervenes the toilet revolution, it goes beyond inspiring eye-catching forms for the city's construction works. Of greater importance is contributing to the continuing urbanization of modern-day China through the integrated innovation of products, services, and systems, and thus realizing social, ecological, and design sustainability. Throughout this process, architects play a crucial part in the way they focus on the complexities of urban settings, integrate negative spaces such as public toilets, respond to the needs of residents, and conceive construction systems.

Notes

1. Rem Koolhaas, *Elements* (Italy: Marsilio, 2014), 1557
2. David Leatherbarrow, "Responsive Construction: The Building as a Network of Topographical Relationships," trans. Mai Li, *Architectural Journal*, no. 10 (2019): 21–26.

ARCHITECTURE
CHINA

Projects Highlight – Other Built Projects

Riverside Passage

Atelier Deshaus

Location: No. 2524 Yangshupu Road, Yang Shupu Gasworks Wharf, Shanghai
Architect: Atelier Deshaus
Principal architect: Liu Yichun, Chen Yifeng, Shen Wen
Landscape design consultant: YIYU Design, Laurent Landscape & Architects Firm
Area: 268 square meters
Completion: October 2019
Photography: Tian Fangfang, Chen Hao

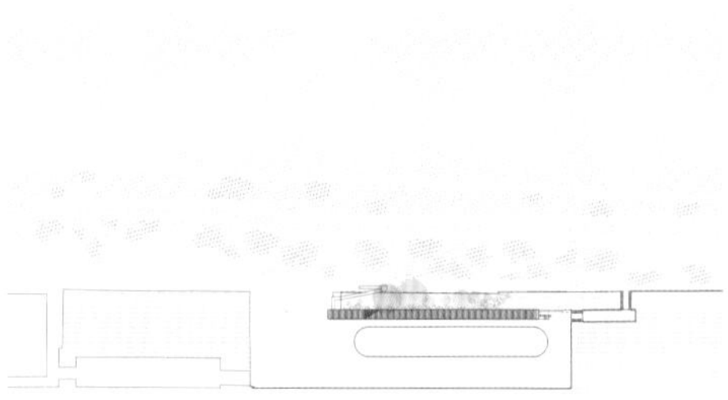

Site plan

The site of the Riverside Passage was previously used as a coal unloading wharf for transport connected to the old Yangpu Gas Plant. A reinforced-concrete wall, which is 90 meters long and 4 meters high, was built to prevent coal from falling into the river. When the coal wharf became out of use, this long wall became abandoned and fell into a state of solitude. Before this wall, there were originally two walls on the wharf. The one along the river had been removed long ago, and in its place emerged a gap in between the wharf and the flood control wall. In that gap, covered by dust, coal debris, and concrete blocks, seeds sprouted and grew into trees that now accompany the long wall—a scenery of beauty, woven with ruins. This scenery has gradually vanished in the gentrification-oriented urban regeneration of Shanghai in the recent years. It is important, even urgent, to retain the characteristics of this existing scenery in the regenerated waterfront that was turned from an industrial area to an open, public space as it has been witness to the prosperous industrial activities in Shanghai over the last fifty years.

The project adopts the long concrete wall as a platform for new construction. The wall is regarded as significant solid earthwork and serves as a foundation for a sloping bridge that extends from the wharf to the flood control wall, traversing a small pocket of trees along the way; it makes for an impromptu elevated, long open corridor, as well as a resting pavilion. A single-pitched roof is designed to demarcate the space inside and outside the wall. Facing the shore side of the wall is an opportunistic garden that time has planted in the gap between the wharf and the shore; there is also a low corridor on the ground level. On the river side (outside) of the wall, is a cantilevered corridor for visitors to take in the view of the Huangpu River. The difference between the two corridors—one is lowered and the other is elevated—implies the changing scales in the different distances and viewing sceneries.

The coal factory wharf before the renovation
© Atelier Deshaus

The coal factory wharf after the renovation © Tian Fangfang

The wall turning into the boundary between the manufactured and natural environments © Tian Fangfang

An aerial view of the Riverside Passage and the Huangpu River © Tian Fangfang

The roof and the support attatched to the existing wall © Tian Fangfang

The gap and the halo © Chen Hao

Detail of the Riverside Passage © Chen Hao

The wharf devoid of coal unloading is now polished into a roller rink, which makes a close spatial relationship with the cantilevered corridor. The ground, the concrete wall, and the inserted structure are integrated into a new leisure attraction, where people might choose to linger or intentionally pass by. The former coal wharf is now turned into an urban place for flaneurs. The slender post-and-beam steel structures act as a series of makers that frame the many witnesses of the passing eras—the chimney of the old gas plant, cranes in bright colors, concrete blocks embedded in mud and washed repeatedly by tide, high-rises across the river, and bridges far away—against the tireless movement of the people.

Looking toward the Huangpu River from the entering platform © Tian Fangfang

The slope-bridge that crosses the gap between the wharf and the flood control wall © Chen Hao

The turning roof, the slope-bridge, and the tree © Tian Fangfang

The wall, the opening, and the roof forming a new integrity © Tian Fangfang

The fusion of the rock ruins and the landscape © Tian Fangfang

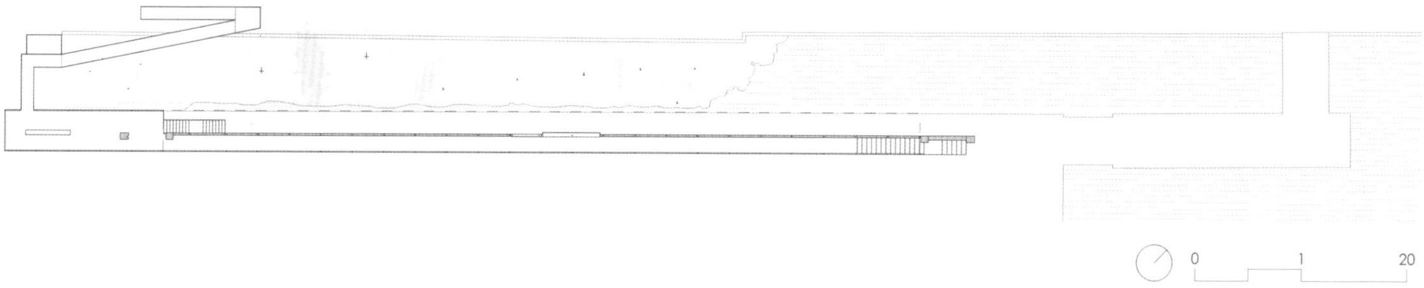

Upper-floor Plan

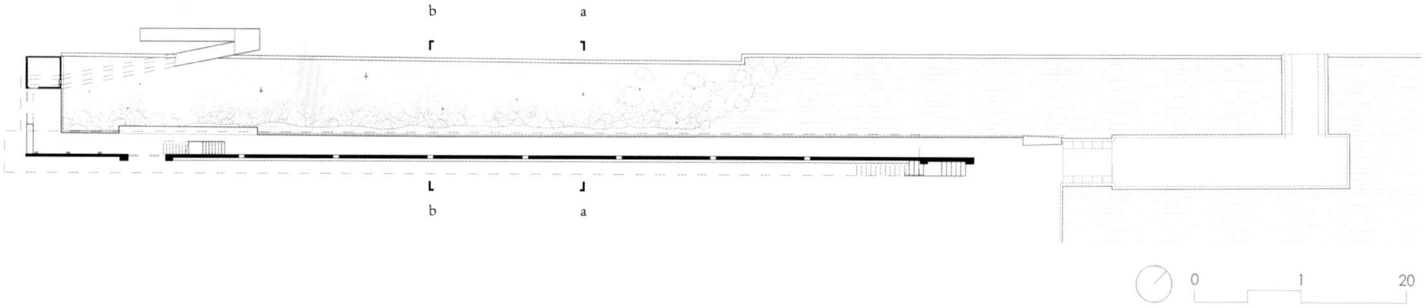

Ground-floor Plan

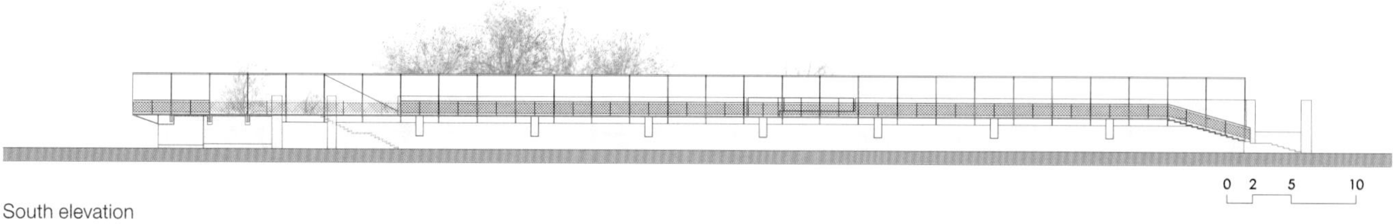

South elevation

North elevation

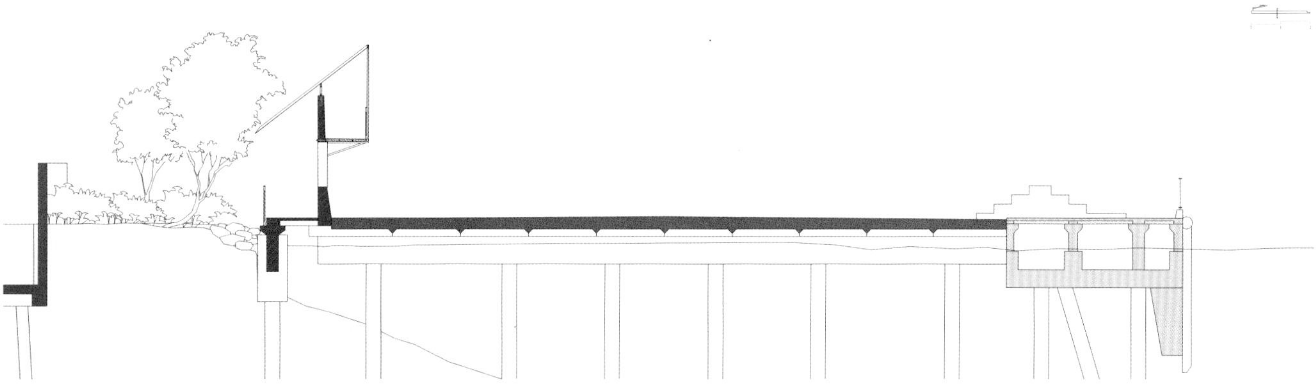

Section A-A

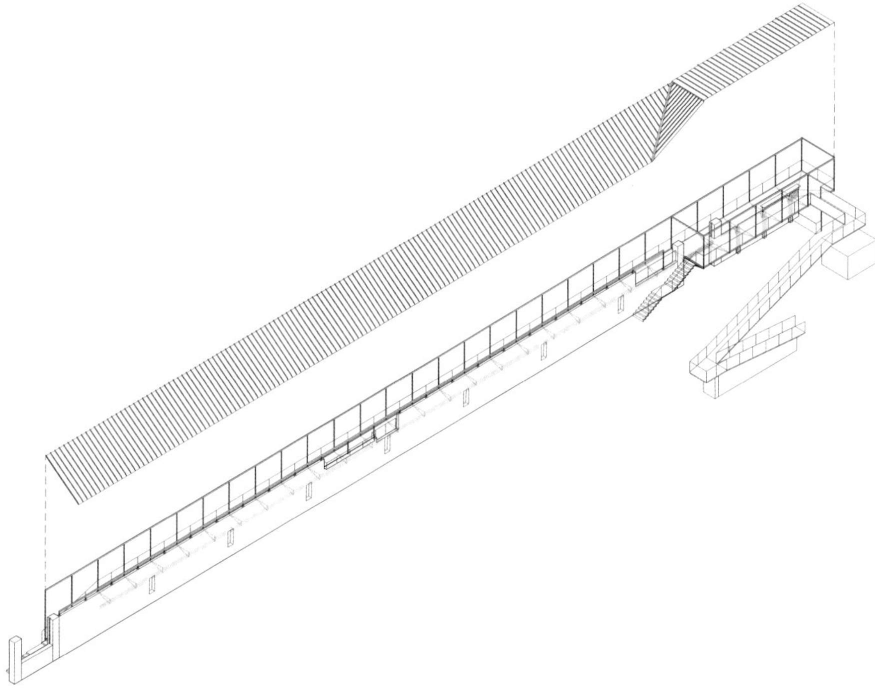

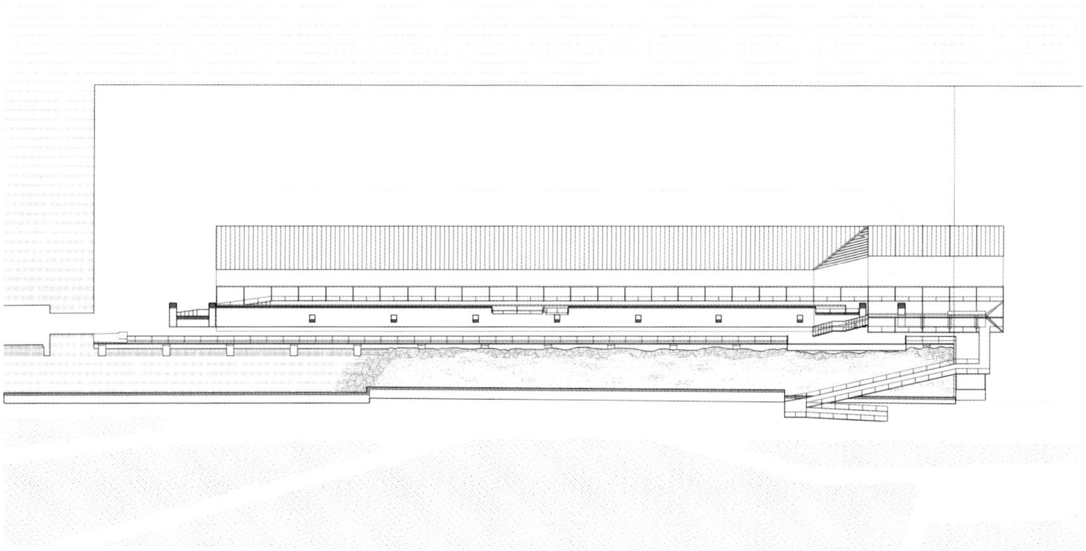

Axonometric diagram

Pocket Plaza

Atelier Archmixing

Location: Lane 390, Yongjia Road, Xuhui district, Shanghai
Architect: Atelier Archmixing
Principal architect: Zhuang Shen, Ren Hao, Tang Yu, Zhu Jie
Design team: Li Lide, Ding Xinhui, Yin Jidong, Chen Hongbang, Lu Shuijuan (intern), Qiu Xin (intern)
Structure: Shanghai Wildness Structural Design Firm
Area: 767 square meters
Completion: March 2019
Photograph: Wu Qingshan

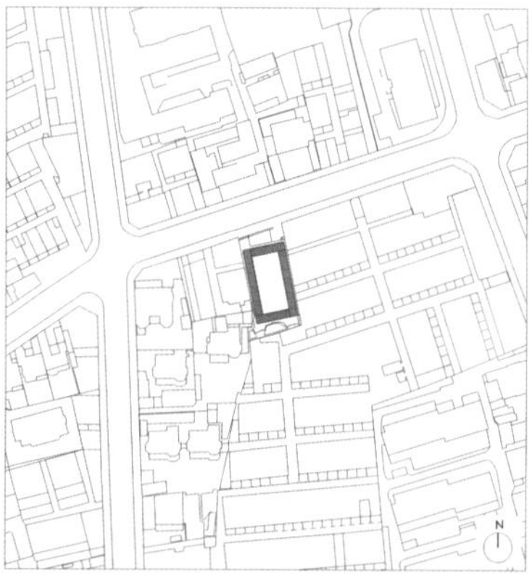

Site plan

Located in the center of Shanghai, the public space around Yongjia Road is dominated by lines of streets and characterized by the typical urban vitality of the eastern Chinese metropolis: dense neighborhoods, crowded spaces, a large residential population, pleasantly-sized roads, trees lining both sides of the streets, small businesses serving the needs of everyday life, and a rich lively atmosphere. The site of Pocket Plaza at Lane 309 is located in the middle section of Yongjia Road. Seizing the opportunity to reconstruct the road, the Government decided to demolish two rows of old lane houses, which posed a fire hazard, and transform the area into an open, public space for the use of the local residents.

Inner courtyard of the Pocket Plaza

Elevation alongside Yongjia Road © Tang Yu, Chen Pingnan

The demolished area forms a rectangle with one short side connected to the street. It's about 18 meters wide, 40 meters deep, and is surrounded along the south, east, and west by old-style houses. With its straight rectangular boundaries, the space creates a pocket, giving the project the name Pocket Plaza.

The design concept was to create "an open space with a sense of privacy and territoriality" for the surrounding community. The design uses linear open corridors along all four sides, built close to the solid wall around the perimeter of the site to form a new rectangular "courtyard" that echoes the strong quadrilateral boundaries formed by the architectural fabric of the historic district. With the height of the corridors deliberately lowered to 2.1–2.7 meters to create an intimate scale and the windmill-shaped connections, the four sections of open corridors enclose a small square of hard pavement in the center. The ground of the "courtyard" square is raised 50 centimeters above street level, enabling better visual communication between the corridors, the square, and the street, while increasing the number of spatial levels. These spatial treatments create an appropriate sense of privacy and territoriality for the community in the open urban space.

Rest space

Temporary market in the Pocket Plaza

The open corridors feature a light and delicate wood-and-steel structure, with each unit consisting of steel columns, wooden beams, and steel tie bars. The main timber beams are made up of stacked squared timber that project 2.46 meters into the central plaza. The detachable connection nodes of the structural form between the timber beams and the steel columns are specially designed to rotate in only one direction, thereby limiting the rotation of the beams and balancing the upward force of the wind on the roof. At the same time, stainless-steel tie bars fixed to 40-centimeter-tall concrete blocks balance the weight of the overhanging section of the gallery. The purpose of this paradoxical and conflicting treatment is to add a dramatic element and an interesting tension to the design's rational shape, in turn providing a light tone to this everyday space.

Enabling the future use and effective management of this public space is important. To this end, a wall made of rusted, partially foldable panels was installed at the backside of the square, blocking off a secondary, auxiliary space, which can serve a range of different uses. When the plaza opened, a cozy coffee shop fittingly named Pocket Coffee moved into the site and actively participated in organizing small events such as temporary markets, adding to the liveliness and attractiveness of the space. Its owners love the plaza and actively manage and maintain its use and safety.

Being used well and well-used is the greatest result that can be wished for on this project. A year after its completion, the Pocket Plaza at Lane 309 of Yongjia Road has been utilized in a variety of ways and has become a popular place for the residents of the surrounding community.

Detail of wood-and-steel structure

Detail of wood-and-steel structure

Entrance of Pocket Plaza at night

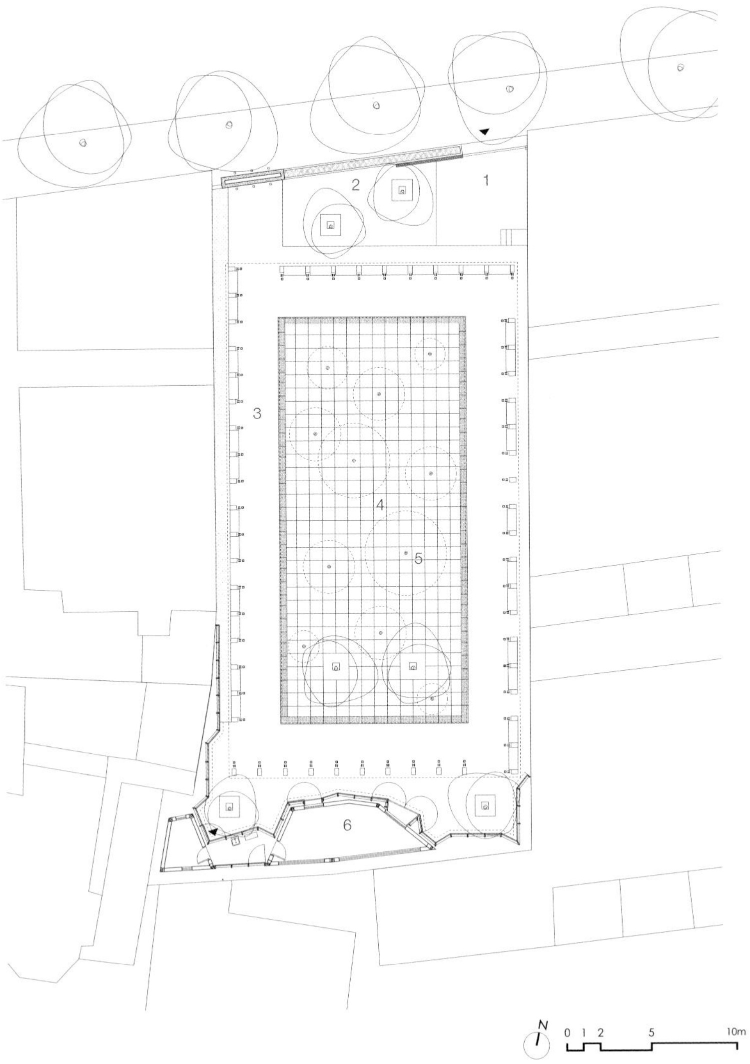

Ground-floor plan

1. Entrance
2. Ramp
3. Gallery
4. Courtyard
5. Fountain
6. Café

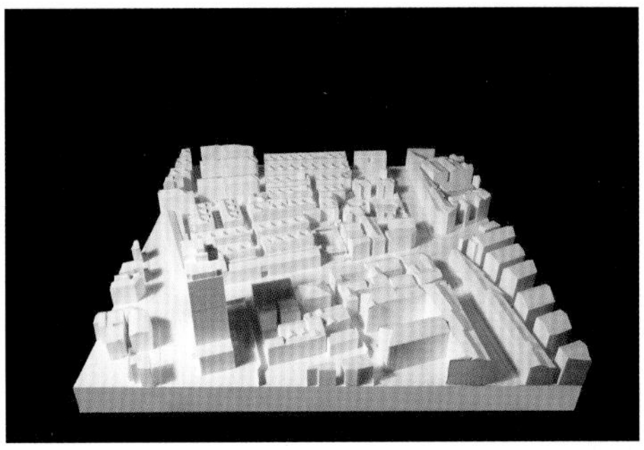

Model of adjacent district

Aerial view of adjacent district

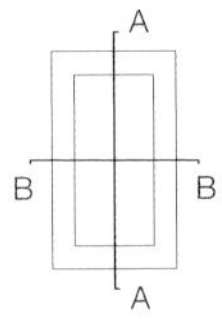

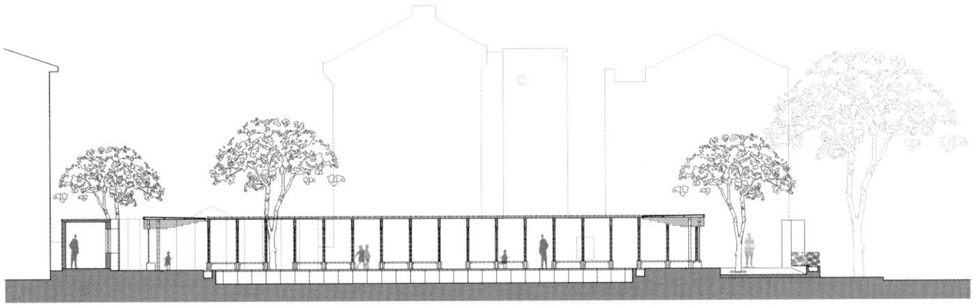

Section A-A

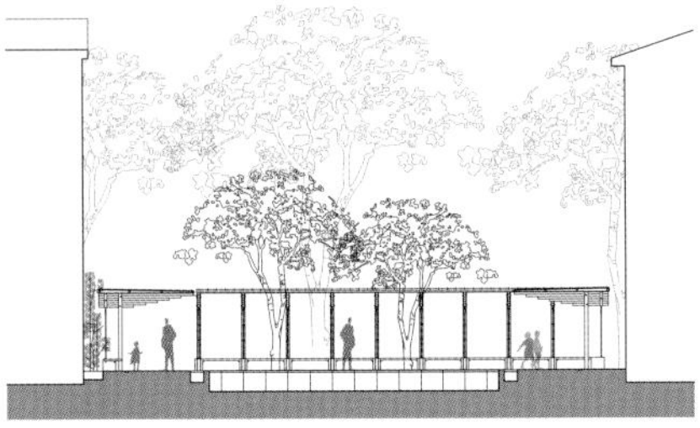

Section B-B

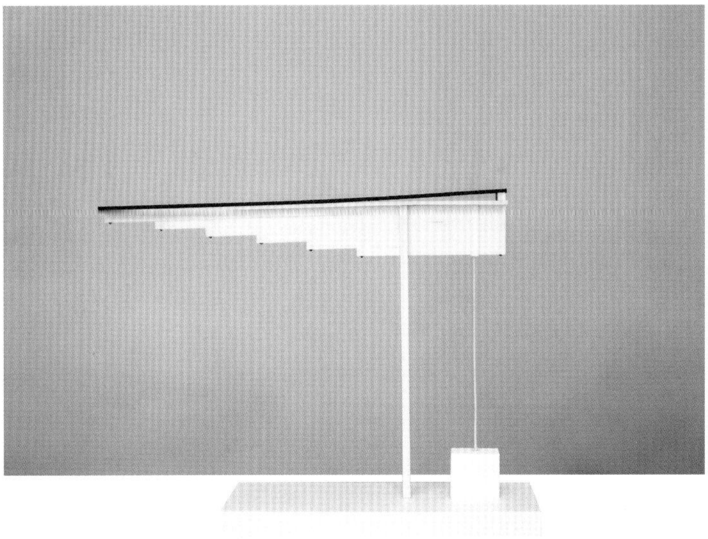

Structural model

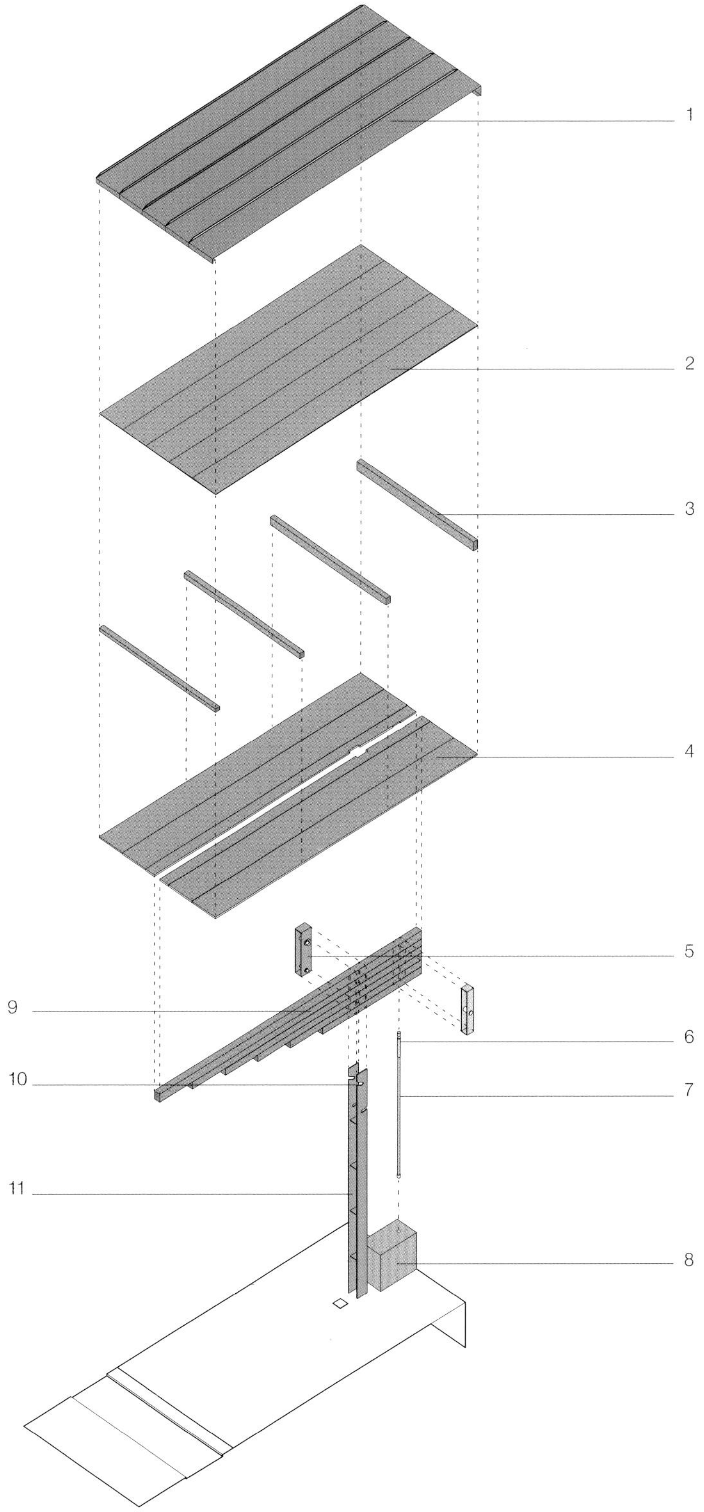

Axonometric diagram of wood-and-steel structure

1. Seaming metal roof
2. Roof backing panel
3. Timber purlin
4. Roof backboard
5. Steel hoop
6. Adjusting rod
7. Steel tie
8. Concrete block
9. 70/76 timber tie
10. Latch
11. Flat steel columns

Wetland Research and Education Center

Atelier Z+

Location: Dongtan National Nature Reserve, Chongming Island, Shanghai
Architect: Atelier Z+
Principal architect: Zhang Bin, Zhou Wei
Project Team: Liu Yu, Hu Liyao, Liu Yi, Zhang Yanan, Sun Jiaqiu, Xue Chujin
Area: 4,092 square meters
Completion: June 2019
Photography: Chen Hao

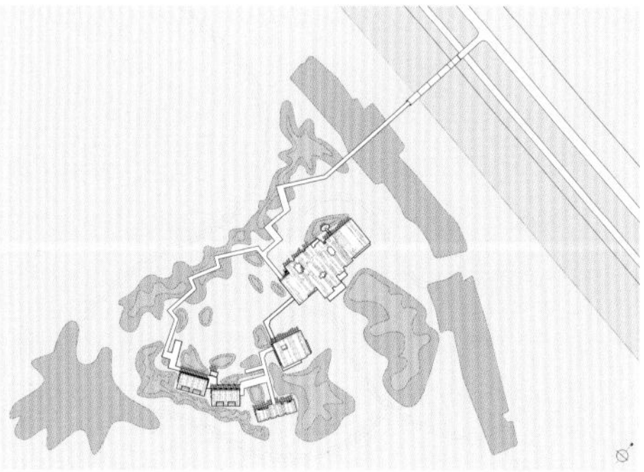

Site plan

Located at the easternmost point of Chongming Island, at the mouth of the Yangtze River, Dongtan Wetland is an estuary tidal flat. This wetland sits in the middle of the East Asia–Australia route, which is known as one of the eight migration routes of birds around the world. As a very important migration corridor for waterfowl in the Asia-Pacific region, Dongtan Wetland is also among one of significant gathering places and habitats for wild birds. In the 1990s, an invasive plant species, spartina alterniflora, was introduced to reinforce the tidal flat, however, it unexpectedly resulted in the ecological deterioration of the wetland. To deal with the issue, in 2013, Shanghai Chongming Dongtan National Nature Reserve initiated ecological control on spartina alterniflora, as well as directed efforts toward the environment optimization of bird habitats. As a supporting facility of that project, the Research and Education Center was built to accommodate scientific research monitoring, bird banding, law enforcement of management and protection, and science education. It also served to showcase ecological and environmental protection, while promoting worldwide cooperation and exchange.

The site is situated in a restored reed wetland northeast of the nature reserve, where water and sky merge at the horizon. In being respectful toward nature, the building is conceptualized to be in harmony with nature, taking inspiration from the description by fourteenth-century Chinese landscape painter Wang Meng, of secluded shacks scattered between the mountains and waters. To minimize the impact on the local ecosystem during construction, or when the space is in use, the architectural volume is divided and scattered, forming a group of settlements above the pile platform that float on the water, hidden among the reeds. Five buildings forming different volumes for a conference and exhibition center, canteen, research facility, and dormitory are cross-connected by a zigzag trestle bridge. Through prototype conversion and the control of scale, the atmosphere of indoor and outdoor spaces are enabled to be in response to the environment specificity, such as sky, wetland, reeds and flying birds. Led by the design of the "shack with double-pitch roof" in Wang Meng's painting, the design team flipped the double-pitch roof, made a Y-shaped cantilever structure, juxtaposed the two independant Y-shaped units and created a new double Y-shaped (YY) space. This creative idea brings this prototype new spatial meaning. First, the space covered by these two Y-shaped structures is given a sense of shelter and the

Aerial view of Wetland Research and Education Center

structure creates a fixed horizontal vision toward the vast wetland, while extending the openness of ridge toward the sky. Second, the inverted peak of the "Y" creates the feeling of living in a micro-valley and also designs a view to match as the periphery is cropped and re-composed by the eye to be broader and more horizontal. Out on the veranda, it feels like the space first presses down then lifts up, creating the image and impression of opening up to the environment.

View from north side

1
2 | 3

1. North façade of conference and exhibition volume
2. View from north of research zone
3. View from under the roof, south side

With juxtapositions and different variations of the Y-shaped units, a series of continuous saw-tooth roofs is designed, creating covered spaces with scale difference for multifunctional programs. With the organization of circulation, distribution of courtyards, transparency variation of enclosures, and differentiation of structural span and height, together with the combination of ridge skylights, no clear boundary between different functional spaces is stipulated, and people are encouraged to use them in a flexible way. This special linear pattern of space organization brings a unique indoor experience to in-position view and in-motion view. In certain units, people enjoy a body-enveloping experience under the roof, with the view parallel to the structural unit and the external natural scenery right before the eye; while walking through different space units accompanied by a fluctuating rhythm of varying height and light, they will feel like they're walking in a garden-courtyard house. This unique experience is strongly intensified on the roof of the conference and exhibition building: in response to site features, a flashback interpretation is evoked by alternating and combining the distant eye-level view of the wetland (as seen from the roof "valley") with the more immediate view of the indoor scenery observed from the skywalk under the roof. The scattered building volumes are fragmented by the overhanging saw-tooth roofs with deep eaves, successfully eliminating the scale difference between buildings—which are also blurred by overlapping deep shadows and reflections above the water.

Considering that weather-proofing and maintaining the facility will be challenging work in high humidity and salinity conditions, light steel or wooden structures are abandoned in the design. Instead, reinforced-concrete is selected to build with, using the simplicity of tectonics. Buildings A, B, and C were built by Y-shaped cantilevered reinforced-concrete bent frame structures with crisscross sections and partial folded plate. Among these buildings, the cantilever of building A was so large that the whole structure had to be constructed by steel-reinforced-concrete and the exhibition hall had to be partly designed with steel mezzanine. Buildings D and E were constructed with a concrete folded plate structure. In order to expose the crudeness of the concrete structure against the wetland, long pine timber formworks were used in the as-cast finish concrete construction to obtain a natural wood texture. The non-structural enclosure and partition walls were also coated with refurbished recycled timber formwork to unify the material expression. Bird-friendly, floor-to-ceiling windows with vertical grilles, which provide visitors maximum field view

Multipurpose hall in conference and exhibition zone

are used for most of the external envelop. The trestle bridge and the water platform are paved with precast concrete battens with cracks left in between each other; this not only enhances the feeling of walking over water but also makes room for reed growth. All the roof "valleys" are also filled with slightly undulating soil and low-maintenance planted miscanthus and shrubs. For the purpose of environment integration and sustainable recycling in the future, all the pitched roofs which are trimmed with titanium-zinc sheets are covered with indigenous reed straw, reaped and processed under the supervision of local, experienced reed weavers.

Indoor of dormitory zone

Conference and exhibition zone

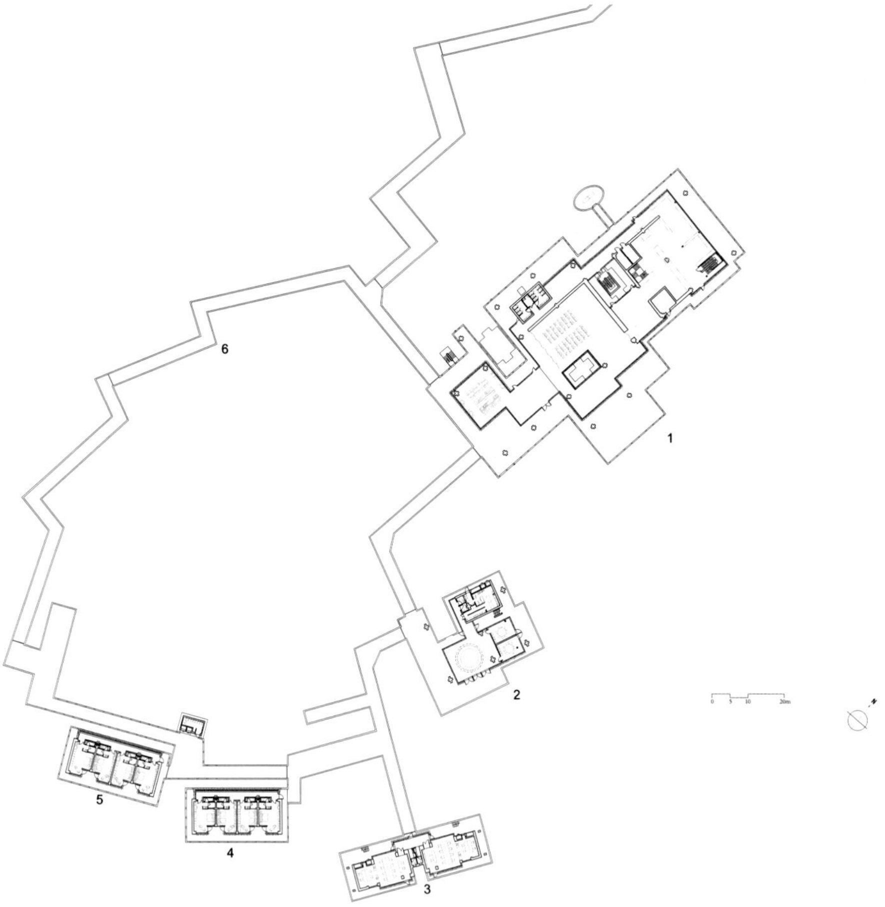

Plan of the entire group of buildings

1. Conference and exhibition
2. Canteen
3. Research
4. Dormitory
5. Dormitory
6. Trestle bridge

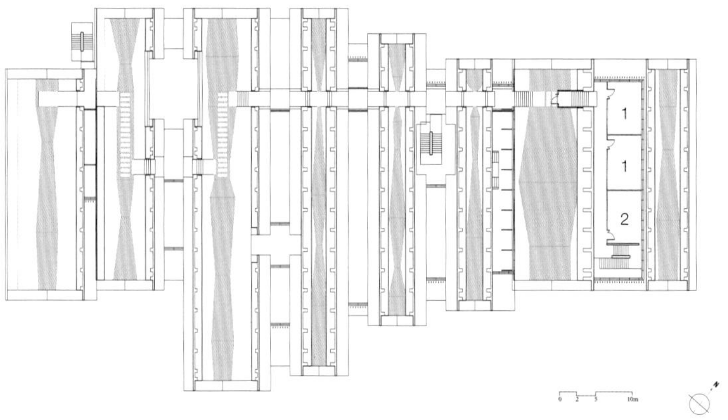

Second-floor plan of conference and exhibition zone

1. Office
2. Security room

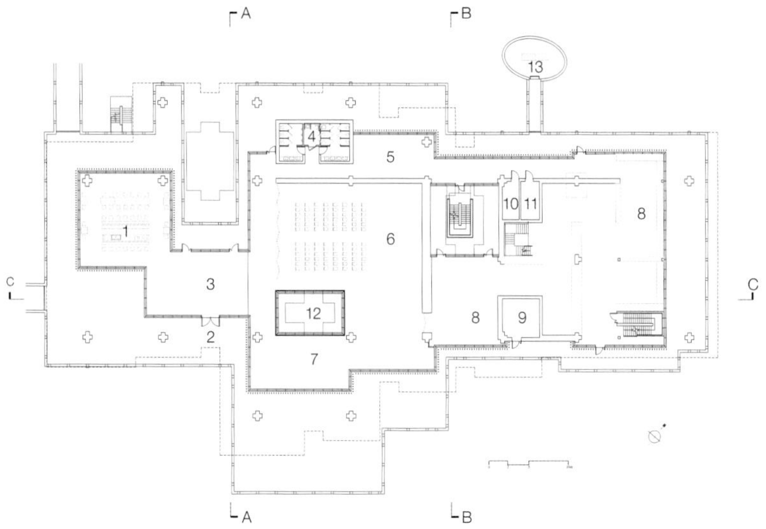

First-floor plan of conference and exhibition zone

1. Café
2. Main entrance
3. Entrance hall
4. Restroom
5. Rest area
6. Multipurpose hall
7. Foyer
8. Exhibition area
9. Fire control room
10. Storage
11. Reference room
12. Courtyard
13. Equiptment

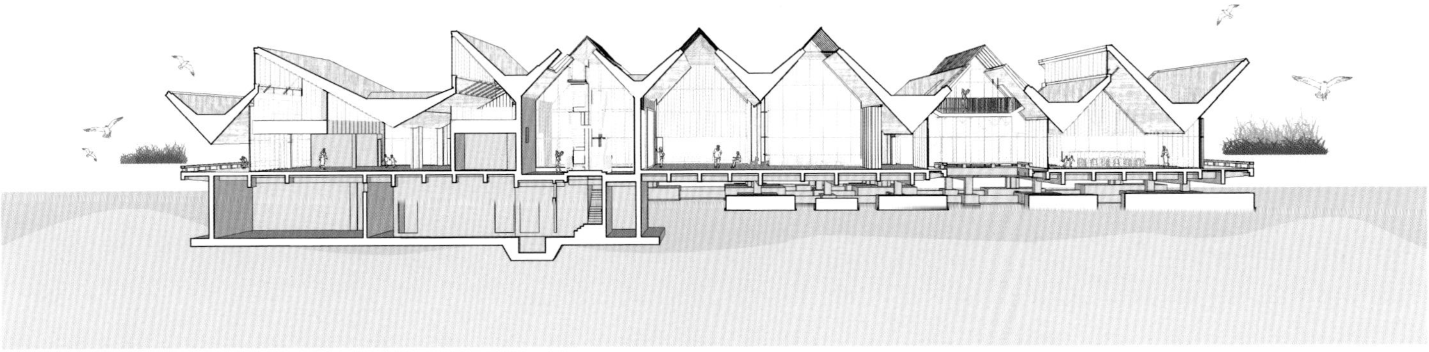

Perspective section of conference and exhibition zone

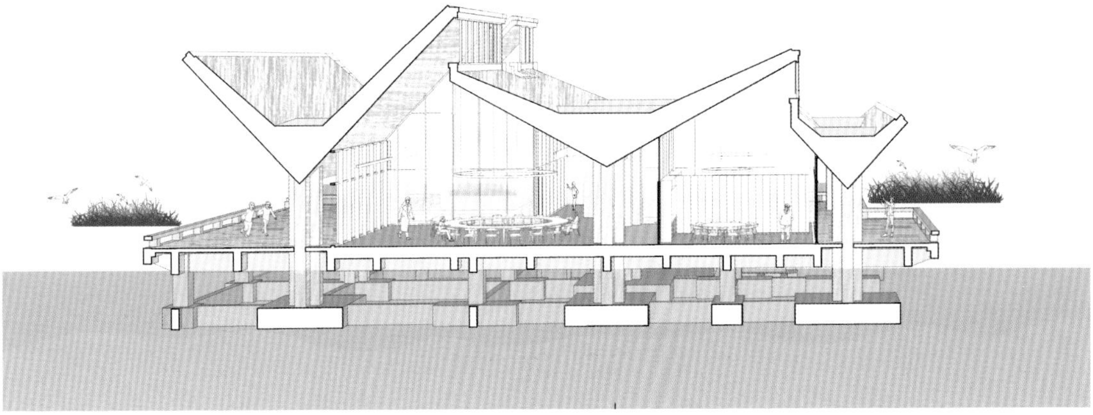

Perspective section of canteen

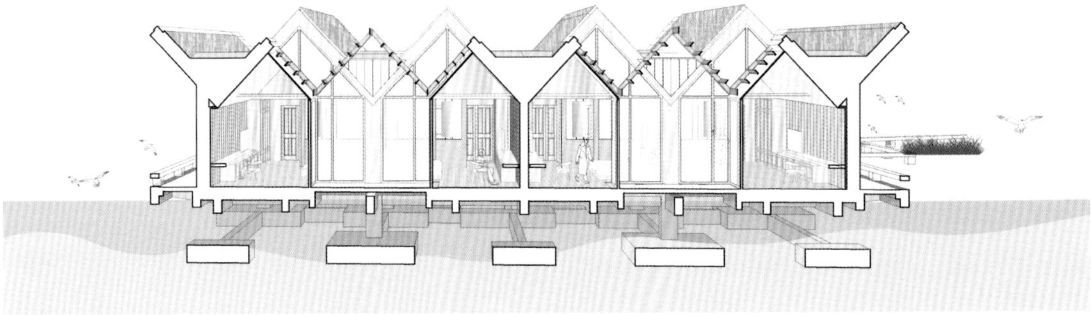

Perspective section of dormitory

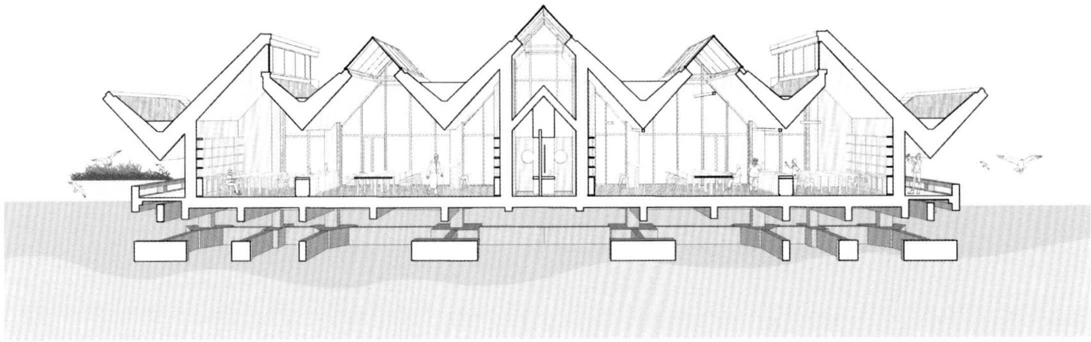

Perspective section of research volume

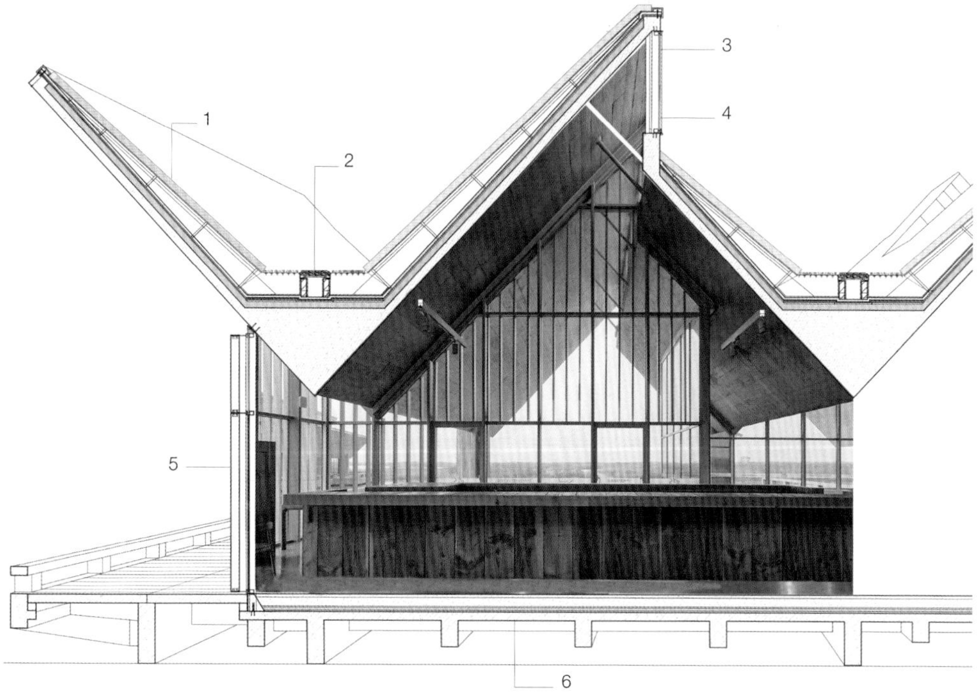

Construction Details

1. Pitched roof with thatch as insulation
2. Roof platform, accessible for strolls
3. Aluminum cover
4. Double-layer glass
5. Pine door panel
6. Concrete floor

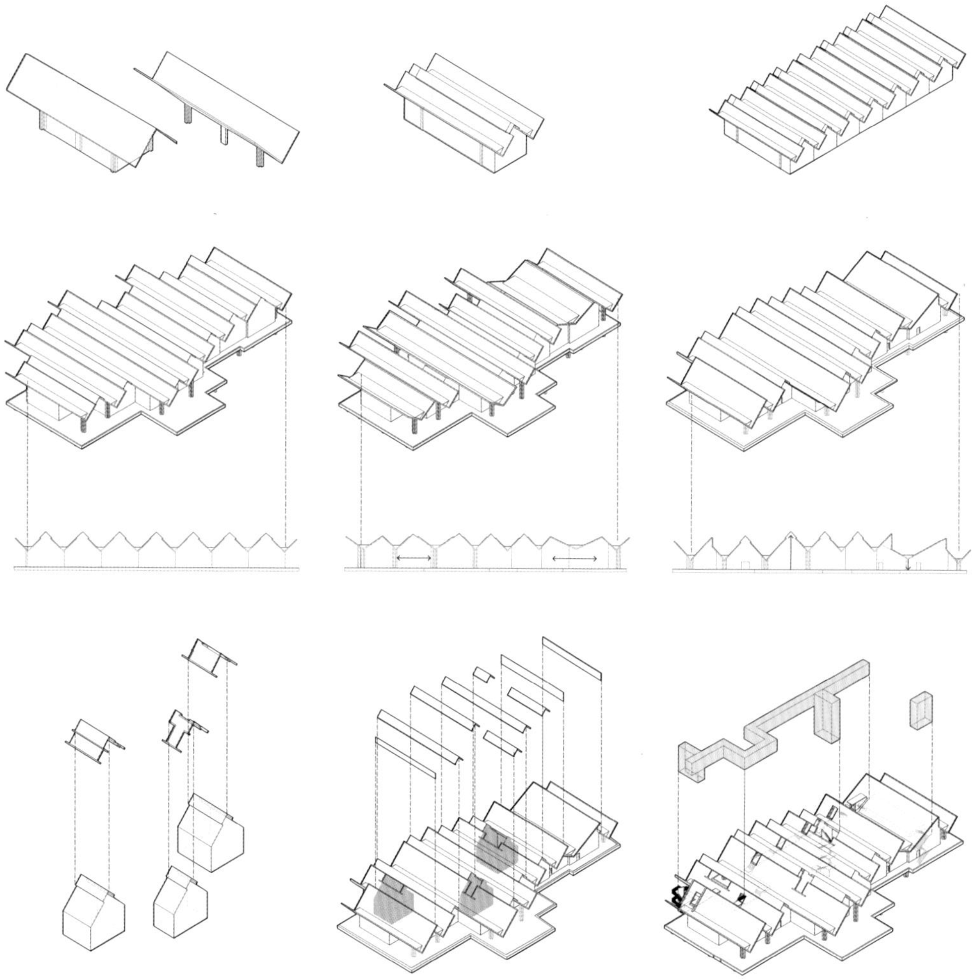

Axonometric analysis of architectural volume

Details of building materials

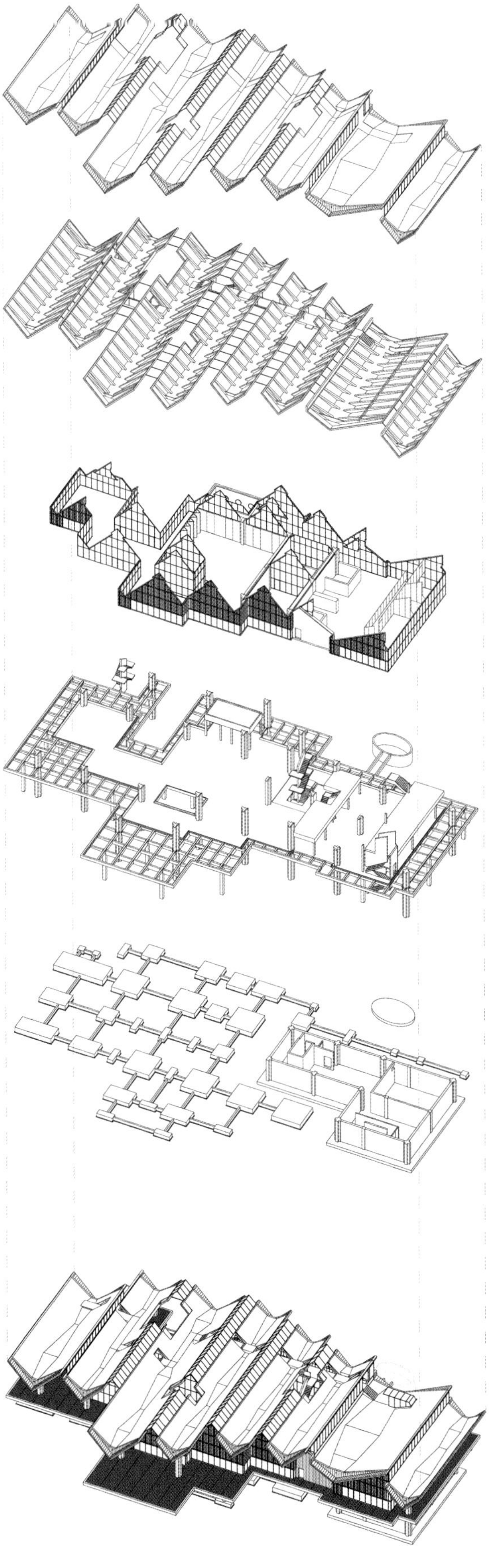

Axonometric analysis of structure

Ash Gallery

Original Design Studio – TJAD

Location: No. 2800, Yangshupu Road, Yangpu District, Shanghai
Architect: Original Design Studio – TJAD
Principal architect: Zhang Ming, Zhang Zi, Qin Shu
Design team: Li Xuefeng, Wu Yunsong, Zhu Chengzhe, Zhang Yichen, Liu Jingyi
Structural design: Nan Jun, Cao Linyong
Area: 3,840 square meters
Completion: 2019
Photography: ZYARCH Photographer

Site plan

The first coal-fired power plant of the Far East sat on the site of the former Yangshupu Power Plant, which was built by British investors in 1913. The industrial remains abundant on the site, such as the 105-meter-high chimney that became a landmark for ships entering the port of Shanghai, suspension cranes along the riverside, coal trestles, conveyor belts, freshwater ponds, wet ash silos, dry ash silos, and other such operation items have unique, impressive spatial volumes and forms, and occupy an important position in the Yangpu Waterfront project.

The site was formerly an industrial zone

The dry ash silos found at the easternmost part of the power plant were converted into Ash Gallery. Plans for the redesign of the silos began in 2015, but uncertainty over their final function led to multiple rounds of changes. Finally, it was the idea of converting the

View from Huangpu River

structure into an art gallery, a more flexible and open strategy, that went into design and implementation.

The addition of two observation platforms united the three ash silos that had once stood independently. The original sealed ash silos, measuring 15 meters tall, were renovated with an ambiguous interface. The use of the entire space was envisioned as a cluster of public promenades that curled from the concrete framework at the base all the way to the top of the ash silos. After the creation of this roaming expanse, six spaces—their functions still undetermined—were connected via staircases and plugged into the structure. The intervention of artworks subsequently formed a mode of spatial connection that intertwined artistic discussions and public wanderings.

Ash Gallery served as the eastern station during the Shanghai Urban Space Art Season, held September 9–11 in 2019. Built into a public artwork by Portuguese artist José de Guimarães, Japanese artist Keisuke Takahashi, and Chinese designers Han Jiayin and Zhang Ming, the gallery became a significant component of the entire art season.

Details

Aerial view of Ash Gallery

Connecting bridge in between silos

Spiral ramp inside silos

Entrance on the first floor

Stairs to promenade in between the concrete structure

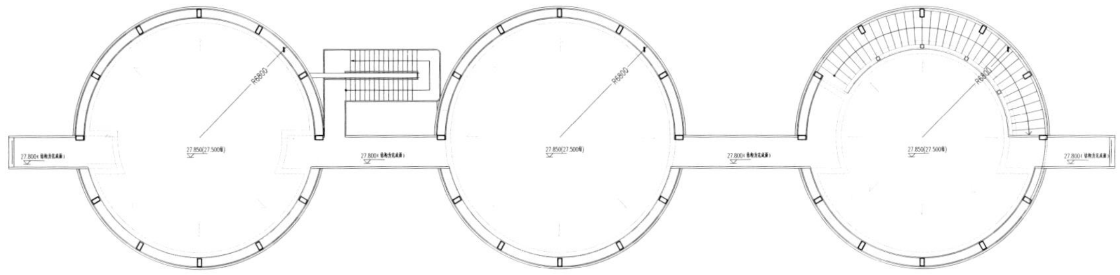

Roof plan

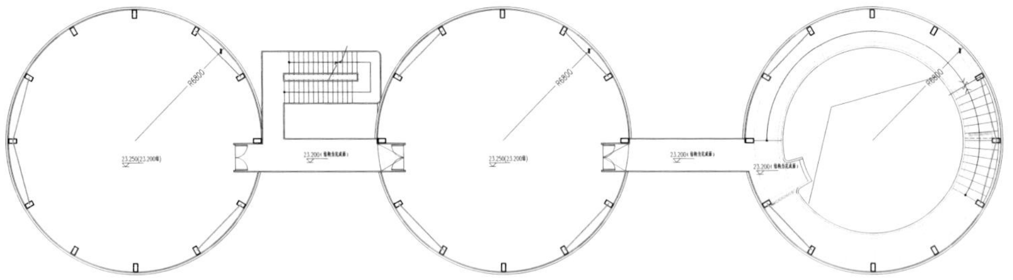

Upper-floor plan

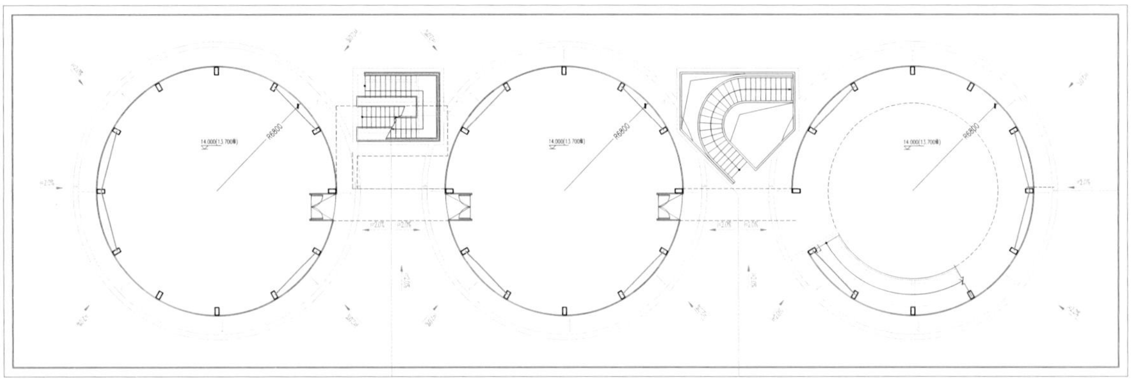

Second-floor plan

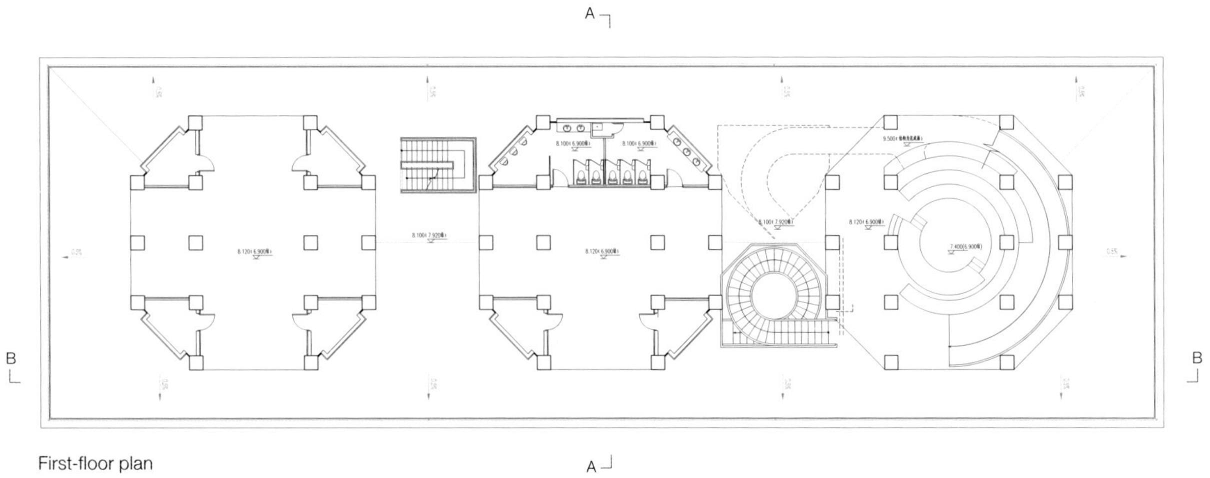

First-floor plan

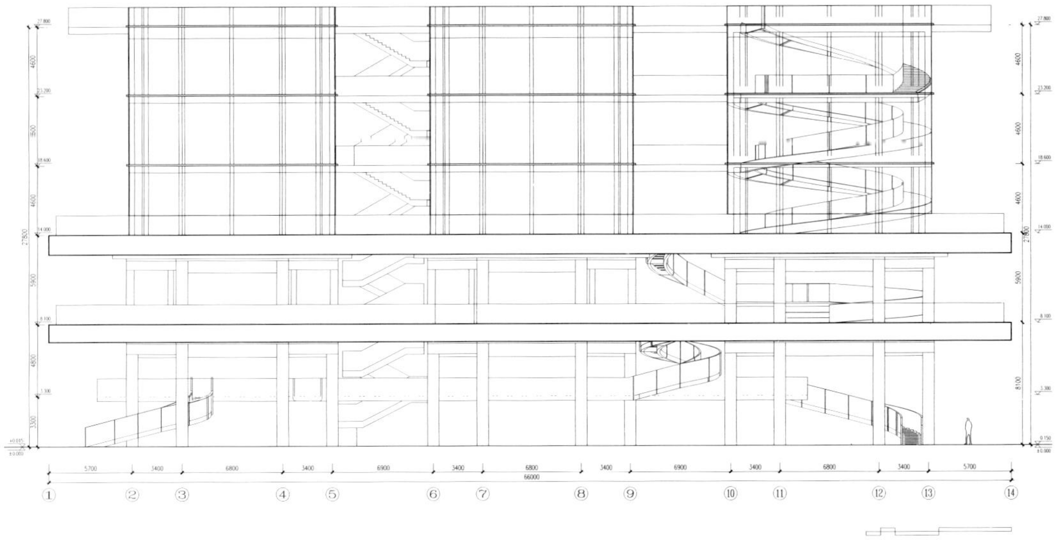

South elevation

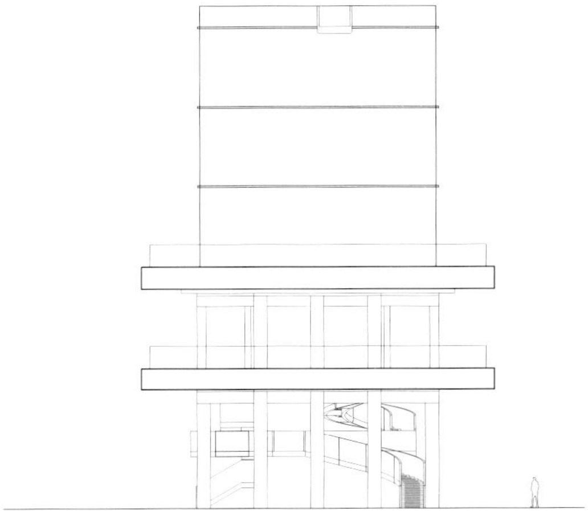

East elevation

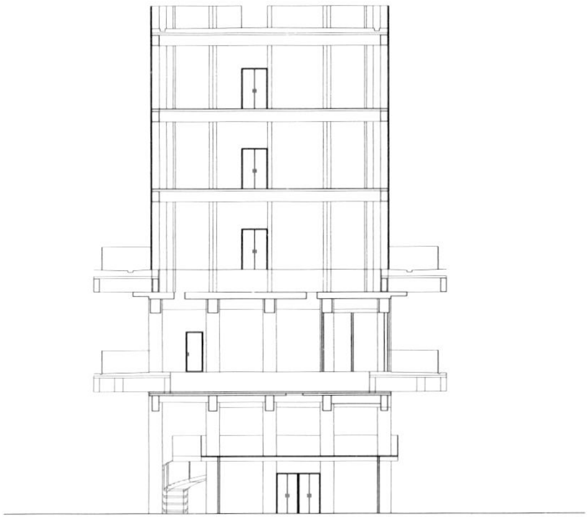

Section A-A

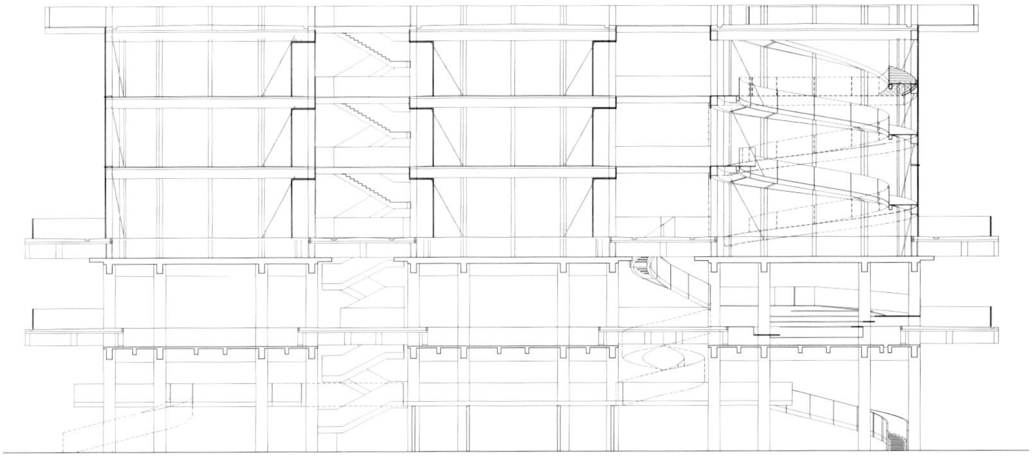

Section B-B

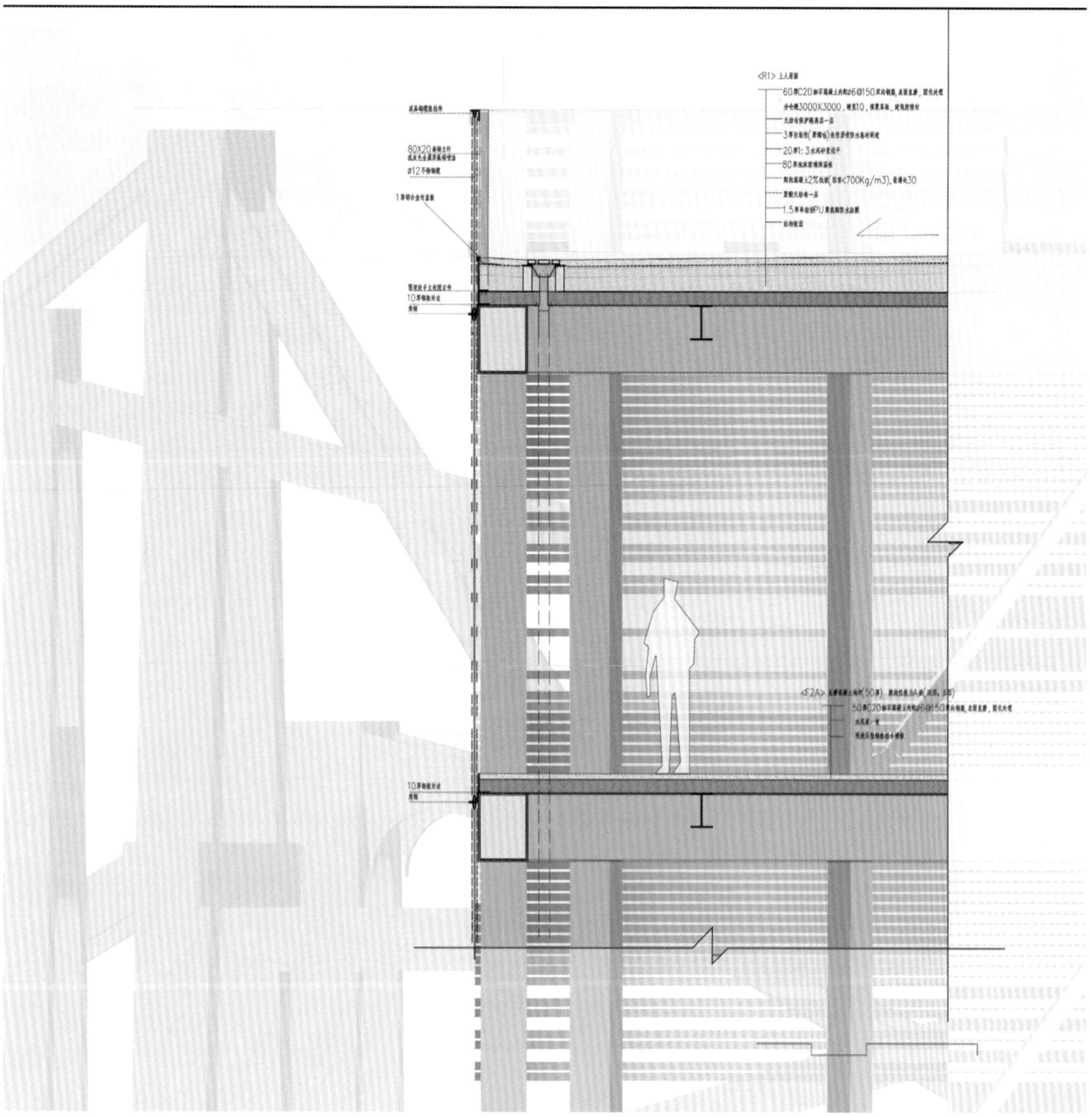

Construction detail of floor

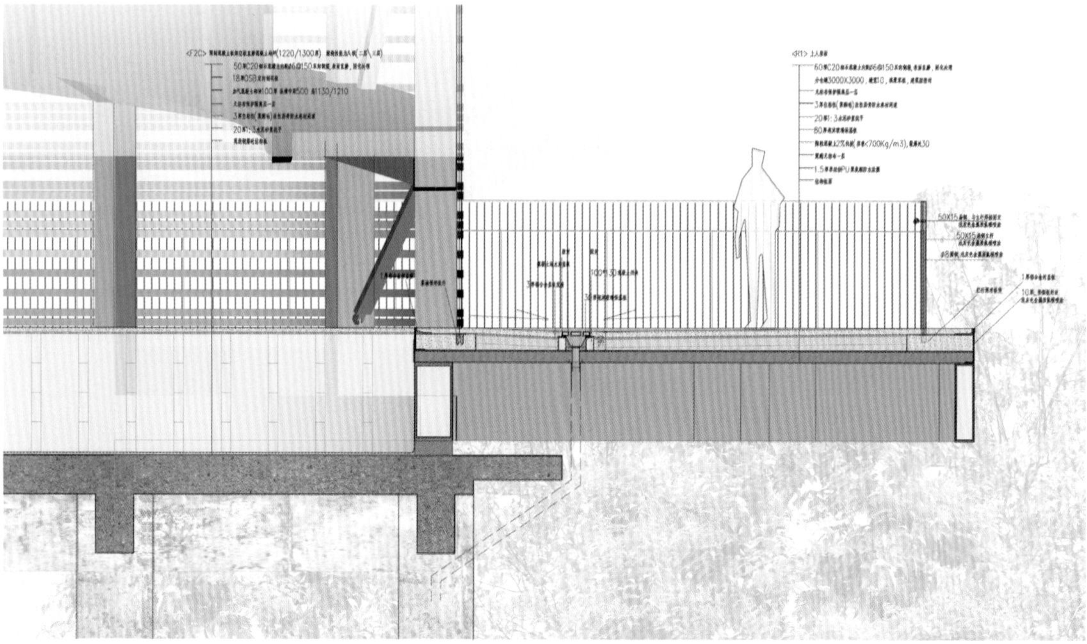

Construction detail of outdoor platform

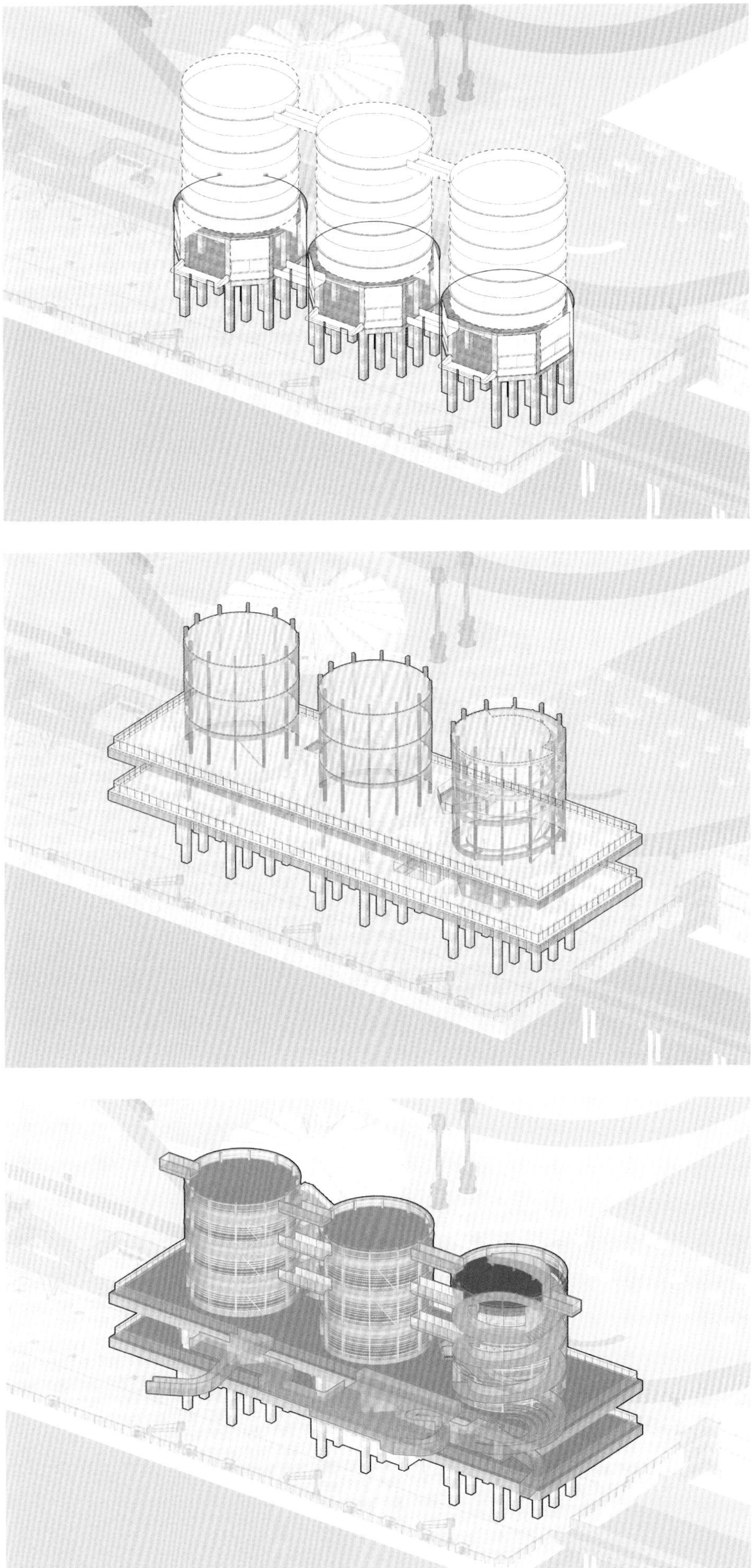

Axonometric diagrams

Visitor Center of Changping Future Science City

Hu Yue Studio (BIAD)

Location: Entrance Square of Changping Future Science City, Changping, Beijing
Architect: Hu Yue Studio (BIAD)
Principal architect: Hu Yue
Design team: Tai Fangqing, Xiang Xi, Wang Xixi, Feng Jingxuan
Structure: Jiang Yang, Liu Yang
Equipment: Lu Dongyang, Zhang Cheng, Pei Lei
Interior Design: BCEG Decoration Construction Engineering Co., Ltd.
Area: 847 square meters
Completion: June 2018
Photography: Chen Su

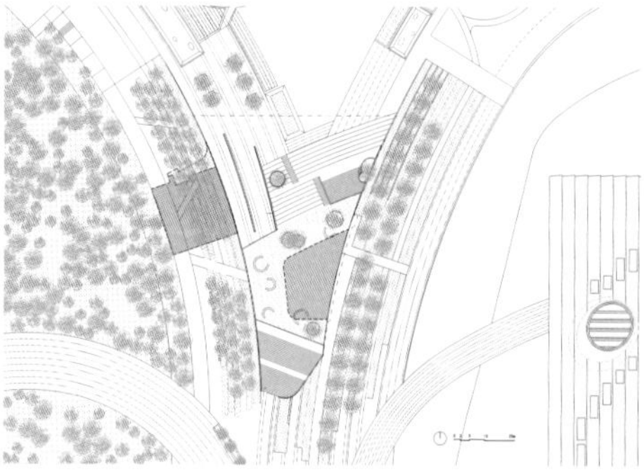
Site plan

Built along an old river, this project is located at the entrance of a central park within a large-scale industrial park in the suburbs of Beijing. Early plans had considered creating a central lake district based on the river, but the park still bore the artificial marks of small service facilities and landscape designs that clashed with the surroundings.

The park entrance is located on the south side, bordering the city expressway and situated across from a dense construction area. Like many of China's new developing areas, the original villages of the area have all been relocated and in their place, modern buildings and wide streets are currently under construction. The visitor center perches at the junction of the construction area and the park.

Café area of the visitor center

Night view

Before getting involved in this project, the landscape planning team had already proposed plans for the visitor center: it would take the form of a gate, with dining facilities above the entrance. Impressions of the completed construction had stuck with people and they had grown to look forward to the actualization of the gate. The proposed character of the gate also fulfilled managerial expectations of iconic entrances, but this design would unfortunately have a negative impact on its natural surroundings, hence the priority became designing a visitor center that matched the setting. Thankfully, a 6-meter difference in height between the entrance plaza of the park and the lakeside turned out in favor of the design as it is used to mask the building and blend it into the environment to great effect. Two rows of large trees still stood on the east and west side of the visitor center, so two sloped, curved pathways were set-up alongside those trees, extending from the entrance plaza down to the lake; the visitor center is placed between these two pathways. From the entrance plaza, people can see a descending flight of stairs leading to the visitor center.
The center is split into two parts. One part, located beneath the western slope, includes the restroom and changing rooms. The other part, located at the eastern side and enveloped in glass, encompasses the information desk, café, supermarket, storage room, and offices.
A wide passage runs between the two buildings from the entrance plaza to the lake. As people look toward the visitor center from the lake, the only visible elements between the ramps and the trees are two concrete walls partitioning the flow of visitors and a viewing platform adapted to the terrain. In that way, the visitor center takes shape as a micro-intervention in the natural landscape, interwoven with the natural surroundings and its visitors.

Entryway seen from roof terrace

Detailed view

The project started with coordinating the relationship between the artificial objects and the natural environment; it then fully integrates traditional buildings and the external environment by shattering their geometric boundaries. The building's subtle embedment into the terrain creates a new kind of architectural landscape that negates the strong contrast between the site's history and the buildings as it spotlights the design paradigm of the sculpture-like buildings. At the same time, the simple, dexterous geometrical relationship of the visitor center fittingly conveys the traditional values of modern architecture. More importantly, it helps city managers realize that environmentally friendly and de-monumentalized buildings are the way forward.

East side view

Sunken channel

West side view

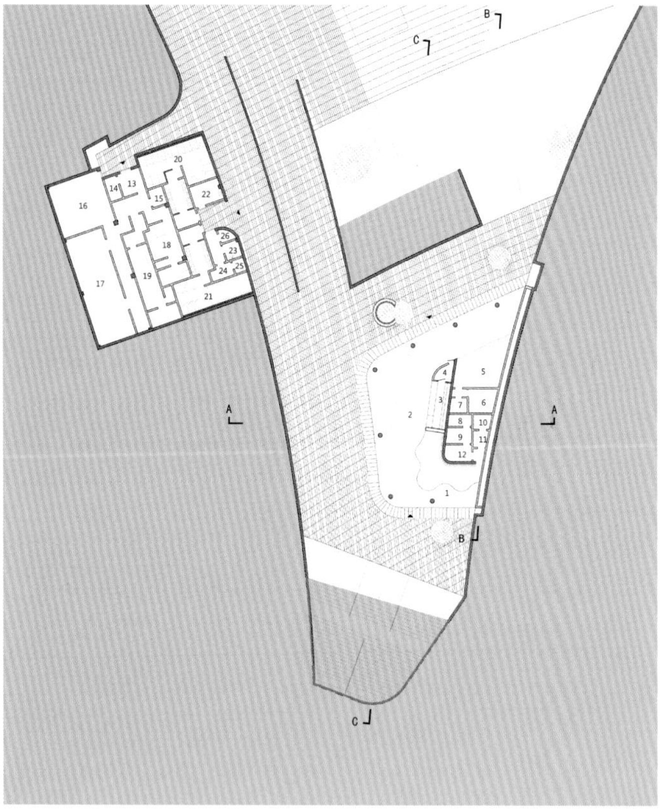

First-floor plan

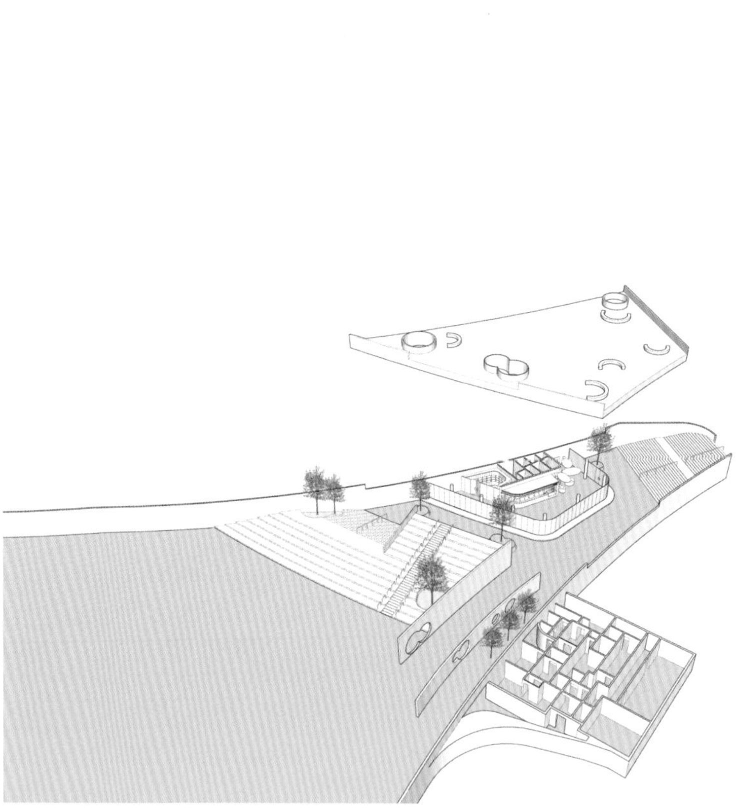

Axonometric diagram

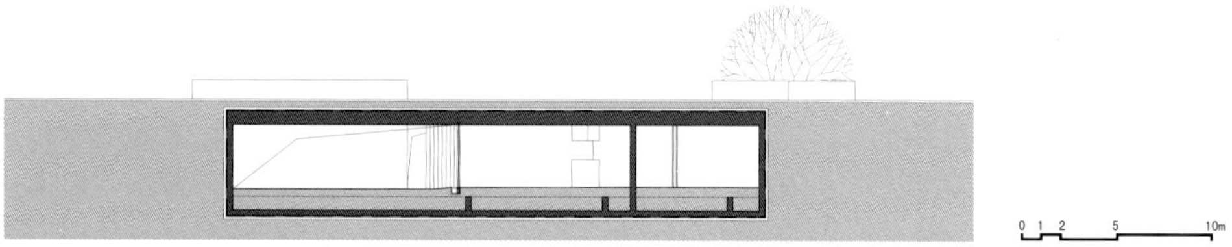

Section A-A

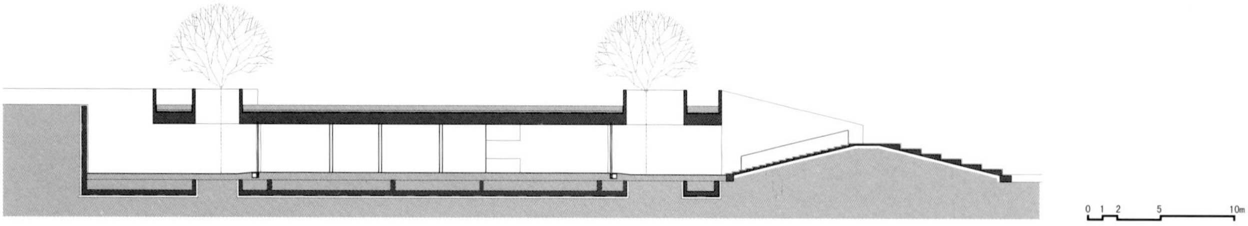

Section B-B

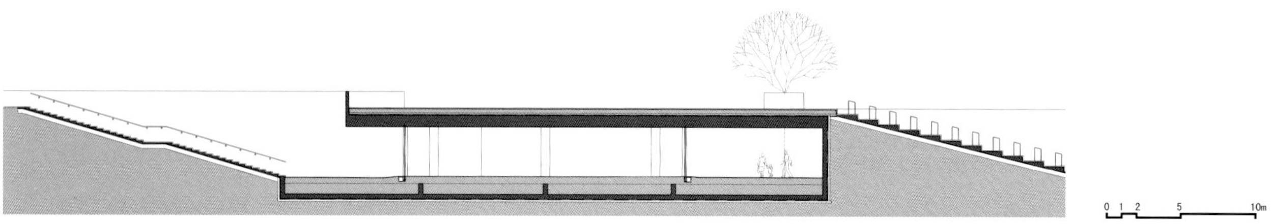

Section C-C

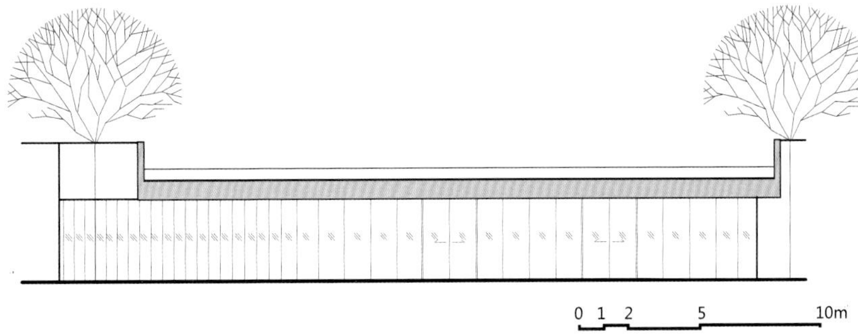

A Zone west elevation

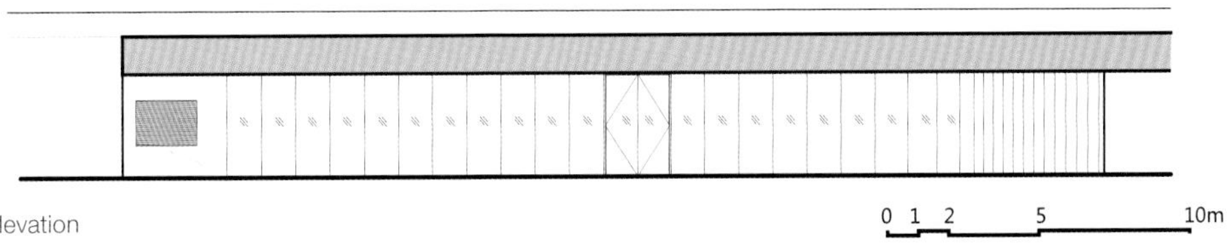

A Zone north elevation

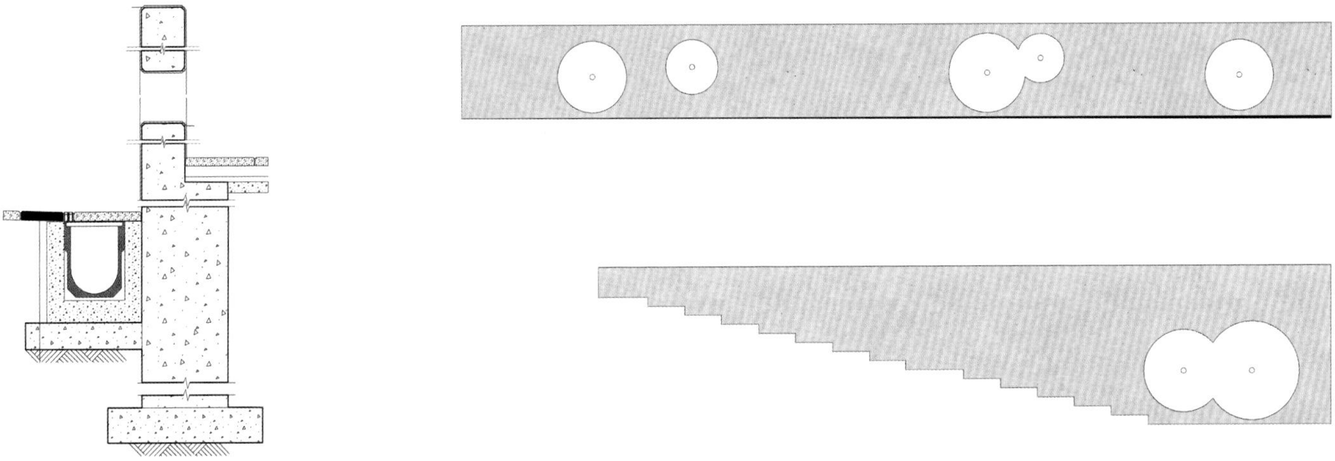

Detailed construction of the concrete wall

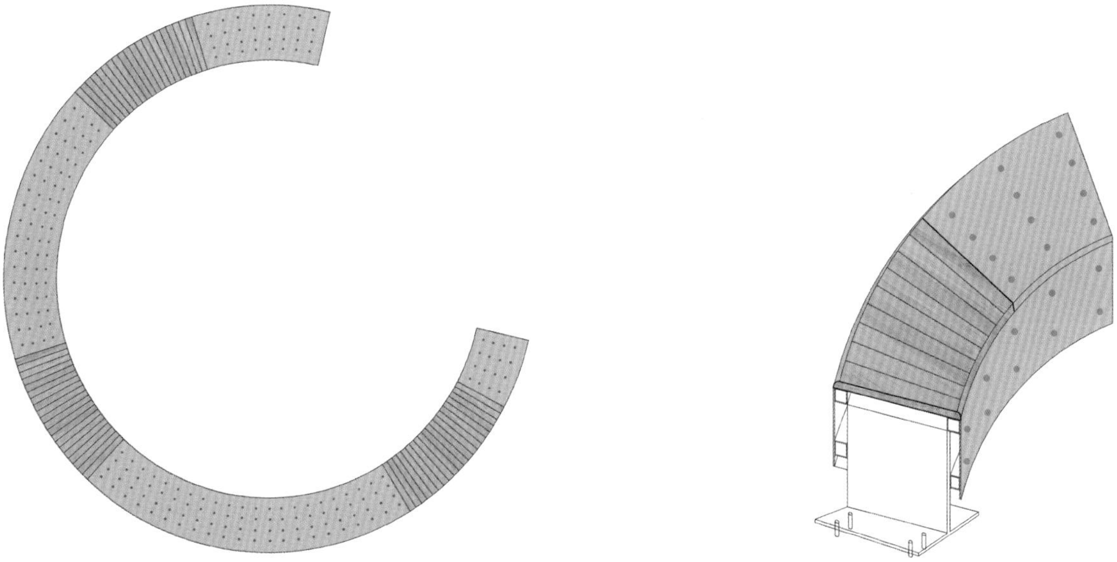

Detailed construction of the seat

Opening Exhibition at the Jingdezhen Imperial Kiln Museum

On September 19, 2020, *Metamorphosis – A Joint Exhibition of the Four Contemporary Masters of CAFA*, the opening exhibition for the Imperial Kiln Museum, officially kicked off in Jingdezhen, China's renowned porcelain capital in Jiangxi Province. Fan Di'an, the president of the China Artists Association and the president of the Central Academy of Fine Arts (CAFA) served as the chief curator of the exhibition, while the well-known architecture scholar and critic, Zhou Rong acted as the curator, and Wang Mingxian, a scholar of architecture and art history at the China Academy of Art, served as the academic director. A forum titled *Symposium on the Jingdezhen Imperial Kiln Museum* hosted by the editorial board of the Architectural Journal was also held at the museum later that day. The symposium was chaired by Li Xiangning, professor and vice president of the School of Architecture and Urban Planning of Tongji University, who was joined by well-known professionals, including academicians Cui Kai and Zhuang Weimin from the Chinese Academy of Engineering; Wang Mingxian, scholar of architecture and art history at the Chinese National Academy of Arts; Zhang Jie, award-winning master of design and engineering; Zhou Rong, associate professor of the School of Architecture at Tsinghua University; Huang Juzheng, executive editor of the *Architectural Journal*; Liu Kecheng, professor of the School of Architecture at Xi'an University of Architecture and Technology; and Hu Qian, founding partner of ISOZAKI + HuQian Partners. Zhu Pei, the lead architect of the Jingdezhen Imperial Kiln Museum opened the symposium by elaborating on the design concept of the museum. The guests then delved into a discussion on the museum's design from three diverse perspectives: the building itself, the connection between the architecture and art, and the connections between the architecture, the city, and nature.

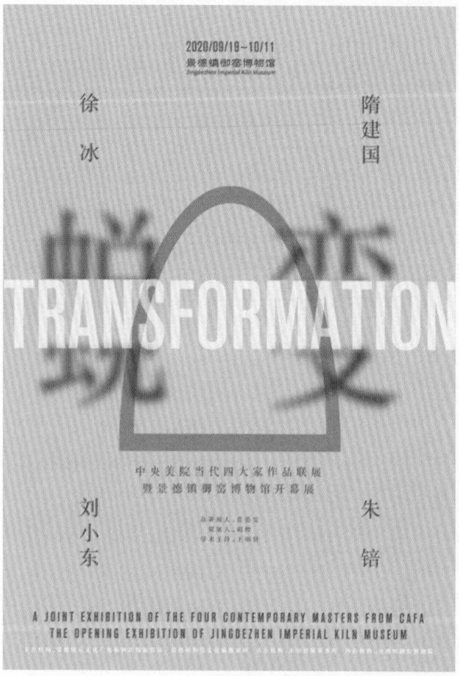

Photos courtesy of *Architecture China Journal*

Award Ceremony for 2020 Building with Nature: Architecture China Award

In the afternoon of December 5, 2020, the award ceremony and academic conference for the 2020 Building with Nature: Architecture China Award was held at the Museum of Contemporary Art in Shanghai, also known as the Power Station of Art. A total of four awards were presented: the Practical Achievement Award, the Technological Exploration Award, the Youth Exploration Award, and the Special Project Award of the Jury.

Wang Shu, jury chairman of the 2020 Architecture China Award and winner of the 2012 Pritzker Architecture Prize, as well as jury member of the Pritzker Architecture Prize and dean of the School of Architecture of the China Academy of Art and Cui Kai, honorary president of the China Architecture Design & Research Institute and chief architect and academician of the Chinese Academy of Engineering jointly announced the 2020 Practical Achievement Award—the highest distinction of the 2020 Architecture China Award. The prestigious award was taken home by Liu Jiakun, founder and lead architect of Jiakun Architects. In their statement, the jury remarked: "Liu Jiakun's practice embodies a certain direction of contemporary Chinese architecture. His works focus on the social reality, local culture, and low-tech strategies, and he strives to inject the power of nature and humanity into them. With a clear understanding of the diverse Chinese traditions and an ability to perceive and grasp the current reality, Liu Jiakun expertly addresses the contemporary propositions of Chinese architecture."

The winner of the Technological Exploration Award was unveiled by Yung Ho Chang, a former Pritzker Architecture Prize jury member who is also professor at the School of Architecture and Urban Planning at Tongji University and lead architect of Atelier FCJZ. The award went to Luo Yujie, founder and lead architect of LUO Studio. The jury had this to say: "Luo Yujie's practice explores sustainable construction methods and ways of creating more versatile spaces with fewer materials. With prefabricated structural steel and wood components as the main focus, he combines the rationality of different structural prototypes with the characteristics of contemporary culture to create a spatial structure with a sense of strength and growth."

The Youth Exploration Award was presented by jury member Ge Ming, vice dean of the School of Architecture at Southeast University; Wang Lu, architect, architecture scholar, and professor at Tsinghua University School of Architecture; and Lu Wenyu, a member of the organizing committee for the Architecture China Award and director of the Sustainable Construction Lab at the School of Architecture and Art at the China Academy of Art. The prize was awarded to Wang Hao, co-founder and lead architect of Anonymous Architects; Atelier XÜK (Liu Kenan, Zhang Xu); and Sounding Architecture (Liu Chang, Gao Qin, Kong Dezhong). Congratulating their win, the jury commented on each of the work of these three young groups of architects, respectively: "While steering clear of simple nostalgia, Wang Hao's practice explores the revival of traditional building culture, creating a tense and differentiated spatial experience with the forms of modern architecture and the techniques of traditional craftsmanship."

"The practice of Atelier XÜK combines the rational logic of European modernist architecture with the inquiry into places in the contemporary Chinese context, creating spaces connected to everyday life and communal memories through the selection and combination of different construction systems."

"The practical exploration of Sounding Architecture seeks a poetry in everyday materials. The focus on the materiality of architecture and their delicate spatial organization allows them to reinstate the human body as the primary medium of perception in a world that is increasingly dominated by visual experiences."

The Special Project Award of the Jury was presented by Gong Yan of the Shanghai Museum of Contemporary Art and Li Hui, founder of Fengyuzhu, the main partner for the award. The winning projects are: Bingding Wood Kiln (AZL architects), Taizhou Contemporary Art Museum (Atelier Deshaus), In Bamboo (Archi-Union Architects), Gymnasium of New Campus of Tianjin University (Atelier Li Xinggang), Rong Garden (Yinyuan Studio), Soft Matter (NATURALBUILD), Tai Kwun Centre for Heritage and Art (Herzog & de Meuron), and M2 Tourist Port at Bai Lianjing (TJAD Original Design Studio).